# The Man Who Lives with Wolves

# The Man Who Lives with Wolves

## Shaun Ellis
### with Penny Junor

 HARMONY BOOKS / NEW YORK

Copyright © 2009 by Shaun Ellis

Published in the United States by Harmony Books, an imprint of
the Crown Publishing Group, a division of Random House, Inc., New York.

www.crownpublishing.com

Harmony Books is a registered trademark and the
Harmony Books colophon is a trademark of Random House, Inc.

Library of Congress Cataloging-in-Publication Data

Ellis, Shaun

The man who lives with wolves / by Shaun Ellis with Penny Junor.

p. cm.

Includes index.

1. Ellis, Shaun.   2. Wolves—Behavior.   3. Human-animal relationships.

I. Junor, Penny.   II. Title.

QL737.C22E59 2009

599.773092—dc22

2009021819

ISBN 978-0-307-46453-8

Printed in the United States of America

Design by Leonard W. Henderson

page i: The author with Tejas and Nataa, age six months *(Roger Cooke)*.

page ii: The author with Tamaska *(Roger Cooke)*.

page v: The author with grandfather at harvest time *(Shaun Ellis Collection)*.

10 9 8 7 6 5 4 3 2 1

First Edition

I would like to dedicate this book to the memory of my grandfather, Gordon Ellis. Thank you, Old Man, for your patient teaching; your wisdom and knowledge is with me wherever I go. I was once told by my brother Levi's people, the Nez Percé, that someone only dies if you forget them. You will be in my thoughts forever.

# Contents

# Author's Note

When you are living with wolves, all that matters is staying alive and protecting the pack; days slip into weeks, weeks into years. Time, as we know it, has no relevance and I want to apologize in advance if I am a little fuzzy about dates and times. I have never kept a diary, never been a letter writer, and have never hung on to anything. For much of my life I have lived out of a rucksack so have very few possessions of any sort. There is very little, therefore, to remind me about when the various events that took place in my life actually happened. If I have attributed something to the wrong year, please bear with me. The events themselves I remember as if they were yesterday.

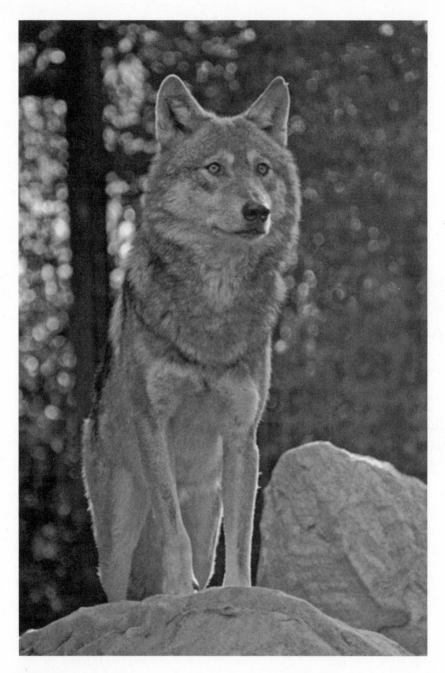

Matsi. *Roger Cooke*

# Touching a Nerve

I was helping out at a wildlife center in Hertfordshire, one of the home counties, just north of London. A man appeared outside the wolf enclosure one day, pushing a child in an old-fashioned wheelchair that looked almost Victorian, with a large rectangular tray on the front of it. I was immediately struck by how out of place it looked. He told me that he and his son, who may have been thirteen or fourteen and who, I could see at a glance, was severely disabled, had driven all the way from Scotland, a distance of around five hundred miles. He had heard that we allowed members of the public to interact with the wolves and he wanted his son to meet one.

I was surprised that this man had gone to such lengths to show his son a wolf. The child didn't look as though he would get anything out of the encounter. He sat immobile, silent, staring into space, and I doubted that he would even be able to stroke the animal's fur. Normally, I loved this part of the job. Children arrived with such preconceptions. They pulled back and screamed when the wolf came near, convinced by all the stories they'd read and the cartoons they'd watched, that wolves were sly, vicious creatures that ate grandmothers, blew down the houses of little pigs, and ripped the throats out of little girls. I had grown up with exactly the same terror. It had taken me many years to discover that wolves are actually shy, intelligent animals with a very sophisticated social structure, whose bloodthirsty reputation is not deserved. I found nothing more gratifying than watching children touch the wolves and listen to what I had to tell them about these animals, and watch their prejudice and ignorance fade away.

I felt almost evangelical about this. I thought that if children could feel their coats and look them in the eye, they could make up their own minds about them so that in time, future generations will perhaps be ready to give back to wolves the place in our world that is rightfully theirs.

Once upon a time wolves and men lived alongside one another, each respecting and benefiting from the other's way of life. Sadly, those days are gone and I believe that we are the poorer for that. The natural balance in nature that they promoted has been whittled away and several species, including our own, have been allowed to go unchecked and become diseased—in the truest sense of the word.

This may be a little fanciful but I believe that as well as healing the natural world and restoring its balance, human society could benefit from having wolves roaming the forests once more. We could learn a lot from the loyalty they display to family members, the way they educate and discipline their young, the way they look after their own, and the circumstances in which they use their considerable weaponry to kill. The world is not yet ready for that but I like to think that in some small way my work of the last twenty years might have begun the process.

Whenever I introduced a child to the wolves, it was vital that the child did not become frightened. I had to watch their reaction carefully so that I didn't do more harm with this exercise than good.

This boy didn't speak. His disabilities were clearly mental as well as physical and I guessed he might have been autistic. I could immediately see there would be a problem and asked the father, as tactfully as I could, whether the child would be able to indicate when he no longer wanted to be near the wolf, explaining how important this was. "He won't be able to," said the man, bluntly. "He has never spoken, and never reacted in any way to anything. And he has never expressed an emotion in his life."

Common sense was screaming at me to tell this man to turn around, to take his poor child all the way back to Scotland, but for reasons I can't explain, and a few I can, I agreed to go ahead.

There was a young wolf called Zarnesti in the enclosure that had been handled a lot in his first few months of life and was perfect, therefore, for introducing to children. His mother had stood on him or rolled on him soon after birth, crushing his jaw. As a result he had been hand reared and was not as nervous around humans as most wolves. I loved him; he had the most wonderful character, but he looked a bit like Goofy, the dog in the Mickey Mouse cartoons.

Questioning my sanity, I went into the enclosure and came out carrying Zarnesti. He was then about three months old, the size of a spaniel and a wriggling, struggling bundle of energy. It was all I could do to hold him; he was almost flying out of my arms as I put him down onto the tray on this old-fashioned wheelchair, in front of the boy. I had the pup in a viselike grip, but something miraculous happened. The moment Zarnesti saw the child he became still. He looked into the boy's eyes and they stared at each other. Then the pup settled down with his back legs tucked under him and his front legs stretched out in front. I took one hand off him and I realized very quickly that I could take the other hand away, too. After a few moments, still looking into his eyes, the cub reached forward and started to lick the boy's face. I lunged to intercept him, terrified that Zarnesti would nip the boy's mouth with his needle-sharp teeth, which is what cubs do to adult wolves when they want them to regurgitate food. But Zarnesti didn't nip; he just licked, very gently.

The scene was electrifying. As I looked at the boy I saw one single tear welling up in his right eye, then trickle slowly down his

cheek. Guessing this had never happened before, I turned to his father. This big, strong, capable Scotsman was standing, watching what
was unfolding in front of him, with tears streaming down his face. In
a matter of seconds, the wolf cub had gotten through to this boy in a
way that no human had managed to do in fourteen years.

# CHAPTER ONE

# A Special Relationship

I t was early morning. I had crept out of my bed, as I often did as
a child, and gone out into the barn where the farm dogs slept, to
curl up with them—something to which my kindly grandparents turned a tolerant eye. I was a loner; the dogs were my closest
friends and the nearest I had to siblings. I woke up to find the oldest
of the dogs standing over me, his head facing the door. When I
stirred, he turned to look at me and raised an eyebrow. I could tell
immediately that something was wrong. His mouth was open and
saliva was dripping from his tongue. The younger dogs were lying
curled up by my side, which is where Bess, the oldest, should have
been, too. I could hear a great commotion in the yard outside and
my grandfather was calling my name. I can't have been more than six
or seven years old, but it's a memory that has stayed with me, and although I had no notion of it at the time, it was the beginning of a
very long journey for me.

Bess had bitten one of the farmhands, whose arm was crudely
bandaged with a handkerchief and spots of blood were seeping
through the flimsy material. He was complaining bitterly. He had
come into the barn to collect a chain saw that was on a shelf above my
head, and without warning the dog, who knew him well, had gone for
him. Bess wasn't a vicious dog; he had been on the farm all his life

1

and had never been known to attack before. The man was highly in-
dignant, but my grandfather, a wise and wonderful old man not given
to hysteria, soon managed to calm the situation. He had lived in the
country alongside animals all his life, as his father had before him,
and he knew at once what had happened. My bond with the farm
dogs had become so close that Bess, the oldest and most dominant
dog, had come to regard me as one of the pack, and a young member
at that. When the farmhand burst into the barn, waking Bess and
probably the other dogs, too, Bess thought I was in danger and he
was protecting me in the only way he knew how, the way that his wild
relatives might have protected their young.

My grandfather decided that in the interests of safety it was time
to ban my nighttime excursions to the barn, but he recognized that
the dogs played such an important part in my well-being that I
should be allowed to have one of my own, which could sleep with me
in the house.

The dog of a neighboring farmer had had pups and not long
after this incident, my grandfather took me to choose one from the
litter. We had no car in those days; my grandparents were simple
folk who lived from hand to mouth. A lot of what we ate came from
the wild. We would shoot rabbits, hares, pigeons, and pheasants but
I was always taught to hunt in moderation, to respect nature and
never to take more than we needed or more than the population
could sustain. Whenever I made a kill, I knew to cut the animal open
lengthways to remove the innards and throw them into the
hedgerow for other creatures to scavenge. I had no qualms about
killing or skinning rabbits and hares to prepare them for the pot.
Life and death were all part of the natural world and on the farm we
were very much a part of it.

Although the farmer with the puppies was a neighbor, the defin-
ition of *neighbor* in our world was someone who lived within a day's
walk, and we set off right after an early breakfast, when it was barely

light. It was a cold morning; I could see my breath in the frosty air, and I had on a warm coat and boots. Over my shoulder was a poacher's bag that carried cold tea and thick cheese sandwiches that my grandmother had made for us. I was used to long walks—I often accompanied my grandfather when he went to pay his respects or do business with neighboring farmers—and I used to relish time spent alone with him. There were no other children around the farm for me to play with, no television, no video games or any of the other things that keep children amused these days. We were miles from anywhere; there was just me and my grandparents, the dogs and the farm animals. Occasionally—or so it seemed to me then— my mother would appear, but it was rare and my father was never mentioned.

But I was not unhappy. I adored my grandparents and never thought for a moment that I was missing out. My grandfather and I would take the dogs with us on our walks, and we would never get far before he'd be stopping to point out something of interest. It might be an abandoned nest in the hedgerow—he would tell me all about the birds that had inhabited it, and how many young they would have produced, how far their territory would have extended. He would dissect the nest so I could see the skill with which it had been con-structed. He'd spot a broken bird's egg lying on the ground, and would explain how it might have got there, stolen from the nest by a predator maybe; or he'd pick up an owl's pellet deposited on a wooden gatepost, and pull it apart, exposing the tiny fragments of bone, all that remained of the rodents the great raptor had feasted on during the night.

He might make me close my eyes and tell him what I could hear; I'd thought it was quiet until my eyes were closed and then there would be such a deafening noise—birds singing and chattering, in-sects rubbing their legs, small mammals scurrying, even sheep bleat-ing in the distance or a cow coughing three fields away—so many different sounds and songs. Or we'd investigate a rabbit burrow for signs of activity or identify the prints left by deer and other animals on the muddy tracks. He made every outing an adventure, made every discovery exciting. I loved listening to him talk, hearing him explain, in his rich Norfolk accent, which birds preferred which berries, or why foxes killed more than they could eat or carry away; and sometimes, if I asked, he would talk about himself and about his childhood and how different life had been when he was my age, when there were no modern conveniences like refrigerators, tractors, or electricity; when they'd harvested with scythes and milked the cows by hand.

When we'd reach our destination, he would never take me inside with him. He would leave me to wait with the dogs a little way off while he went to see whomever he had come to visit. Sometimes he would be gone for several hours while he and his friend shared a bottle or two of stout, but I had been taught to wait patiently. It would never have crossed my mind to complain; I adored this man and I never questioned his authority, enjoying nothing more than his approval. Besides, I knew that no matter how long he was gone, he would always come back. He would suddenly appear, saying, "Come on then, boy," and I'd slip my hand into his great rough paw. We'd retrace our steps and find new things to look at and talk about on our way home.

One day we made just such a trip to choose my puppy. My grandfather and the farmer greeted each other warmly, like long-lost friends, and disappeared together into a barn, where mother and pups were kenneled, leaving me alone in the farmyard. "Wait there, boy," he said. "I won't be long." And so without question, despite the excitement and my impatience to see the litter, I found myself a comfortable spot and sat down to wait.

Suddenly I heard the barn door creak as a gust of wind took it, and a large dog escaped through the open gap and came charging toward me, barking ferociously, ears flat against its head. I knew enough to know that this was not a friendly greeting. I sat still, kept my hands by my side, and waited; it didn't occur to me to be frightened. Bess and the farm dogs had often charged at me and however aggressive they sounded in a pack, I always held my ground and once they had sniffed me, they were never anything but friendly. The dog's hackles were raised, her tail was erect, and she was growling as she reached me, her teeth bared. I didn't move. I let her sniff my legs, feet, hands, and head. Soon the growling stopped and I turned my hands over to expose the palms, which smelled of the cheese sandwich I'd eaten during our walk. She licked them and looked up at my face with soft eyes. I started to scratch the long fur under her chin, which she obviously enjoyed because she sat down and leaned her body into mine, allowing me to rub the rest of her silky body.

The barn door creaked again and as my grandfather and the farmer emerged, the dog by my side growled deeply, gave a sharp bark, and charged the two men. I guessed she was the mother of the pups, and from the panic that ensued, I gathered she did not welcome visitors. The farmer shouted angrily at her, "Get in that barn, now!" The dog lowered her body and slunk back toward me. "Keep still, boy," warned the farmer. "Don't move and she won't hurt you." But as he ran over toward me, yelling at the dog to get back to the barn, it was clear he didn't trust the animal an inch. By the time he reached me, the dog had tucked her frightened, shaking body into mine and, ignoring his command to stay still, I had started scratching her again while speaking softly to her.

"Well, bless my soul. Come and have a look at this," said the farmer, cap in his hand as he scratched his head in disbelief. "I've never seen anything like it. No one has ever been able to get near that bitch. The only reason I keep her is because she's so good with the sheep, but she's always been a real liability with strangers."

"Ma always said the boy has some sort of gift with dogs," said my grandfather, still keeping a safe distance. "She'll swear he knows what they say."

Not trusting the dog to remain calm, the farmer shut her up while we went into the barn for me to choose one of the puppies. They were fenced in behind straw bales—five in all, four girls and a boy—curled up in one big bundle of black, brown, and white fur. They were lurchers, a greyhound cross breed, so would be good hunters. I knew I wanted a female; my grandfather had taught me that bitches were far better than dogs at providing for their families, and I wanted this dog to earn her keep.

Tied on the end of a length of bailing twine was a rabbit's foot that the farmer dangled in front of the bundle while he squeaked as an alarmed rabbit might. Immediately the sleeping pups' ears went up and they looked around. When they spotted the foot dangling within their reach, they sprang to life and, sure enough, it was the bitches that were there first, two of them ahead of the others. It was one of those two that I chose to take. I picked her up and held her in my arms, and as my grandfather handed over a couple of large bottles of light ale in payment, I could just hear, over the puppy's frantic licking, the farmer say, "The boy's right, you know. She's the one I'd've picked.

"Away you go, boy," said the farmer with a cheery smile. "Take care of her."

"Don't worry, sir," I said, grinning from ear to ear, the puppy warm and wriggly in my arms. "I'll take care of her."

I named her Whiskey and in the next thirteen years, she scarcely left my side.

# CHAPTER TWO

# A Childhood in Rural Norfolk

The English countryside is not an obvious place for a child to develop a passion for wolves, and it wasn't immediate, but animals have been in my life for as long as I can remember.

One summer's evening my mother came home from work. She had been picking carrots or some other vegetable out of the ground all day and was exhausted. "There's a job waiting for you in there," said my grandfather. "Shaun's been busy again." She opened the door and recoiled in horror. Frogs were hopping, croaking, and climbing over every surface in the room. I had spent my afternoon collecting them from the pond up the road, steadfastly walking back and forth with a bucket, and the room was alive with frogs. And I spent that evening going back and forth with the bucket once again, putting them all back.

Another time she went into the coal shed, after night had fallen, to get some fuel for the fire and screamed as five black chickens started flapping and squawking. I had found them on my travels across the fields—and the very next morning I was dispatched to take them back.

And then there was the time I brought home a Muscovy duck, complete with its nest filled with eggs. My mother was too scared to touch the duck—an ugly brute, she called it—so I carried the duck under my arm while she carried the nest and the eggs back to the pond, where we reinstated the whole lot among the reeds. My poor mother; I was always giving her heart failure, coming home with some creature that I'd find a home for somewhere about the house.

I grew up on the land and I was fascinated by the natural world. There was no money for outings, treats, or toys when I was a child; the hedgerows, fields, and forests were my playground, and the dogs were my companions. I roamed for hours; I explored the thickets for bird nests, I knew when rabbits had young, I watched hares boxing in the springtime, I knew where to look for fox dens and badger setts. I could recognize owls in flight and knew the difference between kestrels and sparrow hawks. I couldn't have crossed a busy London street or found my way around a subway at the age of ten—and to be honest, I still feel uneasy in big cities in my forties—but there was not a lot I didn't know about the wildlife on my doorstep.

My home was north Norfolk, a remote part of a remote county on the most eastern coast of England, famed for its fens, its pheasant shoots, and its flat, fertile farmland. Those who own the land are among the richest in the country; those who work it are some of the poorest. My family was the latter. They were farm laborers and we lived from hand to mouth, a very simple life. We caught what we ate and ate what we caught; and my job as the youngest member of the family—when I was too young for gainful employment—was to catch it, with the dogs we had on the farm. They were my friends, but they were working dogs. Apart from Whiskey, they lived outside in the barn, and I was never allowed to be sentimental about them. In our world, every animal had a purpose. We couldn't afford to feed any creature that didn't earn its keep—and Whiskey was a skillful courser.

Our neighbors lived in the same way. Country folk were caring but not sentimental. When I was about eight, I remember going with my grandfather to visit a gamekeeper friend of his. This man had the most beautiful black Labrador. He was the gamekeeper's pride and joy. His coat glistened and he had the softest mouth; he could pick up an egg or anything else he was asked to retrieve without leaving a mark on it. He was immaculately trained; he seemed to know this man's every thought. One day the man discovered that his two sons had taken the dog ratting in the barn, and all the work and training that he had so patiently done with the dog was lost in less than a morning. The first time the Lab went for a rat, the rat bit him on the muzzle and he was so traumatized he shook from then on. The dog was ruined; so the gamekeeper shot the dog and beat the two boys. He knew that he'd let the dog down, that he'd failed to protect him from his sons, but he couldn't repair the damage and he couldn't afford to keep a dog as a pet. I was horrified; the dog's death seemed so meaningless. But that was the reality of the world in which I grew up.

My grandfather—Gordon Ellis, my mother's father—taught me everything I knew. He was sixty-seven when I was born, but he and my grandmother, Rose, brought me up, and although my mother lived in the cottage with us, it seemed to me as a child that she was never there. As a result, I felt far closer to my grandparents than I ever did to my mother.

The truth, I discovered when I went back to Norfolk very recently, after years of being away, is that she was simply always out earning our keep. She was up and out of the house in the mornings, often before dawn, to work in the fields—long hard days of back-breaking drudgery for very little money. She would be collected by a gangmaster who drove her and the other women of the village to whatever farm had need of labor. Sometimes they might drive for an hour or two to the other side of the county to harvest peas or potatoes or soft fruit, whichever the season dictated, and be delivered home at the end of the day, exhausted. After a meal she would go straight to bed. If she didn't work, she didn't get paid and we struggled. As a single mother, she had no alternative.

I didn't realize as a child just how unremittingly hard her life was; I didn't appreciate what she did for me—and how I wish I had. All I knew was she wasn't there and my grandparents were. My grandfather was my hero. He was gentle, wise, and wonderful, and if he had asked me to walk over hot coals, I would have done it for him without even asking why. He was a thin, wiry man, his face weather-beaten. His hands were gnarled and leathery from decades of hard, manual work, but inside he was a true gentleman and I reveled in every moment spent by his side.

He and my grandmother had had eleven children, six girls and five boys. Most of them had left the village by the time I was born, on October 12, 1964, and I never met them. A few stayed, but apart from one sister, Leenie, who was very close to my mother, I don't remember seeing any of them. I think my arrival, out of wedlock, caused a rift in the family.

The cottage we lived in felt huge to me as a small boy, but in reality it was very modest, with low ceilings that I hit my head on whenever I tried to bounce on my bed. It was a typical tied workman's cottage made of the local red brick, set back from a narrow lane and looking on to a meadow at the back, with dense forest beyond. At night I would lie in bed with the window wide open and listen to the noises of the night—scarcely any of them man-made. There were no major roads or motorways and no railway lines within miles. The only thing that sometimes broke the silence was the noise of jets screaming overhead from one of the many air bases in the county. The air bases are still there, but Norfolk is still, forty years later, one of the least populated counties in England, and is still one of the most inaccessible corners of the country.

In the 1960s, it was like a place that time forgot. While the rest of the country was enjoying postwar prosperity, people in the village of Great Massingham were living as they had lived centuries ago. There were several farms in the locality, most of them mixed: they had dairy herds, sheep, pigs, and beef cattle as well as cereal crops, vegetables, and fruit. The land was broken up at that time into small parcels divided by tall, thick hedges and forestry that kept the worst of the Arctic weather at bay—and provided perfect cover for wildlife. And almost all of the farmers laid down pheasant chicks in the spring and ran shoots during the winter months.

Winters were harsh. The cold blew in from the Urals to the east and the Arctic to the north, bringing huge quantities of snow and ice. The hedges stopped most of the snow from drifting, but at times the roads were completely impassable and the landscape was white for weeks and the ponds in the village turned into skating rinks.

At that time there was very little machinery, although that changed as I grew older. Tractors had already taken over from the heavy shire horses—but it hadn't been so long ago. The old horses from our farm lived in happy retirement in the meadow at the back of our cottage. There were no combine harvesters, no chemicals. The work was done by hand. Each farmer had his own workers, most of them living in simple cottages like ours, on the farms, and during the harvest, gangs of laborers were driven from farm to farm to weed and pick and bale.

My grandfather worked at Ward's farm. Ward was one of the biggest landowners in the village, and my grandfather had had the cottage for as long as he'd had the job. There was no inside sanitation, no hot water and no heating, and the old iron window frames were rusty and ill fitting. The privy was in the garden and I remember Sunday nights were bath nights when the old copper bath tub would be brought into the living room in front of the fire and filled with water heated in a big copper pan that hung over the coals. We took turns bathing, and being the youngest, I was last.

There were people living in our village who had never left it. And they had no reason to. The village was self-sufficient. There was a butcher, where my grandparents traded vegetables from the garden for meat; a baker with delicious fresh bread at any time of the day; a dairy; a shop that sold general provisions; a hairdresser; a primary school; a fire engine; five pubs; and a blacksmith who shod horses and fixed machinery. It was a farming community through and through. And the sort of community in which everyone knew everyone else—and knew everything about everyone else.

There were no tourists in those days, no strangers wandering about the village, except when the circus came. Even the gypsies who came at harvesttime were the same ones who made the journey year after year. And there was no crime. We all left our houses open, and people would come in without knocking and put the kettle on while they were passing through to say hello. It was a genuine community. The worst that might happen was when someone had a chicken go missing and would report it to Phil, the village policeman. He knew everything; he knew exactly where to find the culprit and would pay a quiet visit. The next day two chickens would mysteriously be delivered to the aggrieved party.

Shirley, my mother, had given birth to me at the age of twenty-four, knowing that she would have to bring me up alone and unsupported. At that time and in that sort of tight-knit community, to have a child out of wedlock was extraordinarily brave, but her parents were apparently very supportive. Sadly, I don't know the story; I don't know whether she was in love with someone who was unattainable for some reason. I don't even know whether my father knew I existed. All I know is that she never had or wanted another partner. So I don't know who my father was. Even now, forty-five years later, my mother won't talk about it.

My guess is he was a Romany—not to be confused with the tinkers and travelers who have given gypsies such a bad name over the years. The gypsies we knew were wonderful people, scrupulously clean and honest, with a very strong sense of family and strict codes of morality. They used to travel about the countryside in their traditional prettily painted wooden wagons, drawn by horses, going wherever there was work. They would pick hops and fruit in Kent and vegetables and soft fruit in Norfolk. Occasionally they would graze their horses on the village green, but they had a permanent site on a piece of common land just outside the village, next to an old Roman road called Peddars Way.

Every summer I used to go and play with them. We would go out with the dogs and catch rabbits while the farm workers were combining. They had lots of dogs, big lurchers. One in particular, I remember, was called Scruff; he was crossed with a wolfhound, so huge, and he would chase rabbits until he dropped.

A little farther up the Way was a wagon set on its own that belonged to an old gypsy woman who, it was said, bought illnesses. She was very old and wizened, with long gray hair and gold hoop earrings, and looked like the old-fashioned gypsies you see in picture books. People who were ill used to go to see her. I don't know whether she made them better, but I don't imagine anyone would have dared say if she hadn't because it was said she would put a curse on anyone who spoke ill of her.

I felt very much at home with the gypsies, and although she never said anything, I have a strong feeling that my mother was pleased. I think, in retrospect, that she may have been trying to introduce me to my father's family. It was unusual for village children to mix with gypsies. They were never liked by the village people and were made to feel distinctly unwelcome in the shops and pubs. I knew how it felt to be treated like an outcast.

I was a solitary child. I attended the little primary school in Great Massingham until the age of eleven, but I don't remember many friends from that time although I must have had the odd one because I do remember throwing sticks into the horse chestnut tree in the churchyard to get conkers and being told off by the vicar—and I don't imagine I'd have been doing that alone. But with no father, I think I may have been viewed as a bit of an outcast myself. Maybe I felt I didn't need friends; I had Whiskey and the farm dogs and they were much easier than my peers. Dogs don't pick fights or bully or make unkind remarks.

Not that I had much time for friends. I always had to hurry home after school to chop wood for the fires or bring in coal or feed the animals, and I was often taken out of school for several weeks at a time to help with the harvest or whatever farmwork needed to be done. The school never seemed to mind my absence—I was never going to be top of the class, and I wasn't the only child at the school who was taken out to work on the land at busy times. The teachers seemed to focus on those children who obviously had an academic future and didn't pay too much attention to the rest of us. And so I worked hard at the subjects I enjoyed, which apart from art were animal related—biology and other sciences—and sports. Those were things I really could do and I was in all the teams for soccer and rugby and cricket. I loved anything played with a ball or anything athletic.

I also loved fishing. In the village there were three big ponds we used to fish. One of them dried out one summer and we rescued the fish in buckets and ran to put them into the other ponds before they died. North Norfolk has dozens of little ponds, or "pits," as they were called, often in the middle of fields, with tall trees surrounding them. It was a curious feature of the landscape in that part of the county. There were all sorts of theories about how they came to be there. Some people said they were craters caused by German bombs dropped during the Second World War; others said they were left over from some sort of mineral excavation. Whatever caused them, they were full of fish, such as carp, roach, pike, and bream, and provided hours of entertainment for children like me.

Sometimes we would fish farther afield. One pit we were particularly fond of was in a field by the side of the road about four miles from Great Massingham. It was full of gold-colored fish, but every time we got ourselves set up, the farmer would come running out of the farmyard across the field, shouting angrily and waving a stick at us, and we would leap on our bicycles and race away.

I had a green Chopper, which was just the coolest bike at that time. I think my grandfather must have found it on some rubbish pile. It looked as though it had been run over by a steamroller and was all rusty but he restored it for me, painted it, found it a new seat, and it became my prize possession.

A doctor's surgery was the only facility missing from the village. It was a two-and-a-half-mile walk away, in the village of Harpley, where Dr. Bowden had his practice. It was a route I knew well. I was seldom ill but I was accident prone and often needed to be stitched up after bad falls or being bashed during soccer and rugby games.

I didn't care for doctors much, but dentists I loathed with a passion. I have only been to a dentist once in my life, for a checkup when I was about eleven at a practice in Fakenham, a town about twelve miles away. The dentist said I needed a back tooth removed and although he gave me a local anesthetic, I have never felt pain like it. He had his knee on my chest as he wrestled to pull out that tooth. It was the most horrific experience. I couldn't bear it. I hated the smell, I hated the noise, I hated the injection, and I couldn't stand the pain. I vowed I would never go near a dentist again, and I haven't. On the positive side, it did make me clean my teeth properly and the only teeth I've lost since then have been knocked out by overboisterous wolves.

Hospitals have been less easy to avoid. I fell through a roof in my late teens and broke a wrist, and I went through a car windshield soon after I learned to drive, but my first hospital stay was at the age of nine. I lost my grip on the school climbing frame and fell onto the hard ground beneath, shattering an elbow. I was rushed to the hospital in King's Lynn, where I languished in the children's ward with my arm suspended above my head for three weeks. There was a boy in the next bed who had slipped and fallen under the wheels of a double-decker bus.

I have no memory of my mother's visiting, but she tells me that she gave up work for those three weeks and took the bus early every morning into King's Lynn, which was fifteen miles away, to sit by my bedside until early evening, when she took the bus home again.

One day the sister in charge of the ward came up to her and said, "You've been coming here every day for nearly three weeks and I have never seen you have anything to eat. Today you are going to have some lunch. I have organized it with the kitchen." The sister had rightly surmised that having been off work all that time, with no wage coming in, my mother couldn't afford to feed herself.

But at home we ate well. My grandmother was a good cook. Sundays were her baking days and wonderful smells would waft into the yard. In preparation she would buy eggs to supplement those our chickens laid. One Sunday she couldn't find the eggs she had bought, and after looking all over, she had to abandon her baking. That evening my grandfather came into the house and said, "I've found your eggs, Ma. They're under the chicken at the top of the garden." I had taken them and put them under a broody hen to see if she would hatch them.

My grandmother used to sing as she baked, and I will always remember her wearing a blue floral dress. There was always a big stew or a casserole on the stove, made with vegetables that my grandfather grew in the garden and game of one sort or another that we had shot or coursed on the land. I learned to shoot at a very early age, and could always use a knife. I was never squeamish about killing and could skin and gut.

By the age of eight or nine my job was to bring home our meals. My grandmother would make me coarsely cut cheese sandwiches and some cold tea—we never had hot drinks for some reason—and send me out with a penknife, a piece of string, a ten-pence piece—what that was for I have no idea—and tell me I was equipped to conquer the world. And off I would go with the dogs and not come back until I had plenty for everyone to eat.

I didn't kill indiscriminately. My grandfather had taught me which animals to take and which ones to leave. I knew to leave female rabbits that were nursing their young. From fifty yards, he could spot "milky does," as he called them, by their lack of condition and the absence of fur on their underbellies. He knew they had young underground that would die if their mother was killed. Instead I learned to go for the young bucks that would otherwise overpopulate the area.

My grandfather's whole philosophy was about sustainability and about maintaining a balance in nature. Younger farmers wanted to kill off the rabbits because they were so destructive to the crops, but he wanted to protect them, knowing that if you drastically reduced one species, another would take over. He would say that problems arose only when human beings interfered.

# CHAPTER THREE

# A Wolf at the Window

In bed at night, when I was small and the lights were out, I was convinced I could see a wolf outside my bedroom window. I suppose it must have been the way the branches of a tree fell. As an adult, of course, the idea of a wolf being tall enough to look in through a second-floor window is patently ridiculous, but as a young child, I was convinced. And I was terrified. Every night, to escape, I hid my head under the coarse black blanket that covered me, but then I couldn't resist peeping to see if it had gone, and would scare myself all over again. It was just the wolf's head, ears erect, looking to its left; but by morning, in the daylight, there was no sign of it.

I knew a lot about the wild animals around my home when I was small—probably much more than most children of my age—but I knew nothing about those in the wider world. I didn't see wildlife programs because we had no television, and I didn't visit a zoo until I was in my late teens because there was no money for that kind of thing. So the only knowledge I had of big and dangerous wild animals was from books and fairy stories. And all I knew about wolves was that they were sly, sinister, fierce, and deadly; and the images of the stories my grandmother told me preyed on my imagination. It was a long, long time before I confronted my fear.

Foxes, on the other hand, were familiar and although they also had a fearsome reputation, I was not scared of them. One night I was startled from sleep by the noise of the old shire horses thundering back and forth across the meadow behind the cottage. There was a full moon, as bright as I'd seen. It was almost like daylight outside, so I pulled on some clothes, told Whiskey to stay under my bed, and crept out of the house. I quietly made my way down toward the edge of the forest to see what was agitating the horses.

What I saw was pure magic. By the time I reached them, the horses had begun to settle and playing among their giant hooves was the most beautiful vixen with four young kits. They were so busy leaping on one another and tearing around that they seemed quite unaware of my presence, so I sat down a short distance away and watched their game unfold.

It was the most exciting sight. I had never watched a fox at close quarters before. All I had seen were glimpses of reddish brown from afar or a tail, with its distinctive white tip, disappearing into the hedge as the animal ran for safety when I was out with the dogs. Out there in the dark—in their environment, not mine—I felt as though I were witnessing another world.

I went home and told no one what I'd seen, but the next night I went back and there they were again. I can only assume that their den was just inside the forest and this was their playground. Once again I sat a short distance away and watched, and once again they ignored me, but allowed me to be there. This went on for several months as the kits grew bigger and stronger preparing to take their part in the world.

Every night I went out for my secret rendezvous—it was intoxicating to find myself welcome among creatures that were instinctively so afraid of man. In time, they were playing in a small semicircle in front of where I sat, but although they showed no hint of nervousness, they never seemed to pay me any attention. Until one night there was a rustling behind me and one of the boldest of the four kits had started to play in the bush behind where I sat. He burst out into the open and raced around me and playfully ambushed one of his siblings. I was no longer an observer; I had become part of their game.

I learned so much about foxes in that time. I watched the vixen bring food for the kits. It is a myth that foxes kill for fun, that they go into a henhouse and kill far more than they can eat. We think that only because they are usually caught in the act and frightened away. If left undetected, the fox will take one hen from the coop, which is all they can carry at a time, and then go back again and again until they have collected everything they killed. They will eat as much as their family needs that day and bury the remainder in the ground, where it keeps. Nothing is wasted. I know because I saw what they did and saw how well this mother looked after her young and taught them how to take care of themselves.

Six months later I saw a sight that filled me with grief and horror. Walking in the woods with the dogs I came across the limp and lifeless body of this boldest fox kit swinging from a tree. It was held by the leg in a crude trap, having died a painful and lingering death. The fact that this creature that I had come to know so well over the months, which had been so majestic, so beautiful, so full of energy, could have been deprived of life in this vile and cowardly way made me embarrassed for my species. I felt sick. I was so angry that some ignorant human being had taken this vibrant young life for no better reason than because he could.

Native Americans would say that that was the moment when my fate was sealed. They say that you sign nature's unwritten contract to work with animals at a very young age as a result of some experience, either good or bad, that happens in early childhood. Looking back, there is no doubt that the shock of seeing that magnificent young fox—my friend—hanging from that tree left me with a feeling of revulsion for my own kind and a desire to distance myself from the human race.

My concern for foxes put me at odds with the rest of the community. The farmers hated them because in extremis a fox will take a newborn lamb, and the gamekeepers hated them because they took pheasants. So the local hunt was given a free rein to go wherever the scent took them, and it was a popular sport. The results were sickening.

Many were the times I came across a den where the vixen had gone to ground and the huntsmen had dug her out and gassed and killed the kits. The deadly smell of poison would still be lingering in the air. Sometimes it was a family I had watched for weeks, seeing the kits grow stronger and more adventurous. All of them gone, wiped out, given no chance of escape—all because of a reputation that the fox didn't deserve and a few people's desire for sport.

My gran used to tell a story about how she had been spring cleaning the cottage one day with both the front and back doors open, and a fox ran through the yard and straight in one door, through the house and out of the other. Moments later the entire pack of thirty-odd foxhounds followed. They were like a tidal wave sweeping through, jumping up and over tables and chairs as they followed the scent, and they wrecked the place. She had all her best china out of the cupboard and the whole lot was smashed. Shortly afterward the huntsmen came past on their horses, all dressed up in their pink coats, and when she asked what they were going to do about it, they simply doffed their hats and galloped off.

No one would listen to me when I tried to protest that foxhunting was cruel. And as a young boy it was hard to argue with my elders without being disrespectful, but it seemed to me that if you didn't want foxes to get into your henhouse, then you needed to build an enclosure that was foxproof. It seemed totally unjust to set foxhounds to kill foxes because human beings were too lazy to take proper care of their chickens. Whenever I tried to speak to anyone about it, I was told to mind my manners, what did I know? I was just a child.

It was years before I was vindicated and foxhunting was banned in England and Wales. During the debate that raged beforehand, I was involved in researching the effects hunting had on the fox. The prohunting lobby said that they only caught old and sick animals, but that was simply not true. I examined foxes that had been caught and among them were carcasses of eighteen-month-old foxes—animals in the prime of life—too young to know how to save themselves.

Another myth was that the lead dog brought down the fox and it was all over in seconds with a single bite. The truth was they ran the fox to exhaustion until its brain boiled and swelled, its lungs bled, and the fox drowned in its own blood. They were often dead before the hounds even touched them. It was the most horrific death.

But back in the sixties, as a child no one would listen to, I very quickly grew to be deceitful. I went out with the dogs and as long as I came home with a couple of rabbits or pigeons, I could be gone from very early morning until after dark and no one asked any questions. I spent my days studying foxes, sitting for hours and hours watching and waiting; and all the wonderful things I saw and experienced and learned about foxes and their world I kept to myself. I knew that no human could be trusted, that if I told anyone where I had been watching families at play, they would go straight to the den and kill every creature inside it. Without knowing it, I became what the Native Americans call a keeper of the wild.

It was the beginning of a bad time for me. My world that had seemed so safe and secure, so happy and so loving, began to fall apart. I came home from school one day to discover that my grandfather had had a stroke that left him paralyzed down one side. I had not prepared myself in any way; it had never crossed my mind that he might ever be anything other than fit and strong, teaching me about the lore of the countryside and making the decisions for the family. I couldn't imagine him any other way and didn't want him any other way. But suddenly he looked old and frail and could no longer do all the things we used to do together. His mind seemed to have gone. Sometimes he remembered who I was; sometimes he seemed to have forgotten. And where once I had depended on him, he now depended upon others.

It wasn't long before he had a second, massive stroke and died where he lay on the settee at home. My gran covered him with a jacket and sat with him, refusing to move, until the undertakers came to take him away. They must have been married for more than sixty years and had been so close and loved each other so dearly that I think his death broke her heart. They'd gone everywhere together, done everything together, and I had never once heard them argue or say a cross word to each other. If Gran went down to the shops, he would always go to meet her and they'd walk home together or he'd take his bicycle.

I remember them laughing. On washday she would always take the wet sheets up to the garden to squeeze them in the mangle. She would put them in and my grandfather would turn the handle and one day he said something to her that made her laugh so much she couldn't get the sheets into the rollers.

I was just thirteen when he died. He was eighty and had lived and worked in Great Massingham all his life. He had been a popular man, and St. Mary's Church, where the funeral was held, was packed, but among the familiar faces was a family of strangers sitting at the back. When the service was over, they came up to my grandmother and the stranger explained why they had come. He said that many, many years earlier he and his sister, as children, had been hungry, starving, and my grandfather had taken a loaf of bread for each of them from the back of the baker's cart and told them to stuff it inside their jackets. The man no longer lived in the area but said he had never forgotten the kindness and had wanted to come and pay his last respects.

My grandfather was buried in the churchyard under the shade of the horse chestnut tree where I used to collect conkers.

His death changed everything. We had to leave the cottage because it was tied to my grandfather's job, and for some reason that was never explained, we split up as a family. My grandmother, whom I looked upon as a mother, went to live on her own in a council house on Jubilee Terrace, where she was near her oldest son and his family, and my mother and I went to a tiny new bungalow, owned by the council in Summerwood Estate at the end of a cul-de-sac. I was miserable and angry, and I was grief stricken. I felt as though I had lost everything. My mother had never been the one who cared for me or cooked for me; she hadn't been the one who spent time with me, who'd taken me for walks, or who'd taught me what I needed to get through life. It had been my grandparents and they were both gone. I didn't want to be with my mother and I blamed my grandfather for dying and leaving me when I needed him most. I was terrified; I didn't know how I was going to cope without him.

It was only when I went back, at the age of forty-four, and looked at the headstone on my grandfather's grave that I discovered my grandmother had lived for another thirteen years after his death. I thought she had died within months of him. I have no memory of seeing her again after we moved. All I remember was the need to get away from anything that reminded me of what I'd lost.

I must have been very difficult for my mother. I took out my anger and my grief on her. I was at a secondary school in Litcham by then, which was about seven miles from Great Massingham, and she was out at work every day, working long hours as usual. I became very independent and shut her out of my life. I traveled back and forth on the school bus, which was a big blue double-decker run by Carter's of Litcham. It was the oldest bus in the company's fleet and the only double-decker. The kids from all the other villages came on single-deckers, and whenever there was snow, which could be five feet deep or more, there was just one bus that managed to struggle through, bypassing stranded cars and lorries along the way. To our annoyance, it was ours.

I seldom saw my mother. When I came home from school and on weekends, if there was work going, I went harvesting, baling, driving tractors, plucking turkeys, castrating pigs, helping cows give birth—anything and everything. And if there was no work, I would go off with Whiskey, my dog. I would go off for days sometimes, sleeping in barns, not thinking about how worried my mother might be. I became a bit of a recluse, a bit feral, wandering in the woods, being at one with the wildlife in a world where, increasingly, I felt I belonged—the only place where I was able to cry.

# CHAPTER FOUR

# A Misspent Youth

A part from playing on the school sports teams, which I loved, my time at Litcham Secondary School was undistinguished. I had friends, but my best friend died of an asthma attack. I remember the headmaster calling the whole class together one morning and breaking the news. I felt at that moment as though I were destined to lose everything.

I was a regular visitor to the headmaster's office, so it was unsurprising that I left with no qualifications at the earliest moment I legally could, when I was barely sixteen. I needed to get out and earn a living and I wanted to get away from home. I was still angry and hurting and wanting to forget. So rather than look for jobs on the land, I joined a roofing company called Western and Bolton Roofing. It was hard work, carrying tiles and running up and down ladders all day, but it made me strong and fit and it took me to building sites all over the county. Sometimes we would be on a job for weeks if not months and I'd stay in a bed-and-breakfast or in hostels, only going back at weekends, and then I wouldn't necessarily go home but often would stay with friends.

It was through work that I began to make my first friends and develop a social life, which largely revolved around pubs. There were a lot of good pubs in the area and once every three months, on a Saturday night, there was a disco in the little community center in Fakenham. It was *the* place to go. All the top DJs in Norfolk played there and people came from miles around to hear them. There was great music, drink, pretty girls that we'd take outside and kiss against the wall, and plenty of fights—all the good things in life. Then we'd make our way haphazardly home.

I remember one night the fog was so thick you could scarcely see your hand in front of your face and one of my mates said he knew the road so well, he could do it blindfolded. We all followed him on our little 150 cc motorbikes—I was on the back of one, as I usually was—and he missed a bend. He drove straight into a deep ditch and we all followed him into it one after another, no one noticing until we were up to our axles in water.

Fakenham was the fashion capital of Norfolk. On disco days, we would go into town in the morning and buy all the gear we needed, have a few pints, go home, play soccer for a couple of hours, change into the new clothes, go back to Fakenham, have some fish and chips in the early evening, then move on to The Crown for some beers, then to the Rampant Horse, which was as rough as hell—anytime you wanted a fight, you'd go there—before hitting the disco later.

One of my best friends was a tiler named Benny Elson, who lived in Weasenham, a neighboring village, and through him I met my first girlfriend, Michelle Pearce. Benny was older than I was, as most of the guys I worked with were, and Michelle was his wife Jac's niece. She was visiting their house one day when he and I were getting ready to go out and asked who I was.

I started frequenting the Fox and Hounds in Weasenham, where she lived, and she would come in after school and hide behind the bar, and Skiffy, the landlord, would signal to me and we'd go off into the woods together and sit and talk for hours. We wrote each other little notes and I used to walk her dogs for her. She said all the things I needed to hear, and life didn't get much better. Her father was one of the Queen's pigeon keepers—I built him a pigeon loft in their garden—and I remember arriving at their house one day to collect Michelle and finding everyone in a state of great excitement because the Queen had just been to visit.

I fell madly in love with her, but she was too pretty for me and in the end she left me for someone else and broke my heart. We were both very young, but there was definitely something there and I often wonder how things might have been if I'd pushed a little harder or been less of a prat.

Skiffy's real name was Freddy Scarf and he was a character. He didn't turn a hair when I celebrated my eighteenth birthday in the pub—after years of illegal underage drinking—but then he had been regularly paying me in beer for the game he had on the menu that I and a couple of mates had brought in through the back door in sacks! I had been taught to poach by Pete, someone I knew from working on the land. He was married with a family—I never really knew much about him except that he was an expert on pheasants and how to get them illegally, which he had learned from his grandfather.

Pete had a brother and the three of us used to go out with an old 4-10 double-barreled shotgun, a genuine poacher's gun that broke apart so you could conceal it. It had been handed down in his family from one generation to another. It went off with a terrible crack and smoked like mad, so the safest night of the year to fire it was November 5, Bonfire Night, when everyone was setting off fireworks.

Pete tried to make a silencer for the gun but the first attempt, out of copper pipe and baffling, was too heavy to lift. The modified version was much more successful until one day Pete was shooting a bird directly above him. The silencer must have become misaligned as we climbed through a hedge and ended up right in the line of fire. So when Pete pulled the trigger, flames shot out of the barrel and the burning silencer shot into the air and came straight down on his fore-· head, almost knocking him out.

It was dangerous business—and not just because of flying silencers. If we had been caught, we could have gone to prison—and we came close time and time again. One night I felt a massive hand in the small of my back push me down into the hedge. I knew better than to yell. Pete and his brother were lying flat on the ground beside me, facedown, and I lay there not moving a muscle for several minutes. There was not a sound to be heard; then I saw the outline of two pairs of water boots walk past on the track less than five feet from my face—gamekeepers patrolling their patch. My heart was pounding; I was convinced they'd hear it. It must have been four or five minutes before we dared move again. I asked how on earth they had known the gamekeepers were coming. They knew all the tricks; Pete's brother had smelled the gamekeepers' cigarette smoke.

We always tried to avoid the areas where the birds were released because that was where the gamekeepers expected poachers—they put down traps and they patrolled. And Pete taught me never to shoot a white pheasant, although they were obviously easier to see in the dark. Gamekeepers bred them specially, he said, because they were easy to count and if one was missing, they'd know a poacher was in the area and would intensify their patrols.

So we walked for miles across fields, heading for pits, then we'd crawl through the undergrowth to the bottom, which was usually filled with water, and lie there out of sight. You could look up through the trees above you, where roosting pheasants were perfectly silhouetted against the sky and shoot them straight off the branches. As the youngest, it was my job to pick them up from wherever they fell, which was usually in the water, and put them into the bag. Pete did the shooting and his brother held the torch and did the spotting.

I was enjoying my new life, but there was always something missing. I was one of the lads and I liked getting dressed up to go out and having a good time—they used to say I looked like George Michael in my white jeans—but I never lost the need to go off on my own with the dog and roam the countryside, watching foxes, spotting birds, looking for signs of other wildlife. There was always a part of me that remained separate from my mates.

One day I took the bus and went to visit the local zoo, just outside Thetford. I saw animals I had never seen before. I was so excited I felt like a child—and then I came to the wolf enclosure, and standing less than ten feet away were the creatures that had filled me with such terror night after night.

There was one in particular, a beautiful creamy-colored male with lovely golden-yellow eyes that immediately locked onto mine. We stared at each other, and in those few seconds I felt that he touched my soul. I felt as though this magnificent creature understood everything about me, knew my secrets, could read my deepest thoughts and fears, and could see all the hurt and pain. I felt he had the power to heal those wounds and make me whole again. It was an extraordinary connection and I knew that what I was looking for in life was right there in front of me.

He probably looked at every member of the public in that way in the hope that they might throw him a piece of food, but I don't imagine that everyone would have felt what I felt, or have seen what I saw. Maybe it was all those years spent with dogs and with foxes, living with one foot in their world, always being slightly at odds with the human world. Or maybe it was something deeper. Whatever it was, it was the beginning of a lifelong contract. I knew that everything I had been told about this creature was a lie and that he and I had a lot in common and were both living out of our time.

I felt I needed to get back to the land, so I gave up the roofing business and applied for a part-time job as a gamekeeper's assistant on an estate that ran a big commercial shoot. It was good to be back among the hedgerows, but the work flew in the face of everything my grandfather had taught me. He had ingrained in me that you kill to eat; you don't kill for fun. On this estate, so many birds were laid down, you could scarcely put your foot on the ground without treading on a chick; and when it came to the shoots, there was no skill involved—it was slaughter. It was harder *not* to hit a bird than to hit one. They didn't want to fly; you had to throw them in the air to get them to go anywhere.

I stuck it out for about sixteen months, but when I heard on the grapevine that Morton's farm estate, a much smaller enterprise, was looking for an assistant gamekeeper, I went there. It was one of the farms in the village where I'd worked many times over the years, and the job came with a little one-room cottage, which was perfect. Monty, the head gamekeeper, was a craftsman of the old school, and I knew I would learn a lot from him. He trained me and was very good to me; he put a lot of trust in me, which to my shame I abused. But I was in the wrong job.

He wanted me to kill the foxes to stop them taking the young birds. Instead, I killed pheasants and the rabbits and fed them to the foxes. There was a particular vixen I had watched over for months. She had built a den on the tree line where she raised a litter, and I watched her move the entire litter to another den she built on another tree line in a different field, across a road about five hundred yards away. For some reason she must have decided they were no longer safe at the first site, and so carried them one by one, holding them by the scruff of the neck in her mouth, across the fields under cover of darkness.

It was four months before I was caught. Monty found the evidence one day and confronted me. I felt I had let him down badly. When I told the story to Pete, my poacher friend, he said, "You can't run with the fox and hunt with the hounds." He was right, and the episode did nothing to improve my popularity among the locals. To them, foxes were vermin and I was despised for my views.

I was out of a job and a house, but very quickly found work in the

building trade again and rented a little cottage in the village, which I
moved into with Sue, a girl I'd been seeing for some time. I don't
think it was a passionate love affair for either of us, but we got on well
for a while and we married, without a great deal of ceremony, and
had a little girl together, Gemma.

During that time I started studying foxes in earnest. I knew I
wanted to work with animals, not bricks and tiles, but I couldn't see
how I was going to do it, and the laboring jobs paid the rent. So I
read books and went into the forest at night and on weekends.

One evening there was a knock at the door and I discovered that
not everyone in the village was against me. A woman stood there with
a young fox kit hidden under her coat that she presented to me. The
kit couldn't have been more than two weeks old and she had found
him starving, cold, and close to death. His mother had presumably
been killed. I told her I would keep him until he was old enough to
fend for himself and then release him into the wild.

I named him Barney and made a little den for him in the barn out
of a large drainage pipe lined with straw and set about teaching him
what I'd observed vixens teaching their young. When he was old
enough for solid food, I fed him on rats, mice, and rabbits, which I
skinned and minced, making the meat as much like the nourishment
his mother would have regurgitated, and gradually introduced him to
fur and whole animals. I then showed him how to defend his food—I
opened my mouth wide and made a fast *cacking* sound, which is what
I had seen wild foxes do. He picked it up quickly and was soon defending his food from me. I played with him as I had seen so many
kits do with one another: chasing him, rolling him over, and having
mock fights.

Eventually I decided he was ready to be released, but first I spent
several nights out in the woods with him so he could listen to the
sounds and get his bearings before I left him to fend for himself.
When the moment came to release him, I had no idea whether my

training would be of any use to him. He made a dash for the trees, turned for an instant to look back at me, and was gone.

Imagine my joy when I spotted him again many times in the next few years and knew that all those hours as a child spent sitting, listening, watching, and learning had saved this young creature's life.

# CHAPTER FIVE

# For Queen and Country

Looking back, it seems that everything about my early life was preparing me for my future with wolves, though at the time there didn't seem to be the slightest connection. Not long afterward, I was in King's Lynn with three mates. One of them needed some money in a hurry, so we were in a backstreet stealing car radios—not something I am hugely proud of—when someone spotted a couple of policemen heading our way. We ran off into the High Street with two policemen in pursuit, desperately looking for a busy shop to disappear into. It must have been an early closing day because nothing was open except for the army recruitment office, which had a welcoming light inside. We dived in breathless and panting, and announced that we had come to sign up. I don't imagine they had seen so many people all week; they welcomed us with open arms and ushered us swiftly into a back room to see a video about life in the army. Perfect.

We were all impressed by what we saw, and it became my life for the next seven years. We signed up that afternoon, but I was the only one who went the whole way. I had never considered joining the army and, had I not been dodging the police, probably never would have done so, but the more I learned about it, the more it seemed the perfect career for me.

My relationship with Sue was at an end. I was too wild, too angry, too disconnected. I was twenty-two and I wanted to get away from Norfolk; I didn't feel there was anything left for me there. I liked the outdoor life, I enjoyed physical exertion, I had been used to discipline from an early age, and I was good at taking orders without question. These were all qualities I had learned from my grandfather and all were essential components of a successful soldier. In one of the interviews, I was asked why I wanted to join the army and I told them about the car radios. I think they probably thought I was joking.

I was sent for about eight weeks of basic training at the Woolwich Arsenal, where two of the three trainers were from the 29 Commando Regiment of the Royal Artillery. The one in charge was a man named John Morgan, who had been through the Special Forces selection but had been injured in the last lap. He was a strong man, fair and balanced, never ruffled, able to deal with whatever life threw at him, but he was someone you didn't mess with. If I had to name the role models in my life, and the men I've looked up to—heroes in the mold of my grandfather—he would be one of them.

His colleagues were Lugsy Williams, so called because of his big ears, and a very short man named Corbet, known as Ronnie, after the comedian. Corbet was a human dynamo. The man never stopped—I'm sure he did cartwheels and push-ups in his sleep. They used to take turns taking us out on what we called Bergen runs of four, five, or six miles, wearing boots and all the gear, carrying anything up to sixty pounds in a backpack. These were in addition to the normal training and were designed to get our fitness up. It was crippling and I used to pray for John Morgan's turn because he was slow and steady, as I was. The others ran us all into the ground.

I did sufficiently well in my written tests to be given a choice of which service I wanted to join. Having seen photographs of people rappelling out of helicopters and walking through snow and skiing, and having spoken to John Morgan and Lugsy Williams, I opted for the 29 Commando Regiment of the Royal Artillery. It was based at that time at HMS Drake, naval barracks on the south coast about three miles south of Plymouth. The regiment's usual home was in the Royal Citadel, a beautiful seventeenth-century building in the center of Plymouth, with seventy-foot walls designed to fend off the Dutch in the wars of that century. It had provided England's most important defense for the following hundred years, but when I arrived in 1986 the building was being renovated and all 29 personnel had moved to the modern facility (built in the 1880s) down the road.

The 29 Commando was a close support artillery regiment, part of the heavy-weapons division that supported the 3 Commando Brigade of the Royal Marines. In laymen's terms, when the marines took the beaches, we were there to draw fire; but it felt as though we lived in no-man's-land, between two worlds. We weren't quite the navy and we weren't quite army and neither seemed particularly fond of us. We went anywhere and everywhere the marines went, and since 3 Commando specialized in operating in extreme temperatures and conditions—in frozen wastes, jungles, and deserts—those were the places and conditions in which we trained.

The initial training took place at the Commando Training Centre Royal Marines near Lympstone in Devon. It was the toughest thing I had experienced—this from someone who had spent years as a roofer, running up and down ladders carrying stacks of tiles. We didn't stop; we were running or doing push-ups, sit-ups, or pull-ups—strength and stamina training—all day. It made runs with Lugsy and Ronnie feel like child's play.

It was relentless; day after day after day our bodies were pushed to the limit. We had tests sometimes as often as three times a day. We were worn down, exhausted, beyond exhaustion physically and mentally. I would get into a bath at night and feel as though I'd never be able to walk again—tomorrow couldn't come slowly enough. But it was all done with a purpose. As commandos, we needed not only the physical fitness to get through hostile terrain, we also had to have the mental stamina to be able to fight and defend ourselves once we got there. If we weren't up to it, we were no use to the unit.

And when we weren't pushing our bodies to the limit, we were map reading, doing survival training in extreme weather conditions, taking military tactical awareness courses, learning to look after our kit, taking bearings, and preparing to be dropped into an enemy zone at night "by sea, by air and by land"—the force's motto.

During the training we were known as hats, which was short for *crap* hats because we wore undistinguished black berets. The final test to win the coveted green beret was a thirty-mile trek across Dartmoor that had to be completed in eight hours. It was a combination of running and walking in full gear. The dropout rate at this stage was between 40 and 45 percent. It was as tough as anything we had done, but our team came in on time. There was no heroes' fanfare, no ceremony. The instructors were at the finishing point waiting for us, and as we limped in on the verge of collapse, they flung our green berets at us. I can still remember the feel of the material, the excitement of holding it tightly in my hands as we returned to base in the back of an open truck, tired and freezing cold—and the feeling of incredible pride. It was a sense of achievement unlike any I had ever had.

There was no resting on our laurels. That was just the beginning. We were away from base for eight and a half to nine months a year, and the training we were given in that time and the places we went to were phenomenal. I had thought I knew about outdoor living, but being out in the wild in Norfolk was a far cry from the frozen wastes of Norway in midwinter, when it can be minus twenty degrees centigrade. That place will kill you if you don't know how to take care of yourself. I learned all about survival. I learned how to keep myself warm, how to be healthy by eating the sort of food that the body could use rather than food that simply satisfied hunger or was comforting. I learned how and where to cross frozen lakes, and how to use the environment to my advantage. In those conditions it's possible to go from subzero temperatures to plus two degrees by something as simple as digging a hole in the snow for shelter. I learned where and how to make those holes in the quickest time and using a minimum amount of energy.

If we were traveling long distances on foot in those temperatures and that terrain, the leading person would never break trail for very long. He would lead for about five hundred meters, then taper off and go to the back and the next person in line would lead for another five hundred meters and so it would go on. The logic was that forging a path through deep snow is more tiring than following in someone else's footprints, and on the presumption we would have to fight once we had arrived at our destination, every soldier needed to be as fit as the next.

I always used to wonder how people discovered this, but it wasn't until I was out on the mountains with wild wolves in central Idaho years later that I noticed they used exactly the same technique in snow. After a while the leader would break off and join the back of the line, ensuring that when they came to make the kill, every animal had conserved enough energy to be effective. My guess is that the Inuit, the indigenous people of North America and Greenland, learned from the wolves, and passed on their techniques to our specialized troops when they arrived to train in those areas.

There was nothing I learned during my time in the army that wasn't invaluable in my work with wolves, and many of the survival techniques the wolves also used. In combat I was taught to go for the element of surprise, to fight the enemy in a *known* environment, where the odds for keeping control are in *my* favor. One person alone against twelve on enemy turf doesn't stand a chance, but by taking on those twelve in a familiar environment, the chances of survival go up considerably.

Wolves, I discovered, do exactly that. They will always make sure they change the environment to bring the odds into their favor before taking on an opponent. I've seen three wolves successfully take on a seven-hundred- to eight-hundred-pound bear and remain in control throughout just by waiting until it was pitch dark for the final assault. Being nocturnal animals, the wolves could still see clearly, but the bear, which is fundamentally a daytime creature, was at a disadvantage.

My unit didn't go to Afghanistan or Iraq; the only active duty we did was in Northern Ireland, but we did a number of "hearts and minds" tours with the United Nations. I remember in particular being in Cyprus, where the UN was maintaining a buffer zone between the Greek and Turkish parts of the island. I went to the Turkish side one day to deliver food. I was the driver and I had a mate with me, but once we arrived, we were redundant. Local henchmen stepped in and started handing out the food—and violence if there was any trouble. I felt cynical about the whole exercise; it seemed to me that all we were doing was helping the rich get richer and the poor get poorer.

As I was standing around waiting, I noticed an old lady struggling to wheel a wooden cart down a cobbled alleyway toward the lorry. She had a lined and weathered face and was dressed in black, as so many of the women were. The henchmen didn't seem to be paying her any attention, so I quietly loaded her cart with food and while she followed, muttering, I pushed it back up the hill to her cottage, which must have been six or seven hundred meters away. I didn't speak a word of Turkish and she didn't speak a word of English, but when we reached her door, she thanked me by holding my hand in hers. Then she did the most incredible thing: She reached into the cart and took out a precious apple, which she insisted I take. I tried to explain that I didn't need it, that I had plenty of food, but she wouldn't hear of it. I was so moved; this old woman had nothing and I had three square meals a day. Her generosity of spirit was humbling. Her culture and upbringing made it impossible for her not to repay an act of kindness, and much as I admire the billionaires who give millions to charity, there's nothing quite like the gesture of someone giving away a piece of fruit that could mean the difference between life and death to her.

There were many reasons why I loved the Forces, and moments like that were certainly among them. Having been a solitary child, I also enjoyed the sense of camaraderie. I loved the outdoor Action Man lifestyle and I believed in everything the military stood for. It suited me down to the ground. I felt secure in the routine and discipline. I felt a sense of family among my colleagues in the ranks. I imagined I would be there for a very long stint. I even tried to get into the notoriously difficult Special Air Service (SAS) and the Special Boat Service (SBS).

Normally you could only apply for the SAS if you were in the army, and the SBS if you were in the navy, but the government had begun a trial to allow crossover. I volunteered to take part in the trial. The SBS training was tough but then I went up to Wales for the SAS training and that was carnage. I got through the first stage, but I didn't get to Hereford, where the unit is based. It was disappointing, but I was comforted to have made it past the first day. Out of 150 people who started, 40 had fallen by the wayside before nightfall. Their exhausted bodies were lying over the Brecon Beacons like sheep dung.

I obviously wasn't destined to join the Special Forces but it turned out that I was not destined to make a long-term career of the army either. Instead, it proved to be a valuable apprenticeship for the real job I was going to do in life.

# CHAPTER SIX

# Up Close and Personal

Ever since my extraordinary encounter with that big cream-colored wolf in the zoo near Thetford, I had wanted to see and know more about these creatures that had so preyed on my imagination as a child. I began reading natural history books, and a lot of what I had learned about foxes from years of watching them seemed applicable to what I was reading about wolves. Foxes were being cruelly and systematically persecuted because of a reputation I knew they didn't deserve; mankind had gone one further with wolves and exterminated them from most parts of the world. I began to wonder whether all the negative stories I had heard about wolves as I was growing up were any more reliable than the falsehoods I had been told about their small, red cousins.

Wolves used to be everywhere. Once upon a time they were second only to humans in the breadth of their distribution across the globe, and when humans were hunter-gatherers, they hunted the same prey as wolves and successfully lived alongside each other, to mutual benefit. They were respected as powerful fellow hunters and given mystical and magical properties. Native North Americans still believe that the spirits of their ancestors live on in the guise of wolves. They won't sign a treaty unless a wolf, or these days a dog, is present. There were countless legends through the centuries about wolves suckling human children. Romulus and Remus, the twins who founded Rome, were supposedly rescued and nursed by a she-wolf who found them in a basket floating down the river Tiber.

But when man evolved from hunter-gatherer to farmer and wolves started preying on his livestock, the wolf swiftly turned from hero to villain. They were demonized, persecuted, and hunted, in many places to extinction. Despite being endangered, they are still hunted in some parts of the world and still widely feared as savage creatures that hunt by the light of the moon, snatch babies from cradles, and tear Russian peasants from the backs of sleighs.

I had felt such intense and curious empathy with that wolf in the zoo that on the basis of nothing more than instinct, and a habit of identifying with the underdog, I felt an overwhelming need to find out the truth and do whatever I could to help and stand up for these creatures.

It quickly became an obsession. I discovered the Dartmoor Wildlife Park near Plymouth in the village of Sparkwell, which had a pack of wolves, and at the first opportunity I made my way there and got chatting with the keepers. I went there repeatedly on any free days I had from the regiment, and offered to lend a hand at times when they were short staffed. I came to know the owner of the park, Ellis Daw, who lived in an imposing house in its midst, and was soon volunteering to work over Christmas and during other holiday periods when the regular keepers wanted time off. There was a flat in one wing of the house that the keepers lived in and I was able to stay there. Whenever we had leave, and my friends and colleagues went off home to see their families, I went to Sparkwell. I didn't go back to Norfolk for more than ten years. I felt the wolves were my family.

The park was on a hillside, about thirty acres in all, backing on to Dartmoor National Park. The wolf enclosure was at the top of the hill, running alongside the perimeter fence. It was a small enclosure, not much more than an acre for six wolves, and was fenced with heavy-duty six-foot-high link wire with a double gate to prevent a wolf accidentally escaping when the keepers came and went. Although the area was small, it was quite heavily wooded, and there was a bank toward the back under the shade of the densest trees where the wolves had dug an underground den. Otherwise there was a low rectangular hut by the gate that looked like an air-raid shelter and another smaller structure with a flat roof that the wolves seemed to enjoy lying on during the day. The keepers took carcasses to the animals every few days. Otherwise, their only human contact was when one of the animals needed veterinary attention. The keepers certainly didn't make a habit of being on the wrong side of the wire for any length of time and no one ever went near the wolves at night. The park closed before dusk and the keepers all went off duty.

It was common practice for everyone going into the enclosure to be armed with a broom handle. It was routine with all of the big predators in case anything went wrong, but the wolves were never threatening. On the contrary, they seemed to feel threatened by us. They panicked when anyone went near them; they tore off to the far end of the enclosure or disappeared underground and only came to their food when we were well away. These didn't look to me like vicious creatures that would attack as soon as look at you.

Curiosity soon got the better of me. I wanted to get close to those animals and to know more about them and so I started sitting quietly inside the enclosure. I sat there for hour after hour, for several weeks, hoping that the wolves might start to take an interest, as the foxes had done, and come and investigate me. They didn't. Then I realized what I was doing wrong. I was invading their territory in daylight, when *I* felt comfortable. What would happen, I wondered, if I switched the odds and approached them, as I had the foxes, at night when they had the upper hand? Might I then get a truer understanding of what those creatures were really about? I applied the psychology I had learned in the army in reverse. I wanted the wolves to feel

that *they* had the advantage and I did not. My colleagues had been astonished by my desire to sit in the enclosure during the day and when
I told them that I wanted to go in at night, they thought I was certifi-
able. But to his credit, Ellis Daw, the owner, whom I had come to
know quite well by then, let me experiment.

Even now I have no idea what I wanted from those wolves or why
I felt so compelled to get to know them in that way. Maybe it was a
voyage of self-discovery, to lay the ghosts of my childhood to rest.
Maybe it was because they reminded me of the dogs I had grown up
with and I was hoping that I would find some of the comfort and security with the wolves that I had felt with the dogs—and not experienced fully since my grandfather died. Or maybe I was just plain
nuts. What I do know is that it upset me that those beautiful creatures found contact with humans so stressful, and I hoped that if they
got to know me, I might in some way be able to make their lives in
captivity a little better.

One night, when there was a new moon in the sky, I put on an old
tracksuit and, taking my courage in both hands, went into the enclosure and locked the doors behind me. I was terrified, absolutely terrified; to the best of my knowledge, no one had ever done this
before—and there had been plenty of accidents with captive wolves.
There was no way of knowing how these wolves might react, whether
they would hide away or tear me to pieces. But I had to know. Enveloped by darkness and stumbling over fallen branches and protruding tree roots, I made my way to the bank at the top and sat down to
wait for I wasn't sure what. It was hard to see and the night was full of
strange noises as the nocturnal animals in the park limbered up. But I
soon began to relax. The wolves remained hidden in the shadows and
gave me no cause for concern. I began to feel comforted by the darkness. As a child I had loved the dark and the noises of the forest; they
had made me feel safe as I lay in my bed under the coarse black blanket in Norfolk, and they began to make me feel safe here, too.

Every night for a week and a half I went into the enclosure. I wore the same clothes, knowing the importance of scent from my experience of the wild, although I didn't know at that time that diet was also important. I was eating normal human food, but as I learned more, I discovered that I had to change. For the first three nights I sat in the same spot; although the wolves kept their distance, I could see that they were beginning to be a little curious. The next night I got up and moved to another part of the enclosure during the night. They immediately scattered, as though frightened, but I could see that a couple of the wolves went over to where I had been sitting to investigate my smell and to urinate, or scent, over it. They then re-settled a safe distance away, but I was aware that they were watching me. That went on for a few more nights. They were interested but they just didn't have the courage to come up and face me.

The next night one of the wolves, Reuben, which I now know to have been the beta animal, walked boldly up to me and started to sniff me all over and sniff the air. He didn't touch—he was just checking me out; and he did this for a couple of nights. The next night I was sitting up on the bank at the highest point in the enclosure with my legs out in front of me, knees in the air. The same wolf came over to me and did exactly what he had done the previous two nights: sniffed me, sniffed the air, sniffed down my legs, and then suddenly without warning he lunged forward and in a split second his incisors had taken a hard, very painful nip out of the fleshy bit of my knee.

I sat frozen to the spot. I didn't know what to do. If I got up and ran, would he run after me with the pack and bring me down? If I lashed out at him, would I make him more aggressive? So out of sheer ignorance, I sat there thinking, Christ, this is it, game over.

But he backed off, and stood looking at me quizzically as if gauging my reaction. Then he turned and disappeared into the darkness and I didn't see him again until the following night, when he came and did exactly the same thing. He repeated the behavior every night

for about two weeks, by which time my knees were black-and-blue.
He might bite a different knee or nip my shin, but it was always the
same procedure; he would come close, sniff, then lash out and disappear into the night. Sometimes he did it two or three times a night.

I had no idea what he was doing, but I knew that he couldn't have
meant me any real harm because he never followed it up with any
sign of aggression and he never called over another wolf to join
him—and with jaws that are capable of exerting fifteen hundred
pounds of pressure per square inch, he could have had my kneecap
off in seconds. But he chose not to and that's what kept me going
back for more. All I had to show for his assaults were thin lines of
bruising on my knees and legs, like little wolf love bites. I didn't react
on any of those occasions, which I later discovered is what saved me.

The first thing a wolf will do, I came to realize, is find out
whether a newcomer is trustworthy; the way he does that is by seeing
how the stranger reacts to a bite. The incoming wolf immediately ex-
poses his vulnerable throat area to signify that he has come in peace
and the established wolf will dominate him until he is satisfied there
is no threat. If I had pulled away or screamed, it could have been all
over very quickly.

After two weeks of nips, Reuben started rolling his scent over
me. He started with my feet, rubbing them with the side of his face,
his teeth, the back of his ears, his hackles, and his tail. He then did
the same to my legs, never biting, just rolling on me. If I got up and
moved during this process, he'd nip me, back off, and if I didn't
react—which I didn't—he'd come and start rolling on me again.
What he was doing, I realized, was testing me. That is the beta's role
in the pack: to protect the others and to act like a bouncer at the
door, making sure that no undesirable or threatening individual gets
through. I must have satisfied him that I was acceptable because
after four or five weeks he started bringing other members of the
pack over.

This was the process that happens in the wild when a lone wolf attempts to join an established pack, as I later discovered. The ones that came to meet me were all high ranking and they didn't touch me initially; they just stood behind Reuben and watched and sniffed, as he moved slowly around my body, nipping. He nipped the back of my head, not quite as roughly as he'd bitten other parts, but enough to produce blood spots that turned into scabs. Once or twice I tried moving back to try to rub against him, but any movement, whether subtle or sudden, got me another nip. He was biting me to keep me in place—and establishing that I could cope with their world, in which nips and bites are an important part of their communication.

I knew scent was important and I discovered that if I put on different clothes or washed or ate different food, the beta male would start nipping me again until he was satisfied that the new smell didn't mean I was going to react differently to his approach or that my mood had changed. The other high-ranking wolves did the same thing, but he didn't involve every wolf in the enclosure. The lower-ranking members of the pack, I was to learn, don't question what the higher-ranking members decide; they are foot soldiers—they have an important job to do, but it is not to think for themselves.

# CHAPTER SEVEN

# A Question of Morality

I felt deeply flattered to have these creatures trust me so much that they were prepared to rub themselves against me, and an incredible sense of achievement to be tolerated in this way. It meant more to me than any human relationship I had established. I found myself looking forward to the end of each day when I could go and be with them again, and I stayed longer and longer during the nights. It was such a privilege to be allowed to sit among this family group and to feel that in some small way I was becoming a part of it. I was beginning to need these creatures that I had been frightened of for so long; I wanted to be with them. But what did they think of me? What did they think I was? They were always curious when I arrived, but what did they think when I left them? Did they miss me? I was attributing human values to them, and human emotions, which I came to realize are not part of their world. I had to learn to turn off my own.

After a while, they started greeting me when I went into the enclosure during the daytime and testing me in the same way as they did at night, a sure sign that they recognized and accepted me. There would be some nips and a bit of interaction that the other keepers began to notice. It felt good to see their reaction, to watch the surprise on their faces and to see them revising their view about these creatures that they fended off with broom handles. Little by little the days and nights merged and I found a week had gone by, and the only times that I had been away from the wolves was when I'd slipped out for some food. I once took a sleeping bag in with me but that was a mistake. The wolves tore it to shreds. They accepted my clothing but nothing else; and the truth was I needed nothing else. When I lay down to sleep, they settled down with me and the warmth of their bodies kept me warm. My excitement at what I had achieved with them was hard to contain.

I never allowed myself to feel complacent, however. I knew that anything could happen and there was no guarantee that because my last interaction had been good, the next one would be also. Every time I went into the enclosure I was full of apprehension, wondering what would happen next. I watched the way they behaved with one another—the way they wrestled and played, and snarled and snapped—and knew that if they started to treat me the same way, I wasn't going to be able to cope. My skin wasn't as tough as theirs. I wasn't covered in thick fur and if they were as rough with me as I'd seen them be with one another, it would not only hurt, but I could sustain serious injuries. Would they recognize that my body was completely different from theirs? Their necks and throats, two of the areas they used most frequently to communicate, were also the best-protected parts of their bodies. My throat was one of the most vulnerable. One bite like the ones I had seen them give their fellow wolves would have been it for me.

But that sense of danger was as appealing as it was appalling. It was like watching a horror movie from behind a pillow, not wanting to see, not wanting to turn it off, and not being able to resist peeping. The excitement and the pleasure I derived from being with the wolves outweighed the danger. I felt comfortable with them; I admired the respectful way they interacted with one another, the hierarchy that obviously governed the pack, the discipline they meted out to members who stepped out of line or pushed in to feed before their elders and betters had eaten. I wasn't able to articulate it at the time, but what I felt most of all was a sense of belonging. Here was a group of some of the most feared and revered creatures on earth, and they had accepted me into that group. I had taken a rigorous entry exam and been tested within an inch of my life, and by a mixture of luck and intuition, I had passed.

But I wasn't allowed to bask in self-satisfaction for long. I went into the enclosure one evening, exhausted after a long day, and fell asleep. I was lying flat out, snoring my head off, and without warning Reuben ran over and bounced onto my chest, landing on all four feet. More than 120 pounds of wolf on your chest is quite a wake-up call. As soon as he'd landed, he bounced off again and stood looking at me quizzically before setting off around the boundary, scent marking. He kept looking back, as if wanting me to follow, and I made the mistake of ignoring him and going back to sleep. What I didn't realize until it was too late was that he was trying to teach me to identify his scent, and it was an important lesson because his job was to look after the alpha pair, which included disciplining around the kill. Any food that had his scent on it was reserved for them.

The alphas are the most important members because they are the decision makers and without them the pack is leaderless. So their survival is paramount. If food is scarce, they will eat first and they may be the only ones who do eat. Other members of the pack will go hungry, even the pups, and starve if necessary. And the rest of the pack knows better than to touch something that has the beta's scent on it. As it was, I learned the hard way.

It was customary for the local shoot to drop off birds during the season and one day they delivered three ducks to the enclosure. At that time I didn't know much about the different foods wolves eat or the value they place on them. During the winter months, when it's cold and there's snow on the ground, fatty, greasy ducks are a valuable food source for the high-ranking animals. The alpha pair took the first two ducks and although I didn't want to eat it, I thought I had better protect my share, so I picked up the third, unaware that the beta wolf had laid an arc of scent around it.

Within a split second I was on the ground. Reuben had come at me from about ten meters away with such force I felt as if I had been hit by a train. The duck went up in the air, and I fell onto my back and lay there, completely winded while he took my face in his jaws and squeezed. He was growling all the while, a deep menacing growl, and saliva was collecting around his lips. I could feel the bones in my cheeks bending under the pressure. It sounded like a handful of dry twigs being crushed. I thought, this is it—no question. He's going to kill me, and I fleetingly wondered what I could do, but I was being pinned to the ground with such force that my options were limited. So I decided to do what he'd already taught me: show him respect and trust, knowing that if he had wanted to kill me, with the amount of weaponry he had, I'd have been dead by now. He was teaching me a lesson. So I tried to tilt my head to display my throat, which I'd been taught was the vulnerable trust area, and as I did so, he moved his grip from my face to my throat, still growling. He held me in a viselike grip for a few seconds longer and then he let go and backed off, still growling, his teeth bared.

If I had read the signs properly, and known what to look for, I would never have taken that duck in the first place. I would have noticed the progression in his behavior to that high-energy snapping and snarling, which should have drawn my attention to his weaponry, as it's designed to do. He was warning me off and I would have seen his ear posture telling me that he was protecting the duck from afar. They would have been flat, going out like airplane wings, to indicate that he was covering something that belonged to him.

It was an experience that changed my entire perspective. I came out of that enclosure wondering just who the monsters on our planet really are. Humans have branded wolves as ruthless killers, but real strength comes in having the weaponry and not using it. How many humans, with that kind of killing power at their disposal, would have had the restraint not to use it?

I had spent seven years in the army being a part of man's brutality to man and becoming increasingly sickened by it. If I had been a religious man, I might have turned to the church for forgiveness for my sins and for the sins of my species, as many army veterans do. Instead I looked to these creatures and I felt what I can only describe as a spiritual bond with them. That wolf in the zoo had looked into my soul and seen the grief that had marked my childhood. These wolves seemed to sense my anguish and my shame and in some way I felt they were the key to my redemption.

There were so many things I loved about the army; it had taken me all over the world. I loved the challenges, loved being part of a crack team. It was exciting to be in control of heavy weaponry, but modern warfare is so removed from reality that much of the time I didn't know what I was fighting for. I became more and more disillusioned. I had been brought up to kill for the right reason and to respect the animal I killed and to respect its place in the world. As a soldier I was part of an organization that killed for other reasons and I didn't have an appetite for them.

The final straw for me was in Northern Ireland, where I did several tours of duty. The province was like a war zone. I remember walking down a street one day in uniform and having to defend myself from a group of children, no more than six or seven years old. They were screaming abuse and hurling broken bricks and anything else they could get hold of. I am sure the only reason they were doing it was because they had seen their parents and grandparents do the same, but there was so much hatred in their eyes. Those children should have been at home playing with LEGO, dressing dolls, or watching *Sesame Street*; they should have been anywhere but out there on those streets, because today's bricks will be tomorrow's bombs.

I don't know whether I killed people in Northern Ireland. I fired in the course of battle and people died, but I'll never know whether it was my bullets that killed them, and I don't want to know. It was sickening enough to have been part of it. It was not the right battle to have been fighting and I found that very difficult to cope with. The people who wanted the army there didn't appreciate us, and the people who didn't want us hated us with such passion that all we did was fuel the situation. There had to be a better way and in the end, years later, they found it: they talked.

In the short time I had spent watching wolves I could see a stark difference between their aggression and ours, and I suspect that at one time, hundreds of years ago, there had been very little difference. Wolves have the power to kill and threaten to use that power all the time, but they only use it when they must. They will fight to the death to save their family and to preserve the food sources that will get their family through the winter, and they will be archrivals with other wolf packs, but they also respect their rivals and value them for what they do. We don't value our enemies; in modern warfare, we don't even have to see our enemies—we can kill them at the push of a button and most of us who are engaged in the fighting don't even know why they are our enemies. The killing is pointless and needless—and the morality highly questionable. I had had enough.

# CHAPTER EIGHT

# A Ticket to a New Life

Wolves had got under my skin and my mind was in turmoil. I felt nothing but contempt for my fellow man and nothing but admiration for these creatures that had admitted me into their world. Theirs was the world I wanted to stay in. It was safer than mine, more disciplined, and I had a greater sense of belonging.

So shortly after I left the army I found myself on a plane to America. It was insanity by any standard. I was going to meet a man I had never met, to work on a program for which I was not qualified, in a country where I knew no one, and I had sold every possession I owned to buy the ticket. The man was a Native American I had heard about, a member of the Nez Percé tribe named Levi Holt. He ran the Wolf Education and Research Center on tribal lands near Winchester, in Idaho, with a captive pack designed to teach people about wolves and give tribal members a chance to connect with their culture. He was also managing a controversial reintroduction program of wild wolves into the Rocky Mountains. It was run by a team of highly qualified biologists, and I didn't have so much as an O level in woodworking.

It all began when I saw a documentary on television called *Living with Wolves*, which featured an American couple named Jim and Jamie Dutcher. They spent six years living with a captive pack in Idaho. The film was riveting; this couple had done everything I had done and had drawn all the same conclusions about pack structure, hierarchy, and the importance of family to these creatures. It was as though we had been living parallel lives. After six years their permit to house the animals had expired and they needed to find a new home for the wolves. The Nez Percé tribe had come to their rescue and in particular, Levi Holt.

I had never met Levi, but I had spoken to him on the telephone and told him I would like to go across to Idaho and study. He said that was fine but since it was a scientific program and I had no qualifications, I would have to do an internship so they could be sure I knew how to record data correctly and be able to support the biologists in the field. Then he told me what it would cost and mentioned a figure that audibly took my breath away. It was several thousands of dollars, and Levi picked up my reaction down the line.

"What's the matter?" he asked.

"I've sold everything," I said. "I barely have enough money for the airfare."

"So what are you going to do?"

"I hear you have a captive pack that you use as ambassadors to teach people about wolves. I've worked in wildlife parks with captive wolves and maybe I could help out with them and that would pay my way through the internship."

"There are only so many hours in the day," he said. "How are you going to do it?"

"How about if I work all day and study at night?"

"Hang on a second," he said. "Let me get this right. You want to come over here and work all day and study all night for your internship?"

"Yes."

The phone went dead for what felt like hours while he went away to consult with colleagues.

"Okay," he said. "Buy your ticket, come over, and we'll see what we can do." It wasn't until later that I discovered how much they'd laughed at this mad Brit who was prepared to come over on a wing and a prayer on the promise of nothing but a tent to sleep in, but my idiocy had appealed to them.

A week later I was on the plane, and I admit I was terrified. I didn't know what I had let myself in for. I had sold my car, my trinkets, my knives, most of my equipment and clothes, and had scraped together the money for the fare. If it all went wrong, I had nothing to return to.

I flew into Boise, the capital of Idaho, which lies in the southwest of the state, where I was met by a tall Texan cowboy named Rick who was married to Cathy, a volunteer at the Center with Levi. I was to spend the night with them and the following morning she would drive me up to Winchester. After a very pleasant meal and a comfortable night at their home, Cathy and I, and a friend she took along for company for the return journey, set off at first light for the reservation. Rick stayed behind to look after their young child. It was a drive of about 250 miles, and the slight flurry of snow we left in soon became a more serious storm. We stopped several times along the way to put snow chains on and take them off again when the road was clear, but by the time we hit the Rocky Mountains we were into deep snow and the chains were on permanently. We were now into wolf country—rocky terrain, lodge-pole pine forests, and snow-capped mountains—and most of the traffic on the road was associated with the logging industry: huge lorries driving back and forth moving timber. We were in the car for most of the day and as we drove, Cathy explained the work that was being done at the Center and how the release program worked.

This program had been a political hot potato for many years, ever since the U.S. Fish and Wildlife Service, which was responsible for protecting endangered species, proposed a recovery plan for the wolf in 1980. The wolf was officially classified as endangered in forty-eight states in 1978. The plan was to reintroduce wolves in northwestern Montana, central Idaho, and Yellowstone National Park, but it had been thwarted again and again by legal action, largely by farming communities afraid that wolves roaming wild would kill their livestock. Finally, in 1994, after much argument, the secretary of the interior signed the release plan, which called for state agencies to manage the wolves once they had been released, but all three states declined to cooperate. Finally, the Nez Percé came up with a management program for Idaho, and in January 1995, after fifteen years of debate, fifteen Canadian gray wolves were released into about thirteen million acres of national forest in the Rockies. Two years later they released another twenty and they were doing so well that the biologists were already predicting that it would take no more than seven years before they could be taken off the endangered species list.

We arrived at the Center just as it was getting dark and everyone came out to welcome us. I think they were keen to take a look at the madman who had traveled all the way from England. It was about half an hour's drive out of the town of Winchester up a windy mountain track. The whole area was breathtakingly beautiful, with mountain trails through forests of giant ponderosa pines and Douglas firs. The main attraction was a big lake that brought tourists to the area as well as eagles and fish-eating birds. In summer the lake offered canoeing and water sports and in winter, ice-skating and ice fishing. The population of this little town was less than three hundred people and the facilities amounted to a canteen, a pub, a grocery store, and a gas station, and that was where we went each week to stock up on supplies and to have a shower and launder clothes.

There was no running water in the camp and no electricity;

drinking water had to be carried in and cooking was all done on propane gas appliances. One of the biologists showed me around. The accommodation comprised a cluster of individual tepees, one smaller one that was the toilet, and one larger tent, set apart from the main living quarters, which was the kitchen and canteen, where there was always a big pot of coffee available. It was set apart because bears frequently came out of the forest in search of food, and any food had to be either buried or hung up to try to prevent them from taking it. The tepees were allocated in order of seniority, those at the heart of the camp being the most prestigious. There was one, I noticed, that couldn't have been farther away. It was right on the edge of the forest; it had a hole in the roof, moss growing up the sides of the canvas, and a door that was hanging off. Pity the poor devil who has to live in that one, I thought to myself. And yes, I was that poor devil.

The tepees were semipermanent. Each one had a wooden floor, a wooden platform bed about three feet off the ground, and a little wood-burning stove, which was essential in those temperatures. That night I sat in my tent listening to the wolves that I would meet in the morning, and stoked the fire with logs. I was broke, I had none of the right equipment because I'd had to spend everything I had on airfare, and I had borrowed a friend's sleeping bag that was far too short. I had no pillow and no creature comforts like those that adorned the other tepees, but by the time I put my head down, my nerves had dissolved and I had a very good feeling in the pit of my stomach. I felt that this could be what I had been searching for.

The next morning I was awake before anyone else, too excited and too uncomfortable to sleep. I pulled on my army boots, put on fewer layers than I would have liked, and stepped outside into the cold of first light; it must have been about minus fifteen degrees. I thought that I could compensate for poor-quality clothing by my knowledge of survival, the golden rule for which is to be aware of your body temperature and resist the temptation to put on every garment you have. If you warm up and sweat, everything becomes wet and then icy cold. As the sun started to rise over the Sawtooth Mountains, I could see the full beauty of my surroundings. The snow was two to three feet deep and crisp underfoot and lay heavily on the tops of the trees—the most magnificent trees with huge trunks that rose more than a hundred feet above my head and smelled faintly of vanilla. It was so silent you could have heard a pin drop; I had arrived in paradise.

The wolf enclosure was at the center of the camp, near the visitor center, where members of the public came to see the wolves and learn about them and the history and culture of the Nez Percé. It was one of the main tourist attractions of the area, but also very useful as a way of countering the fear and prejudice that so many people held toward these creatures. They had eleven timber wolves in captivity living in forty-eight acres of forest that was double fenced with a strip between the two fences. It became my job to walk around between the fences in the early morning looking for breaches or for frozen drifts of snow that could bring the ground high enough for the wolves to escape over the top.

After the small enclosure at Sparkwell it was good to see these wolves had so much space to roam, although on subsequent visits I realized that even these wolves could suffer from the behavioral problems I had seen in small enclosures and always attributed to the cramped conditions. On the face of it, these animals had everything that nature intended and yet they began to have difficulty living with one another. It was a valuable lesson that space was not the most important factor. What was missing, I came to realize, was a rival pack. Just as human beings pull together in the face of a common threat or enemy, so do wolves. If life is too easy for them, food is plentiful and there is no immediate danger, they start to turn on one another.

Once back from my dawn patrol I would go into the cooking tent and fill in the log book, noting any unusual findings. Then I'd pour myself a mug of hot black coffee, or if no one else was up, I would brew the first pot of the morning. Coffee was the only thing that was provided. Everyone bought and cooked food individually, but there was coffee ready throughout the day and for the first three weeks, I lived on black coffee and Jujubes, a sugar jelly sweet that I discovered I could buy very cheaply in the grocery store in Winchester. I used to go down there—the walk took about two hours—and buy three pounds at a time, which only cost a few cents, and which saw me through the coming week. They were packed full of sugar, of course, which gave me an instant high followed by a terrible low. It wasn't an ideal diet to be living on when working eighteen-hour days in sub-zero temperatures, but I didn't have enough money for anything else and I knew that it was only a matter of time before I wouldn't even be able to afford the Jujubes.

We were about twelve people in all, most of them the tribe's people. There was a permanent animal manager, a couple of Center managers, two or three biologists, and about five or six students at any one time. They were graduates or people needing to complete course work before graduating, and they stayed for about three months. Academically I was way behind everyone, and I knew I had been given the opportunity of a lifetime. I lived in fear that they would send me packing at any moment and I was desperate to learn as much as I could before that happened. There was so much to learn; and it was an incredible privilege to be among these Native Americans who had lived alongside wolves for centuries and viewed them not as an enemy or a lower life form but as brothers, sisters, and teachers.

Levi Holt was everything I could have hoped for. His age was hard to guess, but he must have been in his fifties and looked like an archetypal Indian chief. His face was creased and lined and framed by jet-black hair that hung in two long plaits down to his waist. He had the air of one who knew everything and gave away nothing. Every now and again for special occasions he would get dressed up in the full tribal costume, but day to day he wore jeans, T-shirts, sweaters, and anoraks like the rest of us. Any romantic illusions I might have nursed about how the Nez Percé would be living on the reservation—based on cowboy films I'd seen—were quickly shattered. There were no painted tepees, Appaloosa horses, loincloths, or buffalo grazing in the background. *We* lived in tepees at the Center, but these were a very poor people and elsewhere on the reservation they were living in desperately poor housing, dressing in cheap American clothes, driving beat-up cars, and scratching a living in any way they could. They were a shadow of their former selves, but they still had great respect for the earth and the rivers—the environment—because they had never lost touch with the elements that sustained them. They drank from the rivers and took their food from the land and the creatures that roamed on it.

I have never met people who, even in extreme adversity, were so ready to laugh. With them, every day begins and ends with a miracle and to be part of that even for a brief period was amazing. They were so connected to their families, their ancestors, and to the natural world around them. They couldn't understand the way the white man has mistreated the earth, poisoning it with intensive farming and crop spraying, polluting rivers, destroying forests, and upsetting the delicate balance of nature. They wanted to own the land so that they could purify it and show future generations how to live on it, with it, and for it. I remember one night in the town we watched a documentary made by a Frenchman in which one of the neighboring farmers was asked whether he thought the Nez Percé should have their tribal lands returned to them. His attitude, which they felt the government shared, was no; the Nez Percé lost the war, they lost the land, they have to live with it.

I asked what could be done, what help anyone could offer, and Levi's brother said, "What we really need is another messiah who would speak up for the Nez Percé. The problem with us is we have too many chiefs and not enough Indians." They all fell about laughing.

One day the elders invited me to a powwow to ask my advice. They were expecting a visit from a young member of Congress. There was an important bill going through the House and they rightly guessed he was hoping to secure support for it from the Nez Percé. It was a great honor to be consulted and after some hesitation I decided to tell them the truth. I told them to be wary, about how these people often promised the earth but didn't deliver and how they spoke in half-truths. They sat around the fire, smoking and warming their hands, nodding from time to time as I spoke, not looking as though they were very much interested in what I had to say. And why should they have listened to me? I went away feeling rather low and dejected, and when the congressman arrived, my fears seemed to be confirmed. They appeared to be taken in by his demeanor, to be sucking up to him; they were feeling his suit and admiring his shoes and patting him on the shoulder. It was like something out of a novel—the poor barefoot savage overwhelmingly impressed by the white man. They invited him to see all the most important areas and introduced him to all the most important people. The icing on the cake was when they gave him a tribal name, which was the biggest honor they can bestow on an outsider. They called him Walking Eagle, which seemed to me to be about as noble as a name could get until I discovered that it meant he was so full of shit he couldn't fly. Far from being taken in, they had seen right through this man and played him at his own game.

They would always complain that we Western people were too serious, that we should look for coyote medicine. The coyote is the trickster, the spirit guide who walks the path of the dead and the living to embarrass us and make us laugh. They told me a story about a white man who came to the reservation once. He was there on a voyage of self-discovery, hoping he might find some answers from the wise Indians to help lift his depression. He was an earnest young man and wore the weight of the world on his shoulders. One of the tribal elders told him he must go off into the forest for three days to find scats, the droppings from deer, bears, mountain lions, coyotes, foxes, and wolves. He returned with a great collection that the elder then said he must mix with water and make into a paste. That took him another two days. It was now day five and in the heat of summer; the smell and the flies were appalling. Next, said the elder, he must inscribe a circle around himself with a stick in the sand and pour the paste he had made into the groove made by the stick. Finally, the elder told him to sit inside the circle for as long as it took for the coyote to come and tell him what to do next. It was several hours before it dawned on the white man just what he'd done. He'd spent three days gathering other people's crap and was sitting right in the middle of it, and he finally realized the irony of his situation. He sat there roaring with laughter, released from the worries of the world.

It would be wrong to say the Nez Percé lived as their ancestors did, because they blatantly didn't, but they hadn't lost all the old ways. The shaman was still an important part of the spiritual well-being of the community as were the sweat lodges where people went several times a week to pray and connect with the Creator and the spirit world and be healed and cleansed of impurities. The shaman led the ceremony, summoning visions of past tribal members or creatures to guide him. No drugs or hallucinogens were used, but the heat was so intense I found it had much the same effect.

These sweat lodges were dome shaped, usually made of willow—the wood of love, which bends but doesn't break—and covered with animal skins and blankets. Inside each one there was a fire pit in which red-hot stones were placed, set slightly off center to represent the heart, which every now and again was sprinkled with herbal water to intensify the heat. It was the dry heat of a sauna, which made you sweat profusely. The lodges were very claustrophobic, not tall enough to stand in, and with eleven or twelve people inside, very cramped. They were supposed to resemble the womb, dark and warm with a small entrance facing either east or west depending upon where you wanted the prayers to be heard. You went into it naked and backward to symbolize reentering the womb, and you might stay in there for five hours or more, talking, offering prayers, and giving thanks to the spirits, the elements, and the sacred powers. When you finally emerged, you were reborn, both physically and spiritually.

It was the most amazing experience. I remember sitting there knowing the tribal elders were talking about important issues and knowing that I should be concentrating but feeling so spaced out I couldn't focus; but it was almost as though the information skipped the usual route and went straight into my long-term memory. That night I would dream about the conversation and wake up the next morning able to remember everything.

# CHAPTER NINE

# *Found Out*

About three weeks after my arrival at the Center I went into the cooking tent for yet another cup of black coffee to insulate me against the cold, and one of the biologists, who was busy cooking, turned to me and said, "Don't you ever eat?"

"Of course I eat," I lied. "I just do it at different times from everyone else." As I turned away, I saw Levi, that all-knowing Indian, standing in the doorway, arms folded, with a look on his face that said, "I hear what you're telling me, but it isn't the truth."

I thought no more about it until I was in the grocery store in Winchester a couple of weeks later buying my supply of Jujubes. As I turned, clutching my three pounds in a brown paper bag, there was Levi again, standing some feet away, arms folded as before, with the same look on his face. "We eat at different times, do we?"

Oh, God, I thought, he's found me out; he's going to put me on the first plane home.

"When you get back up to the camp," he said, "I want to see you in the office."

I had a long climb back up the mountain track—plenty of time to think about my fate—and when I had reached the top, I had come to the conclusion that I would have to hold my hands up and say I was sorry. I would pack my bag and go without any argument, asking for no more than a lift to the local airfield at Lewiston. What awaited me in England would be anyone's guess. But I had had nearly four weeks of the best time of my life and, given that I wasn't qualified and I wasn't paying my way, it was four weeks longer than I'd expected.

Levi stopped me in full flood. "I've had a word with the biologists," he said, "and they like what you're doing around the wolves; they find it very helpful. So I'm going to give you a small wage, but I'm not going to give you the money; I'm going to credit it to the shop, so that every week you can go down to the town and buy yourself some proper food that you can store in the tent and eat like everyone else."

I was so happy. In the time it took him to say those magic words, my fortunes were completely reversed. I had an income, however small; I had somewhere to live, among people I respected, doing work I loved; and I would be able to eat properly again. It was more than I could have hoped for, and I stayed for a further five months. Looking back, I think the fact that I was prepared to struggle and live off jelly beans in order to live and learn alongside these people went a long way to cement my relationship with Levi and the biologists at the Center. I heard them on more than one occasion say to students who arrived clutching every last comfort, "Look at that guy down there. He doesn't have anything; he lives off the bare minimum and he works all day and studies all night." But I was used to hardship; I had been used to sleeping on the barn floor as a child, and if anything, living as I was in Idaho—out of a Bergen day sack with no spare clothes, no pillow, and no furnishings—took me back to those happy days that I had tried so hard in the past to re-create. This felt comfortable; this felt like home.

After I had patrolled the perimeter, checked the fences, and had breakfast, other tasks for the day followed, including collecting wood for the camp stoves, driving out to pick up carcasses from farms or

road kill people had reported for feeding to the captive wolves, looking after the wolves' welfare, preparing tepees for the arrival of new
students, clearing snow from tracks, and doing general maintenance
around the camp. When the visitor center was open, I might have to
take groups on tours of the site and give talks and presentations or
man the shop to sell souvenirs and booklets. Sometimes I would go
out with the biologists monitoring the movement of the wild wolves.
They were electronically tagged so we could find them in that vast
area and study their behavior—and also warn farmers if they seemed
to be heading too close to livestock. We would often camp out on
these trips, and it was always in the dead of night, when the temperatures plummeted, that I wished I had come to Idaho equipped with
the right gear and a warmer pair of socks. The only savior was my
army survival training.

After my daytime duties were over, my nighttime studies began.
The internship covered everything from the welfare and security of
captive wolves to wolf behavior and communication to field biology,
which involved data collection and record keeping. I read books,
studied maps, listened to talks given by tribal elders. I would go and
sit between the two fences or walk around the perimeter, getting to
know the animals inside and listening to the sounds they made,
watching their communication and behavior. I was learning from
everything I smelled, heard, and saw—getting to know the individual
pack members and building up their confidence in me.

The captive wolves had been brought up in a very sociable environment and were well used to humans—they were ambassadors for
their species—so it was no great challenge to go into the enclosure
with them. The biologists did it frequently, albeit during the day, but
they went in, in a dominant role, and that was how they told me to
behave around the wolves. They said I must never interact with
them; I must never look them in the eye, never get my body lower

than theirs; and I should only touch them, if absolutely necessary, in the area around the shoulder and neck. They said that if ever I showed any sign of weakness, the animals would take over.

After my third week in the camp I was going into the enclosure during the day and doing everything the biologists said and demonstrating to them that I could be trusted to be around the animals without causing problems to them or me. But I didn't get the sense that these were wolves at all. They were like the shadows of wolves— too domesticated and bossed around and intimidated by humans. What would happen, I wondered, if I went in with them at night as a low-ranking member—as I had at Sparkwell—and allowed them to behave like real wolves and dominate me?

After six weeks I persuaded the managers to let me experiment, so one night I set the combination lock on the big iron gates at four zeros and let myself into the enclosure. Everyone thought I was crazy; it was unheard of to try to join a wolf pack as a low-ranking member—it was a reversal of everything they believed—but the truth was I wanted the wolves to teach me about their world, not vice versa; I wanted to become one of them, and if I tried to dominate them, that would never happen. The biologists would never have understood that. They studied wolves as an academic exercise and they did it from afar. They watched the animals' behavior through the lenses of high-powered binoculars and presumed to interpret what they saw based on their understanding of human behavior.

From the limited time I had already spent with captive wolves, I knew that things were seldom as they seemed and that if you really wanted to understand wolf behavior, you had to live among them. Only then, if you were able to think like a wolf, would you be able to help prevent wild wolves from going beyond the park boundaries and raiding livestock, which is what everyone, including the biologists, feared one day might happen.

I was nervous, although I didn't let anyone know just how nervous; I had no idea how these wolves would react to me on their territory at their time of the day. I was going against my entire commando training. There were eleven of them, one of me, and my human eyes were useless in the dark; I was at a serious disadvantage. Being in that enclosure that first night was scary, although there were much-scarier moments yet to come. I was stumbling around, falling over rocks and into water, tripping over the snow, not knowing where I was or where the wolves were or how to communicate with these creatures. It was like being set down in the middle of Moscow's Red Square and being surrounded by people who didn't speak a word of English with everyone looking at me expectantly.

But then the panic subsided. The mist cleared for me and I stopped thinking the wolves were going to harm me. The following night I went in again and there was a moon and a thousand twinkling stars. The reflection of the snow made it almost light and I was able to make out trees and paths and move about the enclosure this time without too many bumps or falls. The animals stayed away and I sat and listened to the noises of the night. I could hear a gray owl hooting and a lone coyote and the grunting of a grizzly bear somewhere too close for comfort. But having regularly fallen happily asleep as a child with the noises of the forest, these noises, although different, were strangely comforting.

I went in night after night and the pattern was similar to that I had experienced in the UK. They were curious about me but kept their distance at first, gradually coming closer and finally giving me testing bites. They would mouth my hands and arms and then take themselves off to the back of the enclosure for long periods. Sometimes I'd follow, discovering that the more familiar the paths became, the easier it was to move about in the dark. Memory played a big part not just in my navigation but in theirs, too. If something unfamiliar was added, or a tree fell across a track, they wouldn't always see it; and I definitely wouldn't.

This was a big pack, but they were healthy animals in good condition, and among the eleven there was every rank and no indication that any one of them needed to be dispersed. A pack is only a pack, or a family, because they need one another; they stay together as a matter of need, not choice. If you had wolves in a captive environment where food was scarce, with no rivals threatening their territory, the pack might well reduce to one breeding pair. That pair would be genetically programmed to survive and the rest would be seen as rivals for the limited food supply. They would start picking on the other animals, fighting with them, excluding them from the food, and in a natural environment those animals would disperse and join another pack where they were needed. In captivity they are dependent on their keepers removing them, or they would eventually die.

I had the feeling, as the months went by, that they accepted me as part of the family and were trying to teach me about their world. It was as if they were saying, "If you're going to be around, we'll teach you the different sounds we make, the different smells of our family members, and about the territorial boundary that we lay down every single night that keeps us safe. This is where you sleep, this is where I sleep; if you have any problems, you go to him, you don't come to me; you certainly don't interact with her. I'll tell you when you can come over here. You can approach him whenever you want; you can groom him and you can bite and nip the scabs off his body where he's been play-fighting, but if you come and do that to me, I'm going to let you know very quickly by biting you on the face that you can't do that." The body language they used to articulate these rules gradually became clearer and I started making fewer mistakes, but when I made a mistake, I was disciplined as they disciplined their own.

I would have been happy to stay up there in the mountains with the wolves and the Nez Percé forever, but after about nine months I felt the time had come to tear myself away. I had completed my internship and I needed to earn a living. Levi was paying for my food, but I had no source of income and a seriously depleted bank balance. I had no alternative but to go back to the UK. I was very sad to leave what I firmly thought of as home and the people—and wolves— whom I regarded as family, but I knew I would be back.

I now had a clear vision of what I wanted to do with my life; the wolves had taught me about their world, and I knew how precarious it was. Unless someone could teach the wolves about our world and act as a go-between, their release into the wild would be short-lived. I would be that someone.

# CHAPTER TEN

# Earning a Crust

I arrived at Heathrow Airport and headed straight down to Plymouth to see if I could pick up the pieces of a relationship that had begun just before I went to Idaho. Janet Williams and I had met in a pub while I was in the army. Her friend had been going out with a friend of mine at Plymouth and we had been good mates for several years before we got together as a couple. Almost immediately after getting together, I went off to America, but Jan had been very understanding and it was wonderful to see her again.

From there I went to the Dartmoor Wildlife Park at Sparkwell. I was hoping that Ellis might give me a paid job and give me the opportunity to put some of what I had learned in Idaho to good use with my wolf family there. Ellis seemed pleased to see me and was very interested in what I'd been doing since we last met. It was coming to the end of the season, but he had been short staffed during the summer and needed someone to look after the big carnivores. These included lions and tigers as well as the wolves, and the job came with board and lodging. I had a room in the wing of the house where I'd been before along with the other keepers, and meals were included.

It was a perfect arrangement except that Ellis could never afford to pay any of his keepers during the winter months when there were no visitors. So although I had a roof over my head and I was working with the wolves I loved, I had virtually no spending money. But every cloud has a silver lining and the upside of that was that when the summer came around, I was owed a lot of back pay. Not everyone had a high opinion of Ellis, but he was very good to me and I have a great deal of respect for him; he cared deeply about the animals in his care and despised the bureaucracy that went with owning a wildlife park.

He had had the park since the early sixties and was irritated by the new rules and regulations and the health and safety restrictions that dictated his management methods. His methods were unorthodox, but he'd looked after the animals his way successfully for years. He had an old bison, for example, as mean as hell, that he'd ride into the shed it lived in at night. He wasn't afraid of any animal and was infuriated by any busybody who tried to tell him what to do. Whenever inspectors were due to visit, as they did from time to time, Ellis would have to be kept well out of the way, lest he give them a piece of his mind.

Admire him though I did, his methods of moving the tigers would have made even the most liberal zookeeper's hair stand on end. The tigers had two enclosures, one for the day where they exercised and one for the night, and the two were some three hundred yards apart, across the middle of the zoo, past the monkeys, the wolves, and the raccoons. Now tigers are very fond of food and so the way we moved them from one enclosure to the other was thus: one handler would attach a length of chain to the collar of the tiger and attempt to hold it while another handler ran at full tilt from the night enclosure to the exercise area, carrying a big chunk of meat. The object was to reach the gate to the day enclosure before the tiger so you could shut him safely inside. Meanwhile the handler holding the chain would be bumping along the ground behind the tiger like an amateur water-skier in an effort to slow him down, and his success depended upon his own weight on the end of the chain. If the tiger reached the handler carrying the food before that handler reached the enclosure, it would leap on him—all nine hundred pounds of it—bringing the handler to the ground and sitting on him while consuming the meat. On occasions, I was that handler. Once the tiger had eaten, it had no interest in going into the exercise run when there were so many interesting places to visit in the park, and we would be sunk.

That was bad but when Ellis and his grandson went out and bought a whole lot of used riot shields from the police that he wanted us to hide behind while we moved the tigers, we said enough was enough.

The wolf pack was sadly diminished when I returned. When I had lived with them before, there had been six wolves but they were of much the same age—a common problem with captive packs at that time—and they were reaching the end of their lives. Now there were only three: Zac, an alpha male; Lucky; and Dakota. Dakota was a female on loan and shortly after I arrived, she went back to where she had come from; and Lucky died. I spent the last week and a half of her life with Lucky, trying desperately to keep her alive. She lay with her head on my lap and I dropped tiny amounts of water into her mouth, but in the end she quietly slipped away.

Zac was then on his own and so I moved in with him to keep him company and stayed for about six months until some other wolves were found. By day I did my usual work and went into his enclosure at night and slept there. Every time I went in he would go through the ritual of rubbing himself against my feet and legs and then work his way up to my head, and if I wasn't careful, he would get behind me and nip the back of my head, often drawing blood. He was testing me, demonstrating that if *he* could sneak up behind me and bite the back of my head, then so could an enemy, which meant I was not up to the job of protecting the pack.

Before Dakota left, she starred in a television program made in the park. It was called *Talking with Animals* and presented by Dr. Charlotte Uhlenbroek. As part of the title sequence Charlotte howled, and a wolf, which was Dakota, apparently howled in reply. It was all superimposed, of course, but as her keeper it was my task to get Dakota to perform, but she refused to answer Charlotte's howl. The only thing that would induce her to open her mouth was if a lion roared. So I had to run across to the lion enclosure to stir up the lions and get one to roar so that Dakota would howl. That was my introduction to television.

It was also my introduction to the wolves at Longleat Safari Park that came to play a big part in my life a few years later. It was where the bulk of the program was made. Longleat is the most respected wildlife park in the country and probably the world, and I had been there as a visitor many times, but this was my first visit as a professional. Their wolves were in captivity but far wilder than the wolves at Sparkwell because they didn't come into contact with humans at all. Visitors saw the wolves from their cars, and the keepers largely managed them from vehicles, too. I hoped that one day I would be back.

During that time at Sparkwell I took a few months off in the winter, when the park was quiet, to visit Canada. I had been there once before during my time in the forces, when we were stationed outside Wainwright in Alberta. I had hoped to see coyote during that time but only glimpsed one very briefly. They are notoriously shy. This time I was part of a study to try to map coyote migration routes. There had been attacks on poultry and there were fears that this was because their traditional corridors had been blocked by human expansion. Our task, as volunteers, was to sit out for twelve-night stints in various locations to establish where they were and what routes they were taking. I was there for three months and sat night after night, watching and listening, eager to see this creature that the Native Americans call the trickster. But in three months the only coyotes I saw were three dead ones that had been killed on the road. There wasn't a living specimen to be seen.

But the irony of it was that they had seen me. At the end of one of those fruitless sessions, a Native American took me and the other volunteer with whom I had been on watch around to the other side of the rocky outcrop where we'd spent our cold and fruitless vigil. There in the dirt, not more than fifty feet from where we had been sitting, was a collection of neat little paw prints. Wile E. Coyote and his friends had been watching us all the time—and no doubt they had been laughing their heads off. My friends on the reservation would have enjoyed this story.

This trip to Canada made me nostalgic for Idaho and I felt an overwhelming desire to see my Native American brothers again. I telephoned Levi and asked if I could come over. I knew he wouldn't be able to pay me but that didn't matter. I just needed to be there. Thanks to Ellis's erratic payment system in the winter, when he did finally pay me, I had nearly a year's salary that I hadn't touched. I had also done a few stints as a bouncer here and there at nightclubs in Plymouth, so I had enough for another trip.

This time I flew into Lewiston, the local airfield, so there were no long journeys through the snow. It was fantastic to be back—to the feeling of space, to the big skies, the giant trees of the forests, the lakes, the mountains, and the squeak of hard, deep snow under my boots. I reveled in the smell of the clear, crisp mountain air and the sounds of the creatures that shared this magical wonderland. It was even good to be back in my old and tattered tepee.

Levi seemed delighted to see me although he was always hard to read, but apart from him and a couple of the biologists, there was no one there I recognized. It was a shame because they had always teased me about the English drinking strong beer, so I had brought a bottle of English beer with me. It went down well with the new guys, though, and it wasn't long before I had friends among the new intake. The work was unchanged and I quickly settled back into the old routine. It was a true homecoming to a place where I felt I fitted so completely and could be myself. There was something so special about the Native Americans, and I felt that a part of me had stayed here at the foot of the Sawtooth Mountains while I was back in the UK. It was a joy to sit listening to the elders tell their stories again and to go into the stifling heat of the sweat lodge and sit for hours feeling at perfect peace with the world.

The only real change was in the wolves, the last place I had expected it. They had been so well-balanced when I was last there, but this time there were a lot of niggling fights breaking out over food. The hierarchy had changed and the pack was less disciplined than it had been. I didn't expect them to remember me and I am sure they didn't, but they allowed me to join them again. I went through the ritual that I followed every time I went into a wolf enclosure—even among wolves I'd left just a few hours before, paying the high-ranking members respect, allowing them to scent roll around me and test me. It is what all wolves do when they've been away from the pack; they greet one another and in that greeting and lowering of the body, they establish their rank within the pack.

I was given the title of assistant field biologist and in addition to looking after the captive pack, my job was to go out on trips with the biologists to monitor the movements of the wild wolves. Levi had a theory that there had been wild wolves in the Rockies long before the Canadian wolves were released in 1995. He believed that they had come back into the area using the old migratory corridors that run between Canada, Montana, and Idaho, and we were trying to establish whether this was true or not. All indications were that it was. The incoming wolves had been electronically tagged before leaving Canada, but they had then been given a "hard release," meaning that a cage was set down and the door opened with no further human involvement. They had arrived in pairs but had immediately set off in opposite directions, suggesting that they knew there were other wolves in the locality with which they might breed.

Thirty-five wolves were released in all, but the whole program was fraught with controversy. The farmers and livestock owners took legal action at the last minute to try to prevent it, fearing that the wolves would prey on their stock, but the judge turned down their request for an injunction and the release went ahead. The local schoolchildren had wanted to name the wolves, but that met with furious opposition, too. Parents were afraid that if the wolves had names, the children would think they were friendly and be tempted to approach any they saw. So they were given numbers, such as B2M, B3F, B4F, and B5M—the M and F denoted male and female. By 1998, the number of wolves in the area had increased to 121, suggesting again that Levi was right and the original number was more than 15.

The best time to track the wolves was in the winter when there was snow on the ground and their movements were easy to follow. Wolves, like most animals, tend to keep to an area they have marked out as their territory and move about within it. So having established the various packs' territories in the snow, we had little difficulty finding them at other times. Once again my army training kept me alive on those trips in the snow—knowing how to find food, how to keep warm, how to avoid overheating or dehydrating. More people die of heat-related conditions in freezing temperatures than ever die of cold.

The seasons were spectacular and more clearly defined than anywhere I had been before. They took me back to childhood when I had so loved the different times of year and the changes in the hedgerows and the daylight and the temperature that each season brought. In the Rockies, the colors were in a different league—they were sensational. Levi once told me a story about how the leaves came to be such a vivid color in autumn. He was reminded of the story when we were deep in the forest one day. We would often walk together, just as I had done with my grandfather, and he would stop every now and again and drop to his knees to examine a scat or a footprint.

As he was squatting down, I spotted an enormous bear less than forty meters away from us. "Bear!" I exclaimed.

"I've seen it," Levi said calmly; "it's been watching us for the last twenty minutes."

I couldn't disguise the panic in my voice. "But it's a bear, and we don't have a vehicle to jump into and we're on our own."

Bears can run at the speed of a horse and climb most trees. Levi told me to relax—his people had made peace with the bear and we had nothing to fear. Long ago, he went on (while I began looking feverishly for escape routes), a bear was being chased by three hunters. Wounded in the back, it ran up a mountain to the highest, most inaccessible place it could find, but the hunters followed. With nowhere left to run, it jumped off the mountain and carried on running in the sky—and the hunters followed. They can be seen to this day, in the constellation known as Ursa Major—the Great Bear—and every autumn, when darkness falls, the bear is said to run upside down, and the blood that spills from the wound in its back falls to earth and turns the leaves crimson.

The forest was full of potentially dangerous animals. One of the students that year kept herself fit by jogging twice a day. Morning and night she would run down the track in the direction of the town, a distance of three or four miles. One day I had been out collecting food for the wolves with one of the biologists and noticed the girl's tracks in the new-fallen snow. After about a mile, her tracks were joined by the tracks of a big cat. It was a mountain lion that had obviously noticed her routine and, unbeknownst to her, had followed her to within 150 meters of the camp. It had probably followed her before—these cats can watch their prey for days before they strike. She had been taking the same route for three weeks, but she didn't go jogging again.

The dangers were not exclusively from the wild. Every week we used to go into Winchester for a shower and a pint or two, and one night there was a karaoke contest in the pub. Thinking karaoke was a bit of fun, as it is in England—something you did when you'd had a skinful of beer, and got better at the more beer you drank—I volunteered to have a go. What I didn't realize was that they took their karaoke very seriously in Idaho; the singers were semiprofessional and these were the regional championships. So when I went up to the microphone and sang my own version of the Beatles' song "Yesterday," retitled "Leprosy": ". . . I'm only half the man I used to be . . . ," which used to go down a storm among the lads in the squadron, I was practically lynched and had to run for my life.

I was never a very heavy drinker, but one of the handlers at the Center was, and he would often wend his way back from the pub on those nights very much the worse for wear. His tepee was near the wolf enclosure and his route took him right alongside the perimeter fence. We started to notice that every Saturday night when he went past the wolves, reeking of alcohol and staggering as he walked, the wolves went wild. They knew this man well and yet they were prey driving: leaping at the fence, bouncing off it, and running back and forth in a feeding frenzy. We thought it must be the smell of alcohol on his breath that was confusing them because they were never normally aggressive toward people and certainly not toward the people who handled them.

We ran some experiments. We covered him in alcohol and got him to walk in a straight line past the wolves, but they didn't turn a hair. Then we made him stagger as if drunk even though he was, in fact, stone cold sober with not so much as a trace of alcohol anywhere, and they went crazy. We videoed him to see if we could work out what was going on, and then one of the biologists produced a video he had made of wolves hunting among a herd of bison. One of the bison calves was injured and when we played the footage of the calf on a television screen alongside the footage of the handler staggering, we realized that the pattern of their movement was exactly the same. The wolves were not reacting to the alcohol; they were seeing the staggering handler as prey, and the chances are they would have taken him if they had been able to get at him. It left a serious question about whether he would be able to continue working with that pack.

# CHAPTER ELEVEN

# The Call of the Wild

These wolves had been born in captivity but they had not lost any of their instincts. Being in with them was always challenging and unpredictable, and I never felt I could let down my guard for an instant. But I started to wonder how different wild wolves would be and whether I could be accepted by a pack that had never encountered humans. That would be the ultimate excitement. I was also keen to discover whether Levi's theory was right: that there were wolves already in the area that had used some ancient route, one we might identify.

The biologists at the camp were quite forcefully opposed to my plan, and some were downright hostile. They thought my theories and beliefs were misguided, and apart from any scientific objections, they thought it would be a suicide mission. To them I was a maverick from a foreign country with no qualifications—and it was hard to argue against that opinion. What I wanted to do went against every scientific principle; as biologists, they observed but they didn't touch and they followed well-defined methodology. But I wasn't a scientist; I didn't have a reputation to lose, as they did. I didn't have a fear of not succeeding; I had nothing to lose and everything to gain.

They had other concerns, too. They were afraid that I might

change the wolves in some way, stop them being fearful of humans and encourage them to approach people—and therefore farms and communities. This was less easy to dismiss, but my hope was that I might be able to teach them something about humans before they met a mother taking her young child to school, which could result in a bad first experience.

There was no certainty I would even find wolves, let alone get close to them, and there was a strong possibility I might be killed in the attempt, but I was determined to try. The final decision, however, was Levi's, and being the sort of man he was, he didn't stop me. I think that secretly some of the Indians—maybe even Levi—felt slightly envious of what I was doing. They might have liked to take off into the forest, too, but they had families and jobs and responsibilities.

I had prepared myself as best I could. I was physically fit; I had been running, walking, and lifting weights for months. I had studied maps, read books, and talked to the tribal elders about the wolves. And before I left England, I had gathered together some good kit. I had been to a shop that catered to extreme-sports enthusiasts and explained what I needed; they had given me a number of items to try out for them, free of charge. I had three pairs of socks, for example, that were supposed to breathe and not need washing, and a kind of second skin that I wore in place of underwear that was warm in the cold and cool in the heat. The rest I had bought: good walking boots and an all-in-one supposedly waterproof quilted jumpsuit with ventilation panels under the arms. Other than that, I had jeans and a couple of layers on my top, gloves, and a hat.

I didn't take a sleeping bag or any kind of shelter, and I didn't intend to do any cooking. I wanted to be as much like a lone wolf as I could, so a fire was out of the question and a sleeping bag would just have been a nuisance. I took a rucksack containing a water bottle, purification tablets, a knife, some wire and some string to make snare traps, a signal flare in case I needed to alert anyone to my position, a compass, a map, a notebook and pen, and some very salty beef jerky in case I had difficulty finding food.

I set out from the camp as soon as the sun was up one autumn morning and took the old trail that followed the Salmon River. It was the path along which the legendary Chief Joseph took the Nez Percé to escape the U.S. Cavalry in 1877, which ended in his surrender in Montana. It was acknowledged as one of the most brilliant military retreats in American history. With a band of about seven hundred Indians, fewer than two hundred of whom were warriors, he fought two thousand U.S. soldiers and is heralded among the tribe as a humanitarian and a peacemaker. The elders would talk at length about Chief Joseph and the history of the tribe and how their lands were systematically taken from them by the white man. Joseph had promised his dying father than he would never sign a treaty selling the land that held the bones of his father and mother. "A man who would not defend his father's grave is worse than a wild animal," he allegedly said, but in the end he decided that breaking the promise to his father was better than further bloodshed.

It was a track that tourists used during the summer months; the scenery was spectacular, the colors glorious, but I knew it was not as benign as it looked. I would need all the survival skills I could muster to stay alive in that terrain—and a great deal of luck, too. The Rockies were beautiful but hostile and they covered a vast area. I was stepping into the unknown—against all advice—and I wasn't sure whether, or for how long, I would be able to cope. The temperatures dropped to dangerous levels at night at that altitude, and if the cold didn't kill me—or the wolves—there was always the possibility of an angry bear or some other predator. I had had rudimentary lessons on how to deal with bears but they still terrified me. The biologists had talked about taking guns and radios and telephones and arranging rendezvous every twelve hours, but it wouldn't have worked; it would have involved too much contact with humans that would have frightened the wolves away. I wanted to give myself the best chance of success, and that meant taking risks that maybe others wouldn't have taken. I was going against every safety code known to man, but then I'd always gone my own way, trod a different path from the herd.

I would like to say that my apprehension soon disappeared, that the training kicked in, and that I had rapidly focused on staying alive. But that would be a lie. I was in shock for the first two to three weeks—convinced that if I managed to get out of there alive, I'd be very lucky. I barely moved in that time, rather like an animal tentatively exploring a new environment. I stayed close to safety, to what I thought of as my Get Out of Jail Free card. I had agreed to a rendezvous point with Levi where I would leave my rucksack, and he or someone from the camp would drive to it every couple of days to check that I was okay. Anytime I wanted to come home I simply had to wait there; and we both used the notebook as a means of leaving each other messages. The track would be impassable when the snows came, but there were search and rescue helicopters on tap if it became necessary and the team at the camp knew what they were doing. If I had been attacked by a bear, of course, or any other animal, no number of contingency plans would have helped.

Those first few weeks I walked no farther from the bag area than fifteen or twenty miles. I was torn between my determination to find wolves and the very human side of me that was scared stiff and didn't want to commit suicide. I was so frightened of predators that I didn't dare move after dark, and for the first four nights I slept in a tree, although *sleeping* was hardly the word. I was listening for every sound and occasionally nodding off briefly, and it was only when I fell out of the tree on the fifth night that I started sleeping on the ground. I didn't fall far, not more than fifteen feet, but I realized that if it happened again and I injured myself, I would probably die anyway, either from the cold or starvation. The Indians would always say that every warrior wants an honorable death, and I could see myself being known as the only person who worked with wolves who killed himself falling out of a tree.

Gradually I became more confident and began to venture out by day. I analyzed scats and tracks on the ground to establish what sort of animals I was sharing this untouched wilderness with. Then I plucked up the courage to stay up at night. I changed my sleeping pattern, although I still wasn't doing a whole lot of sleeping. I started catnapping and dozing mostly during the day. I thought it was important not to establish any patterns that might attract the attention of a predator. I made rudimentary snare traps with wire and string and a flexible stick and set them in runs where I could see that animals followed the same paths day after day, and caught my first rabbit before my rations of jerky ran out. I skinned and gutted it but only ate the legs. I had eaten rabbit raw before—it was a strong, gamey meat; but I had to be really hungry, which I was later, to eat the rest of the animal—and starving to eat the stomach contents. I also caught birds, rodents, and other small mammals, such as squirrels. I didn't go for anything larger than a rabbit because being on my own I couldn't risk being gored by antlers or injured in any way. That would have stopped my hunting and without food I would have died.

Killing wasn't hard for me. During my commando training, we had each been given a soft, fluffy rabbit to look after for the afternoon. Four or five hours later we were told to kill the rabbits; they were our next meal. My rough, tough fellow recruits were horrified, so I had to do all the killing. The only problem here was the likelihood of other predators finding the kill before I did. I was eating a diet, like the wolf's, that provided quality but not quantity, and one meal of raw meat gave me slow-release energy to keep going for a day and a half to two days. Sometimes I would supplement it with nuts and berries, but I always did a poison test before eating too much of anything.

As the weeks went by, I established a routine and found an area in which I felt comfortable. I could hear deer, badgers, and owls, and a wolf or coyote gave a brief call, but I didn't see a living thing for four weeks. I was in my element—alone with nature and living on my wits—surrounded by the most breathtaking scenery and on the track of wolves. It was like being a student driver—passing my test and suddenly having the freedom to take the car out by myself. I was feeling positively cocky, invincible, as though I could have stayed there forever.

Then I experienced my first reality check: The weather changed and for four days the most horrendous storm raged around me. Nothing moved, the animals sat tight, and my food source dried up. I realized that when bad weather hits, nature closes down and sits it out. I had no alternative but to do the same; I sheltered under a collection of evergreen trees and became bored and depressed. My routine was what had been keeping me happy. I was hungry and my mind and body were beginning to shut down. Then the training kicked in and I remembered what I'd been taught in the military about how vital it is to keep thinking positively. No matter what situation you find yourself in, no matter how hopeless it appears, you have to quickly look for your options—how are you going to feed yourself, what can you use to protect yourself or to patch up your wounds? You have to keep your spirits up or you are dead. Wolves are the same; they never give up, never feel sorry for themselves; even if they are mortally wounded, they keep running. And above all things I wanted to be like a wolf. Most human beings want to make the animals they love be more like them; I had always wanted to be more like the animals I loved.

It was two and a half months before I found the first trace of a wolf. I was beginning to despair when I came across a small water hole with a bank of soft mud around it, and in the mud was the print of one large male wolf. It was an exciting moment but also unnerving. I could see no evidence of any other animals, so I guessed he must have been a lone wolf. I decided to stay there that night and when the light faded, I howled. It was ridiculously brave—or foolish—because it immediately made my position known to any predator. And all for nothing; there was no response. I was disappointed but not really surprised. That night I didn't even doze; I lay under a tree and listened to all the creatures of the forest grunting, hooting, and calling, aware that I had recklessly put myself in danger.

I saw and heard nothing for the next three weeks. I became very depressed and began to wonder what on earth I was doing there. I longed for some comfort and normality, to be able to relax and enjoy a full night's sleep without having to worry when I heard a twig snap. I hadn't had that luxury in more than three months.

And then in the middle of the night I heard the first hint of wolves. It was a low tone, so it was probably a male and I guessed a beta rank and probably a wolf that was away from his pack rather than a lone wolf. It was coming from the tree line, but it was hard to gauge distance. I reckoned he might have been about three-quarters of a mile away. I was tempted to howl back but thought better of it. If I had howled, I would have had to move—I wasn't going to be a sitting duck like the last time—and I didn't want to have to stumble around in the dark.

Another three weeks went by with nothing—not a paw print, not a sound—and then suddenly as I was walking down a track in the middle of the afternoon, a big black wolf crossed about 150 meters in front of me. It stopped fleetingly and looked straight at me with piercing yellow eyes before disappearing into the forest. I didn't have time to see whether it was male or female, or whether it matched the description of any of the wolves that had been released. It was gone in a flash and I was left wondering whether I had really seen it or it had been a figment of my imagination.

I was so excited. The doubts I had been turning over in my mind about the trip vanished. The depression was gone. All I thought about from that moment onward was how close I might be able to get to that creature. And what if I discovered it was a genuine wild wolf, born and bred in the area with no interference from man whatsoever? I hardly dared consider the possibility. Given its response to me, it was obviously not used to humans or comfortable around them. How would I do it? I considered leaving some food around but then realized that although that might attract the wolf, it might also bring other predators into the area. Should I take my courage in both hands and try to communicate with it? If it was a lone wolf, it might respond on the grounds that even though it wouldn't be a pair bonding, it is always safer to be two than one—but it would be alerting others to my whereabouts. I weighed the pros and cons of all my options. Was this the wolf I had heard howl? Was it the one whose footprint I had seen in mud? I had seen no evidence of more than one animal in the area.

I had to take a risk—that was what I had come there for and what the last four months had been all about. If I did take it to the next stage—and it was a completely different stage to take it to—then my routine would have to change; I would have to step outside my comfort zone. I wasn't going to be able to sit tight at night; I would have to sleep through the day and move around in the dark, which was a prospect I didn't fancy at all.

To do anything in that environment, whether it's for survival, recreation, or charity, takes courage. It means exposing yourself to everything we humans fear most: the dark, the forest, the wolf, the bear, and all the dangers of nature. Native Americans had the right idea. They used to send their children onto the mountain alone at the age of eight or nine for five days, and some of them still do it today. It was a kind of ritual to exorcise the childish terror that the rest of us feel even as adults; they made peace with the natural world in the way that Levi had made peace with the bear. He didn't fear it, and it didn't fear him.

Fitness is the key to every creature's survival. No predator will risk taking down another predator that is fit, because there's a chance it might be injured in the attempt, and the minute any animal has an injury or shows weakness of any kind, it might as well be dead.

That first night was terrifying. I knew what I was doing was dangerous, more dangerous than any of the nights I had spent with captive packs. My eyes were not designed to see in the dark, and if I stumbled or fell, a predator could have me in seconds. It was like swimming with sharks where they had all the advantages and I had none. I didn't go far—no more than six or seven miles—stopping after every step and listening, knowing that however quiet I tried to be, with every step I was giving away my position. There was no moon and I was surprised by how much I could see without it, but everything appeared in shades of gray. I scanned my surroundings for movement—that was the key. Every sense I possessed was heightened. I took deep breaths of air to catch smells; I used the wind to bring sound and scent of the creatures around me, something I'd never done before. I could hear every stretch and sigh and, at times, I swear I could hear my own heartbeat—it was thumping that loudly.

Bears were my greatest fear because they were so unpredictable. Since man's interaction with them, their patterns of behavior have changed and they are just as likely to be wandering through the forest at night as in the day. Because of their experience of picnickers and campers, they have come to regard man as a supplier of food, and they will follow humans in the expectation of being given something to eat. That is why they were around the Center so much. They were fast and agile, and if you inadvertently surprised a bear or came between a mother and her cubs, it could be game over very quickly. It took a long time for me to conquer my fear of them, but even today I think my immediate reaction to bears is one of fear, not respect.

The night, which I had thought might be my last, passed without incident. Dawn brought the first light of a new day and I was alive and unscathed and ready to welcome it with open arms. I felt elated. I may have flunked every exam at school and been a failure in so many ways, but suddenly none of that mattered. I had achieved more in this one night in the wilds of the Rocky Mountains, among some of the most dangerous mammals on the planet, than I had achieved in thirty years living among my own kind. The excitement I felt that morning was hard to contain. It was good to be alive—and never again would I be made to feel inadequate.

# CHAPTER TWELVE

# A Waiting Game

It was, however, just one night. I tried to rest the following day but I was too excited, and the next night I wasn't up to it, so I stayed put and went out again on the third night. What I would have done if the wolf had howled, I wasn't sure. Would I have howled in return and let every predator in the forest know where I was? I told myself that I was waiting for him or her to call me, but I think it was just an excuse. I was still very afraid.

I had established a resting place where I felt safe and comfortable, about eighteen miles away from the track where I'd seen the wolf. It was in a clearing. I had a big rock behind me and a good view of the immediate area in front of me, and although I never allowed myself the luxury of sleeping for hours at a stretch, I could sleep in short bursts and feel reasonably secure. It was from there that I went out each night in search of the wolf. A wolf's territory is generally egg shaped, so I walked in egg-shaped circles, growing more confident as time passed and I continued to find myself alive at first light. My senses were improving. My eyesight was never going to be good in the dark but everything else made up for it: I could hear a pine needle drop and smell the different animals that observed me as I crept through their world without needing to see them move.

The one animal I neither saw nor heard nor smelled was the wolf.

He or she seemed to have vanished, and after a while I decided to go back to the bag area, where I had left my rucksack, to see if there was any news for me and to let Levi and the others know what was going on. I felt a huge sense of despair. Having been so up after the sighting and surviving my first night in the forest, I was now as low as I had ever been. I was on an emotional roller coaster and quite unable to control it. I had come so close and yet was still so far. I still didn't know whether this wolf was truly wild or whether I would ever see him or her again. I began to have all the nagging doubts again about the whole mission. There was no note for me at the bag, but from the footprints on the ground around it, I knew that Levi or someone from the camp had been there. So I wrote a note myself, telling them about the sighting, took more of the jerky, putting what I didn't eat into my pocket, and set off to where I had just come from.

It must have been a good four weeks before I saw another wolf—or maybe it was the same wolf. It was early evening and I was resting under a tree in a clearing with the wind toward me. That was the way I preferred to be so that I could smell any creature before it came into my line of vision. I was becoming more like a wild animal with every day that passed—and probably smelling more like one, too. I hadn't changed my clothes in months or done more than splash water from the river every now and again over my face, my crotch, and under my arms. My hair was uncombed and my beard unshaven.

This wolf was big and black and came out of the tree line heading directly toward me. It stopped, looked at me quite calmly for thirty or forty seconds, and then turned to its right and disappeared into the forest. It didn't seem to be afraid of me, which made me suspect that it had been watching me for some time and for whatever reason had finally decided to put in an appearance.

For the next month I saw it intermittently every two or three days. It would appear when I was least expecting it and in every situation. I would be walking through the forest and stop to rest and be sitting, listening to the life around me, and suddenly there it would be in the clearing; or I'd be setting a trap, eating or collecting water from the river, and I would look around and see two big amber eyes watching me. I got the feeling it was following me around and seeing far more of me than I ever saw of it. I never spoke—I didn't want the wolf to think of me as human or to teach it to think that humans were harmless. The plan I had in my head was to frighten the wolf when I left the forest so that the lasting impression it would have of man would be negative. But that was for later. Right now I wanted it to trust me, so every time I saw it, I dropped down low or lay propped up on an elbow to let it know I was no threat.

After another couple of weeks, our courtship moved to a new stage. It was early morning and I was half awake when I heard the magical sound of a howl. This time it sounded more like an inquiry than any of the previous howls I had heard. What should I do? Answer and expose my whereabouts or play safe and stay silent? I weighed the options. I now knew this area well and the only tracks I had seen were deer; I hadn't come across any evidence of predators, although that didn't mean they weren't there. I decided to go for it. I cupped my hands around my mouth and gave the response I hoped the wolf was wanting. I waited with bated breath, my heart in my mouth. Minutes passed, which felt like hours, and then the silence was broken by a long mellifluous howl that made the hairs on the back of my neck stand up. I had a reply. I could hardly believe it; it was a miracle. He or she had called back to me. I still hadn't seen this creature for long enough to know for sure what sex it was but guessed by the size of it that it was a male, although black females also tended to be large animals.

That exchange was the turning point in our relationship. Over the next two weeks scarcely a day went by when I didn't see this wolf—and it was a young male. He didn't come much closer but I would find him standing watching me, and when I noticed him, he would look, linger for a moment or two, and then disappear into the trees. At night we howled back and forth to each other and the distance between us could have been no more than two or three hundred meters.

And then I made the most amazing discovery. This was not a lone wolf. He was part of a pack of five, and my guess was that either he had been curious about me and had taken it upon himself to investigate, or more likely, that he had been sent to check me out by the alpha female.

I was in a clearing late one afternoon, sitting with my back to a rock, when he appeared out of the tree line as he had now done so many times before. As I looked at him, wondering whether we would ever get any closer, a second wolf appeared, and then a third, fourth, and fifth. One by one they wove in and out of the forest, giving me just the briefest glimpse of each. There were three males in the pack and two females. Seeing them together, I realized that the male that had been communicating with me was possibly last year's or the previous year's pup, and one of the females was his sister. The others were all fully grown adults and not one of them matched the descriptions I had of the wolves that had been released; these were not B2, B3, B4, or B5. Unless I was much mistaken, these wolves were truly wild.

I was excited and I could scarcely believe my good fortune. This was the most incredible sighting. I had seen what others had only dreamed of, and I'd seen them because they chose to make themselves known to me. This was so much better than anything I could have hoped for. I was on a complete high. And then as swiftly as my spirits had soared, they were brought back down to earth. The wolves disappeared. I searched for them. On the assumption that they had been watching me for weeks if not months before they let me see them, I repeated my pattern of behavior. I stayed in the area; I called but nothing came back. I started to worry that the young male had been chastised for getting too close to me, that he'd made a mistake and they had punished him by moving away. All sorts of crazy ideas went through my head as I went through the motions of my daily life. Yet I somehow couldn't believe them; I kept coming back to my conviction that the adults had been using him to investigate me.

A month later I was once again sitting in a clearing with my back against a rock when the pack reappeared as suddenly and as silently as they had vanished. They had lost a member; one of the older males was missing and they seemed to be more flighty than they had been when I had first seen them. Even the young male seemed apprehensive and wary. Despite this, they settled down to spend the afternoon resting and playing by the tree line about a hundred meters away from me. The young ones were wrestling with each other and would growl and whimper and break away, then pounce, and they would squeak when the play became too rough. The older ones growled from time to time in a grumpy sort of way and when the pups had exhausted themselves with their mock fighting, they lay flat out and slept while their elders kept watch.

That night I heard the pack howling, presumably for the fifth animal. I wondered where he was and what had happened to him. He could have been lost or killed during the month they had been away or he could have been right here, in the area, patrolling around the back of me, preparing to catch me off guard. I was not foolish enough to think that because they had come back and allowed me to watch them relax that they necessarily thought of me as a good thing. I wondered what they *did* think of me, or if they had any idea that they were the highlight of my day or how incredibly proud I felt to have made such progress with them.

The progress continued. I saw them most days. I had my sleeping area still, but every day I went to the clearing where I had first seen them and that was where I continued to see them, and although they still kept their distance, they seemed to be a lot more comfortable and relaxed in front of me. For the next three or four nights they howled. I assumed it was still for their lost family member, but he never responded. One night I plucked up the courage to respond instead—as a lone wolf might have done when he sensed there was a vacancy—and the whole pack came back to me. It was another memorable moment and I realized I was losing my fear. I was taking comfort in their presence, feeling as though in some way I was coming under their protective umbrella in this hostile environment that I'd battled by myself to survive in for so many months. I didn't feel so alone anymore. I realized I was beginning to need them.

I hoped and expected that the distance they kept from me would steadily diminish, but what actually happened took me by surprise. The brother and sister were playing about fifty meters from me; the adult female was about a hundred meters away. I hadn't seen the other male—or given him any thought. Suddenly I heard a twig snap just behind me. I quickly turned and there was the male, a big powerful animal, standing less than ten meters from me. I was sitting defenseless and he could have been on me in a flash, and I realized once again just how vulnerable and inadequate I was in their world. His presence wasn't threatening, though. He didn't even look at me. He looked over my shoulder at the young ones playing and I felt as though he was including me in the family group, just as the foxes had done in that field in Norfolk. Before, I had been an outsider observing a life that didn't involve me; now, rightly or wrongly, I felt a great surge of belonging.

Things moved rapidly after that. I was squatting on a low rock watching them interact in their usual way when the same big male broke away from the others and came directly toward me, trotting at first before he slowed to a walk. I was expecting him to turn away at any moment, but he kept on coming until he was within about seven meters. His tail went up, and I wondered what he was planning. I was not in a good position to defend myself. My bottom was lower than my knees and if I needed to get up in a hurry, it would be difficult; but if I moved now, I might destroy everything we had been building up to. He eased forward slowly, then crouched down and stretched his head until it was about twelve inches from my legs, as though he didn't want his body any closer than absolutely necessary. Then he began to sniff my knees and then my walking boots, and he seemed particularly interested in the instep. My heart was in my mouth. Where was this going to end? As purposefully as he had arrived, he turned and walked back to the others, moving his tail from side to side as he went. They greeted him as though he had been away for weeks, frantically licking his mouth and muzzle area. In the midst of this frenzy, he turned on the young female, growling and snapping at her, and she quickly dropped down onto her back and displayed her submissive underside for a moment. Then she was on her feet and they all disappeared into the forest.

I heard nothing from them that night and was disappointed. I spent the night trying to figure out why he had broken the pattern and done what he had done so suddenly. What was his next move going to be and how should I prepare? Should I go to the area in the dark? I decided against it. That would have been giving them all the advantages. These animals were built for the dark; I wasn't, and if the big male had come at me in the dark as he had done in daylight, my reaction might have been very different because I would have felt less confident—and that might have had unfortunate consequences. I decided to keep to my routine and return at first light, fully expecting it would be the day when I would meet and greet the whole pack.

# CHAPTER THIRTEEN

# *Worth the Wait*

There was no sign of them, and no sign again on the second day. It wasn't until the afternoon of the third day, when I was dozing, that they appeared. Their energy levels seemed to have changed and they were more assured than before and more purposeful, as though they had some kind of agenda. I was relieved to see them and watched while they interacted with one another. Then the big male broke away from the others and made a beeline for me, as he had done before but more confidently. He didn't crouch down this time; he remained standing while he sniffed and then without warning he lunged forward and nipped the flesh beneath my knee with his incisors. It was exactly what the beta male at Sparkwell had done before accepting me into the pack at the wildlife park. He immediately pulled back and looked at me, quizzically. It was painful and he drew blood but it didn't feel dangerous. I wanted to grin from ear to ear but I didn't react. He lunged forward again and nipped the same place, three times in all, stepping back and looking at me after each bite, and then he turned, walked back to the rest of the pack and lay down with them. The temptation to go and join them was practically irresistible, but I didn't want to do anything that would spoil the magic of what had just happened. An hour later they were gone.

Two days after that we had a repeat performance. Again it was the big male, but this time the two youngsters came with him and stood on each side of him, watching. Occasionally he snapped and growled at them as if to keep them in order. He sniffed my knees and feet, checking for any new smells or danger that I might be bringing to him and the pups. Then he nipped my knee several times, and then he brushed and rubbed himself along my sides, as a dog might do, and sniffed around the back of my head. I could feel his fangs on my neck. I was frozen to the spot, waiting for his jaws to clamp around my throat, which would bring either instant death or acceptance, but it didn't happen. At that moment, the young male gave me a much gentler nip on my knee while the older male knocked me off my perch on the rock. As I fell I put a hand out to steady myself and found it resting on the pup's shoulder. He didn't pull away; he felt like no wolf I had ever touched and in that split second I was overcome by an incredible surge of love for this creature and his family, and an overpowering need to be part of it.

I knew there and then that when those wolves went back to the dominant female, I was going to go with them. It was now or never and I had to satisfy this incredible urge to be accepted. I followed them. I was on all fours, which was clumsy and cumbersome, but they looked back several times and saw me behind them and seemed unfazed, so I kept going. I was confident I had made the right decision until I reached the matriarch. She was hostile, not ready to tolerate my coming any closer than twenty or thirty meters, and was clearly extremely nervous. She barked and growled, and the others immediately looked as though they realized they had done something wrong. The young ones sprang to her side and stood glaring at me. I got the impression that the older male was trying to act as go-between to defuse the situation, but at the end of the day his loyalty was to his leader. She got to her feet, flattened her ears, bared her teeth, and let out low barking noises that warned me to stay away. She then took the young pups and ran into the forest. The big male lingered; the young male reappeared and stood next to him for a second or two, then they both turned and were gone.

I felt a huge depression—and loss—but then I reminded myself of what I had achieved that day. Three of them had accepted me; the female hadn't and her decision had been final, but I had still made great strides. I went back to my nighttime resting place as darkness fell. If the female had accepted me, I might have been tempted to follow the pack and make a bid to join it that evening; because she hadn't, I didn't feel safe staying in that area in the dark. I thought she could be dangerous.

That was the last I saw of them for a week and a half. I decided it was time to go back to the bag area; I had lost track of how long I had been gone by this time—it must have been nearly nine months—and I thought I should leave a note to tell Levi what was going on. It was a journey of two and a half days from my overnight spot and during that time I mulled over in my mind what had happened. On the one hand, I was elated; on the other, I was profoundly depressed. I had no idea where the pack had gone when they disappeared and I was entirely dependent upon their coming back and finding me, and now that I had upset the dominant female, maybe she would never bring them back again.

I reached the rucksack, wrote a note, and spent a couple of nights there chilling and catching up on some real sleep—something I hadn't had in months—before retracing my footsteps. I had enjoyed having a full night's sleep and I was tempted by the idea of a shower, some human company, and a hot meal, but I was too excited and too close to give up now. I had a chance to go further toward infiltrating a wild wolf pack than anyone, as far as I knew, had ever gone before. I had to go back.

I arrived back at my sleeping site two and a half days later and the next morning walked the ten or eleven miles to the clearing in the forest where all this interaction had taken place. No one came. I

repeated the process every day and it was a week before the four
wolves reappeared. There were no calls; they just suddenly came out
of the tree line and were there. Wherever they had been, they
looked well fed. I was sitting on my rock, as usual, and the big male
and the pups immediately came toward me and seemed more confident than before. The female stayed back and I respected her distance. That evening they went into the forest and I went to my
resting site, and the next day we met again. And so it went for two
weeks, if not a month. Every time I attempted to get any closer to
the female, she laid her ears back, growled, and ran off; but slowly,
bit by bit, I managed to get closer before she ran away and eventually she stood her ground and just growled. Sometimes the big male
would push me away.

I continued during that time to interact with the other three
members of the pack, however, and the bond with them quietly in-
tensified. In some ways they were like the captive wolves I had known
and in other ways not. The language they used was similar but these
wolves were stronger, and they were constantly on guard, alert to
every sound and scent and change in the air. One of them was always
on lookout, and even the pups would stop in the midst of their play
every now and again and listen. Their play-fights and games were far
more intense than those of captive wolves. Their bites were more
painful and they didn't pull their punches; they played as hard and
roughly with me as they played with each other. I was covered in cuts
and bruises but it was manageable. My all-in-one suit was quilted but
it didn't protect me from the bone-crushing strength of their jaws,
and it was still scary when they held me down with their full weight
on top of me.

When the pain was too intense, I had to give a shrill, high-
pitched yelp before they would release me, which seemed to get
the female to her feet. She didn't come and help me, but she

seemed interested in what was going on. She still wouldn't let me near her. Whenever I came close, she would growl and lift her lips at me. It was never going to be a friendship made in heaven. The only consolation was that she was as intolerant with the pups as she was with me.

I felt we had reached a bit of a stalemate. I was almost a member of the pack but not quite. They would still go off into the forest every now and again and leave me behind. They would call from afar, but they were locating, not rallying, calls. They weren't inviting me to join them and I still had no idea where they went when they left.

Early one morning I was in the clearing when the four of them appeared after a long absence. As usual, I lowered my body as they came toward me—this time even the female came as if to greet me. She stopped within about ten meters of me and sat and watched as the big male made contact. I could tell that their mood had changed; they were more boisterous, the energy levels were up. He barged at me and covered me with his powerful body; I crumpled to the ground under his weight. I wasn't particularly worried; he had done this kind of thing in the past, but before I realized what was happening, the female had changed places with him and the snarling and growling that she had been doing at thirty meters she was now doing three inches from my face. I could feel the warmth of her breath; her lips were lifted back from her teeth—I thought this was going to be the end. The male tried to muscle in. I didn't know whether he was trying to save me or join the kill, but she snapped and bit his muzzle and he retreated. I lay there helpless. I had no choice but to take whatever was coming to me.

She was on me for the longest two or three minutes of my life, but she didn't harm so much as a hair on my head. When she finally let me go, she loped back to the others; my disciplining was over. The incident didn't seem to change her attitude toward me, but it radically changed my attitude toward her. I knew she could have killed me easily but had chosen not to, and that made a big difference. Up to that point I had believed she was dangerous. Now I thought of her as an intolerant aunt, a creature that was incredibly knowledgeable, rightly respected, and very much in charge, but one of those characters that was always bad tempered. We would learn to tolerate each other.

Every night I battled with my better judgment over leaving the wolves. I had begun to feel safer with them than away from them, but my routine had been to leave them as darkness fell and be back again by first light. One evening, tensions were low, they had all had a good feed, and even Miss Grumpy seemed relaxed. I decided to stay and see what happened. It was a massive anticlimax. I didn't sleep a wink—kept awake by a mixture of fear and excitement—but they all slept soundly until morning. The male pup came and lay alongside me, which was warming even though we weren't touching. It was strangely comforting to have another creature sleeping alongside me after all those months on my own. I could hear his breathing and I felt his every twitch. When morning broke, I was walking on air. I had done nothing more than spend the night with the wolves, but it meant I had been accepted. I couldn't have felt a greater sense of achievement if I'd run a triple marathon.

The next stage was to try to stay with them when they went off into the forest. Like every step I took with these wolves, traveling with them was fraught with danger. If I managed to keep up, which was a big if, and they took me somewhere completely unfamiliar, I might not be able to get back. And if they began to hunt, I knew I wouldn't have a hope of following. I would then be on my own in an area I didn't know with all the vulnerability of being alone. The situation didn't arise.

For the next day and night they were restless, and in the early hours of the second day they took off. I was right behind them and did my best to follow, but as soon as we were among the trees they were invisible in the darkness and they were gone. Dejected and disappointed, I had no alternative but to go back to the clearing and wait and hope that they would come back.

It was a long wait but one morning they not only reappeared, but the young female had brought me food. It was the leg of a red deer. She played with it for a bit then dropped it purposefully by my side. I started to eat it and she sat and watched—so I was obviously doing the right thing. I was hungry and after months of nothing bigger than rabbit, it tasted fantastic. For the next few weeks this became the pattern. They would go off hunting and leave me—even in the daylight I found it impossible to follow—but they would always bring me something on their return. It seemed clear to me that they didn't want me to hunt but were happy to have me around and to feed me.

When they were gone, I would howl and sometimes if they were near enough for my ears to pick up the sound, I heard them call back. And they always seemed to call when they were on their way back. Their voices were familiar and comforting and gave me a very warm feeling. I realized how attached I had become to these wolves and how dependent I'd become on their being around. I would worry that one of them might not come back. It might have an accident or be injured, or worse, killed—as I assumed the fifth member of the pack must have been—and I would hold my breath until I counted them all safely into the clearing. I was even pleased to see the grumpy female. It was like the agony of waiting for loved ones who are late coming home. Then there would be a great greeting ceremony. They licked me furiously around my face and mouth, exactly as they greeted one another, and I was so excited to see them I did the same, running round to each of them like a little pup, frantically licking and nuzzling and vying for their attention. The only exception was the female, who still wouldn't let me anywhere near her—but she wouldn't tolerate the others either.

I sometimes caught myself and thought that if anyone had suggested a year or more ago that I would one day be happy eating nothing for three days and then be so thrilled to see a pack of wild wolves that I'd go around licking their jaws, I would have laughed at the absurdity of the idea. But right now, these wolves were the most important thing in my life; they were my family and I loved each and every one of them. But I knew I had to let them go.

# CHAPTER FOURTEEN

# The Patter of Tiny Feet

A battle had been raging in my head for a long time: I wanted to stay with the wolves and be a part of their world more than anything I had ever wanted, but in my heart of hearts I knew it was time to leave. It was one of the hardest decisions I'd ever made, but I had no doubt it was the right thing to do. I had always had the biologists' concerns in the back of my head and the relationship had now moved on to a different level. I had done what I set out to do and I was worried that if I stayed any longer, they might well get a false sense of security about human beings—and that could be very dangerous for them.

I had taken great pains not to display any human traits, and I behaved in every respect like a low-ranking wolf, but there was no getting away from the fact that I was human.

Spring was approaching and with it the breeding season; what would my role be then? Would they ask me to leave the pack or would they want me as nanny to look after the pups? That would have been a huge responsibility that I wasn't sure I was up to. And would my being human seal their fate in the future? Would they learn to trust humans as much as they did their own kind with disastrous consequences? And so very quietly under my breath I said, "Good-bye and good luck, guys" and set off for the bag.

I walked for two days and two nights, crying most of the way, able at last to display the emotion that with the wolves I had kept bottled up, and able at last to use my human voice. I felt utterly bereft and although I knew the arguments about why I needed to leave and rehearsed them over and over again to myself as I walked, often out loud, I couldn't stop thinking I was making a big mistake. I had come so far, jumped through so many hoops—and had the scars to prove it. I had been on a mental and physical roller coaster for months—living with fear and danger twenty-four hours a day—but all of that was over. I was part of the pack, the wolves had accepted me, protected me, fed me.

No one had ever done this before. There were stories about children being adopted by wolves and walking out of the forest on all fours, unable to speak, but no one had gone into the forest as I had done and become part of a wolf family. By the time I reached the rendezvous point, I realized I could no more leave those wolves than fly to the moon. I wrote Levi a note telling him what I was doing and turned round and retraced my footsteps.

In the time I had been away the weather had broken. Winter was on its way and the first snows followed a few weeks later. That would change everything. It would make getting about more difficult, but on the plus side, the snow would enable me to follow the wolves at my own pace. At last I would be able to find out where it was they went when they were away for so long. But I still had the dilemma of how far to follow them. I could get back to civilization in just over two days from the clearing—I had just done it; I knew the terrain well enough to walk it in the pitch dark and I knew the animals that lived in the area. If I followed the wolves for another two or three days, I would be completely out of my comfort zone and too far away to realistically make it back to the bag area if I broke a leg or found myself with some other kind of injury. But had I really come this far to turn back now because it seemed too risky?

The day the wolves left, I followed. Their pace was slower than on the occasions I had tried to follow them in the past and they seemed to be waiting for me. Even the grumpy female stopped every now and again and looked back to make sure I was keeping up. We must have covered ten or fifteen miles heading toward the northwest, and the terrain was getting steeper and more rugged by the mile. The bag, my security, as I was acutely aware, was southeast, so we were traveling in the opposite direction. I had imagined they might take me to their hunting ground but I was wrong. We came instead to a steep hillside, heavily forested with a river running along the valley about six hundred meters below.

We arrived there before the snow, and the ground was thick with pine needles; the smell, like so much of the forest, was pleasantly aromatic. There was also a strong scent of wolf, and judging by the way the animals relaxed when we arrived, I guessed they came here often. It was possibly where they lived during the winter or it might have been where the youngsters had been born. Whatever it was, they made every indication that we were here to stay.

They never let me follow them to the hunting ground. The big male growled and went for me if ever I tried—his way of disciplining me—but I was never without food. It came thick and fast and I was always presented with as much as I could eat. I was eating much better-quality meat with them than I had ever managed by myself and good clear water was just a short walk away down the track into the valley. I took the opportunity to wash in the stream on occasions when I was left alone, although it was still nothing more than splashing icy water over me. It helped dislodge some of the mud that was caked to me and made me feel slightly fresher. It was hard to feel entirely fresh when I was wearing clothes that I had been in day and night for the best part of eighteen months. They were beginning to fall apart in places and the one-piece suit had taken a bit of a battering from teeth and claws during fights and romps with the wolves, but it was all holding together and even if it was no longer entirely waterproof, on many occasions I was thankful to have had such a sturdy and warm outfit.

We were entering the breeding season and suddenly everyone's blood was up. The energy levels of the males went through the roof as they began their courtship, and my role turned into resident punching bag. They were in deadly competition with each other, desperate to convince the dominant female that they were the one she should choose as her mate—the one who could defend her most effectively—and they were ready to see off any other passing males that might have fancied their chances, too. They prowled about looking for trouble, nipping each other repeatedly on the flank hoping to provoke a response, which for me without the layer of fur they had, was very painful. They simply wanted to get their pheromone and adrenaline levels up to make themselves more attractive to the female, and the harder and more aggressively they fought, the higher the levels rose. So they would pick fights and take their frustration out on the lowest-ranking member of the pack—me.

These fights were infinitely more intense than anything I'd experienced with them before. My all-in-one suit had ventilation patches under the arms and their incisors took great chunks of flesh out of me, the size of 10-pence pieces, that hurt like hell. With hormone levels now brimming, they would go and scratch the ground, roll and scent, leaving a powerful message for the female about their prowess. And while they spent all their time trying to impress her, she was busy trying to suppress the lower-ranking female.

Most of the cuts and bruises I had from these encounters were comparatively superficial. If you live with a pack of wolves, you have to expect to get hurt, but they also had a capacity to be gentle and they would look after me as they looked after one another. They would lick my wounds, which is probably what stopped them from becoming infected. The biggest danger was not the cuts, though; it was the blows to the head that would knock me out briefly, and sometimes they thumped my body or knocked me to the ground with such force that my urine had blood in it for several days afterward.

I was also beginning to question my diet. I had eaten nothing but protein and a few nuts and berries for a very long time. For the first year or more I had felt fitter and healthier than ever before, but now that I needed extra energy to try to hold my own with these testosterone-charged wolves, I realized I had no reserves.

The males were not just pushing and nipping and fighting; they were also trying to mount me, along with every wolf in the pack. This was a whole new experience: 130 pounds of growling wolf on my back with his teeth in my neck and his front legs and claws locked round my neck. I was powerless; there was nothing I could do but wait for him to get off. Sometimes he came at me from the back, sometimes the side, sometimes the head, and he'd be growling and snapping at the younger male all the while. He was displaying his right to be the breeding male, and if I tried to move or get him off me, he just tightened his grip.

This courtship behavior went on repeatedly for two or three weeks, and it was relentless. They were the toughest weeks of my life, and I had been through commando training and an SAS course. I was up day and night, sleeping on my feet, and it was wearing me down. I was becoming a different person; instead of enjoying the calm and balance of their world, I found myself getting angry at the way they were treating me. Every time I moved, there was a wolf on me or nipping me and I was tired and sore. I had gone beyond exhaustion. I had finally found my limit.

Just as I was on the verge of collapse, the pack disappeared and left me alone for a week and a half. I was so relieved I broke down and wept. I couldn't have gone on with that level of brutality for a moment longer; I was shattered physically and emotionally. Where they went is a mystery but I assume that while they were gone, one or the other, or maybe both, of the males mated with the dominant female. I certainly saw no evidence of actual mating when they were on the hillside site, and when they returned, their mood had changed. It was as though someone had turned off the pressure. They were like a different pack: calm, relaxed; even Miss Grumpy was tolerant, her mind presumably on other things. She would come and stand beside me without growling and snarling. It was as though she was aware that she was going to need her family around her in the coming months. It was so refreshing and such a relief. If they had been the same creatures they were ten days earlier, I would have had to leave them.

Life returned more or less to normal. There seemed to be an abundance of food being brought home. I was always given my fair share, but they would take some of it and hide it in caches around and about, mostly in the river bank. The mud was a natural preservative and I assumed they were doing this because they expected lean times ahead. They possibly knew they would be going to lose their hunter, the female, as she reached the later stages of her pregnancy. The other development was that sometimes when the others went off hunting, they left the young male on the hillside with me.

The gestation period for a wolf is sixty-three days and as she neared the end of the second month, it became clear that she was carrying pups. She became lethargic, the hunting trips were far shorter than they had been, and she began to look swollen and pregnant. That was the point at which she started making a den for herself. She took herself up onto a high ridge about four hundred meters above us on the tree line and began digging beneath a small rock formation. She was at it for over a week, and each time she came down for a rest and some food, her coat and paws were covered in mud. I was longing to see how she was doing, but it was a very private affair—the others were quickly seen off if they tried to go near her so I didn't even attempt it. I contemplated instead what my role would be when the pups were born. They didn't make any attempt to get rid of me,

Holding a five-day-old wolf pup. *Roger Cooke*

With Helen and Cheyenne at eight months of age. *Linda Cowen*

With Cheyenne and Nataa at eighteen months. *Linda Cowen*

Inside the main wolf enclosure at Combe Martin giving the daily wolf talk. *Roger Cooke*

Zarnesti, the European wolf injured as a pup who connected so movingly with the disabled child. *Roger Cooke*

Elu at the age of ten, the matriarch of the wolf packs and the mother of Yana, Tamaska, and Matsi in 2004, and of Cheyenne, Nanoose, Nataa, and Tejas. *Roger Cooke*

The wolf pack during feeding. *Roger Cooke*

Matsi displaying defensive behavior during a pack feed. The position of the ears warns others to stay away. *Roger Cooke*

Cheyenne keeps a watchful eye. *Roger Cooke*

With three-week-old pups. *Roger Cooke*

In the omega role during a moment of tension between two adult wolves. *Roger Cooke*

Matsi, Tamaska, and Yana—
captive but far from tame.
*Roger Cooke*

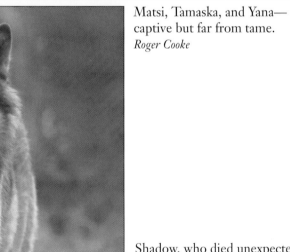

Shadow, who died unexpectedly
in January 2009. *Roger Cooke*

With Levi Holt,
my Native American
brother. *Bernard Walton*

With Tejas. *Roger Cooke*

A traditional wolf greeting from Tamaska, while Yana holds Matsi's muzzle. *Simon Frazier*

A greeting from Matsi. *Simon Frazier*

and I wondered whether they might have been using me as a human in a world that was naturally fearful of humans, as a means of defense.

And then one day she went into the den and didn't come out for a week and a half. The mood among the rest of us was very flat; the males didn't leave the resting site. The only one that moved was the young female that went off by herself every now and again, for short periods, no longer than twenty-four hours, sometimes returning with small bits of food, sometimes not. If the fathers were tense, they weren't showing it, but it was obvious that everyone knew what was happening underground.

When she finally emerged, thin and clearly lactating, she was triumphant. She was a changed character; flirty around the males and even the female, she went running from one of us to the next nipping our mouths, frantic for food. Then she ran down to the river and found two or three food caches and ate ravenously. The only inkling that this was the same wolf was when the older male went too close when she was eating and she went for him. After no more than an hour she ran back up the hill and disappeared underground.

There was no knowing how many pups she had given birth to or if any of them were alive. It looked as though pups had been suckling, but there was always the possibility that she might have rolled on them and squashed them after a few days or rejected them. It was another five weeks before we knew the answer. During that time our routine continued. The males lay around, the female brought back food—not much but what there was we shared. She would come out of the den and as soon as she had eaten and had a drink from the stream, she went straight back. At five weeks she came out looking purposeful and back to her old self, snarling and growling at everyone. She then took the big male and the female and disappeared for the day, leaving me and the younger male to guard the den. They came back full, with their bellies distended, and each one carried a piece of meat in its mouth from what was obviously a big deer that they had brought down. Her priority was to feed the pups and this was the moment when we knew for sure that this had not been a phantom pregnancy. She raced up to the den and called them, and we could hear them squeaking as they scrambled out of the den into the evening light for the first time. We couldn't see them because the area was too well hidden, but it sounded as though there were more than one. She would have regurgitated food for them, then taken them all back into the safety of the den for the night while the rest of us ate the first real meal we had had in weeks. I was so hungry and it tasted so good.

She repeated this process for the next week or so and then one day called the big male up to the den after making him regurgitate food for her by nipping him around the lips. From the bottom we could hear a lot of squeaking and then he came back down the hill, leaving her with the pups. This happened morning and night until one magical morning she came out of the den and tumbling down the hill behind her were two small bundles of black fur.

The excitement among the wolves was unbelievable. They scrambled and fell over one another to get to the pups, to sniff them, poke at them, and generally investigate—and the pups were completely unfazed. They rolled over and exposed their little pale tummies—something their mother had taught them in the den—then wriggled to their feet and went scavenging for food. They didn't even mind me, although I looked nothing like their mother, and in less than two minutes they were nipping at my mouth with their needle-sharp little teeth. Their education had begun underground weeks ago, when they were still blind, and they already knew whom they could trust and how they should greet their elders. Their mother had introduced them to my scent and the scent of every other wolf in the pack. Every time she had come out, she had rubbed herself against us one by one and taken that smell back into the den, so these pups already knew every member of their family and knew without doubt that these individuals were trustworthy.

I realized as I watched that extraordinary scene of nature and nurture just how privileged I had been over the last two years or so to have been accepted by this remarkable family. And just now, with these baby bundles of fur nibbling my face—a human face—begging me to regurgitate food, I had been witness to a miracle.

# CHAPTER FIFTEEN

# A Narrow Escape

What I had always loved about wolves was how important the family unit was to them, but it wasn't until I was with these wolves that I fully understood the social structure and different ranks and the jobs they did within that family. I knew there was one who was more aggressive than the others and I knew there was one that everyone listened to, and there was a lookout, but it was all a bit sketchy. I didn't know what value they put on me, but it seemed that what this pack wanted me to do was interact with the youngsters, and to inform them about our world.

Before they went out on a hunt they were particularly curious about how I moved. They used me as a plaything. They would see how fast I ran and would trip me up by nipping at my ankles from behind to see what happened, as if trying to assess my strength and weaknesses. I could only assume that given the distance they could travel and the length of time they were often away, they might well have gone onto the perimeter of farms and ranches and even towns. Humans were encroaching on their world so rapidly that they were always in danger of coming into contact, and it was as if they wanted to know how to read us, how we would react to an encounter and whether we were dangerous.

The pups were about nine weeks old and their mother and the

big male had gone off hunting. They had been gone for a couple of days and there was no knowing when they would be back. As usual, the young male and I were guarding the den area and, unusually, the young female was prowling around on the ridge acting as lookout.

I had not been feeling particularly well. The weather had changed, spring had come, and it was very hot in the sun. I had been feeling sweaty and very light-headed, almost faint, and was experiencing tremendous thirst. I think my body was in revolt about what I had put it through in the last two years. The stream, fortunately, was not more than six hundred meters away, and I had been wearing a path to it as I went every hour or so for a drink.

It was late afternoon and yet again I felt an overwhelming desire for water. I got to my feet and started down the usual track in the direction of the valley. As I did so, the young male flew at me from the other side of the den area and knocked me to the ground. He was a big, strong wolf and I felt as if I had been rugby tackled by three players at once. I lay there, shocked and winded and unable to move. This was completely out of character but he meant business. He was standing over me growling and snarling, his eyes blazing, ears flat against his head, hackles raised, tail in the air, and teeth bared. I wouldn't have argued with him even if I had been feeling well.

Looking as though he might rip my throat out, he backed me into the blackened hollow of a tree that had been struck by lightning some years before. I crouched, imprisoned, in this bowl of charcoal while he stood over me, and every time I tried to move he growled and snapped the air with his jaws. I knew those jaws could have broken every bone in my body. I had never seen him behave like this. In all our time together, even during the mating season, when he had been so dominant and forceful, I had never thought he wanted to kill me. Now I did and I began to fear for my life. For the next three-quarters of an hour he held me in suspense.

I couldn't work out what was going on, or what I had done to make him so hostile. I began to think that maybe he was planning to wait for the rest of the pack to come back before he killed me. My life flashed before me and I realized I had brought it on myself by being so pigheaded. Everyone had told me it was insanity to try to infiltrate a pack of wild wolves, and they were about to be proved right. They clearly were different from captive wolves and however much I thought I had been accepted, I had been kidding myself. They would obviously put up with humans for just so long but turn on them when they were no longer useful. As the minutes ticked by I became increasingly terrified. I had no means of defending myself; I was on my own, miles from anywhere. I even began to wish the grumpy female would come back; as the leader of the pack she might have saved me. No one would ever find me—they wouldn't even begin to know where to look.

Then suddenly, as dusk began to fall, his mood changed. The aggression vanished and he was balanced and calm once more. He looked at me with soft eyes and blinked. I didn't trust him. I thought, here we go—he's giving me a false sense of security; but he began to lick my face and all around my mouth, as though he were apologizing to me. This was no longer a wolf that wanted to kill me; this was the brother I had known and loved all this time.

Shaking, I ventured out of the hollowed tree, and he made no attempt to stop me. He then started to walk down the track that I had tried to take earlier toward the valley. After a few steps he stopped and looked back, which I knew meant he wanted me to follow him. So I went after him and the pups came, too, and about seventy or eighty meters from the den area, he stopped and scented a scratch mark on the ground. I looked down and there was the biggest pile of bear droppings that looked and smelled different from any I'd ever seen. There were deep scores on the ground and gouges in the bark of the surrounding trees, where a huge grizzly had scraped his claws and left his calling card. What I later learned from the Native Americans was that a bear will indicate his intentions by what he leaves on the ground, and this bear was out to kill a predator.

Suddenly it all became clear. The wolf hadn't wanted to hurt me. On the contrary, if I had walked down that track three-quarters of an hour earlier, the bear would have had me. The wolf had saved me from certain death and prevented the bear from being alerted to the den and the young cubs. I owed my life to him.

About three weeks later I was kneeling at the stream splashing water onto my face when I happened to catch sight of my reflection. I hadn't seen myself in months and I didn't recognize the face that looked back at me. It was thin and gaunt with sunken, darkened eyes; long, matted hair; and a bushy beard. I looked nothing like the fresh-faced youth who had left the Center two years before. I looked like a wild man and it shocked me to the core. I had lost forty-nine pounds and my health was definitely beginning to deteriorate. The pups were doing well. They didn't need me and unless I was prepared to die in the wilderness, I needed to go home, and soon.

I left early one morning, imagining it would take me about a week to get back to the bag. I was drained; I had no energy to do anything other than place one foot in front of the other. I didn't even have the energy to cry. None of the wolves had tried to stop me, but then how were they to know we would never meet again? I looked back just once to see if any of them were following but they weren't. They were making their way up to the den area and the pups for the start of a new day. Life was already going on without me.

I had stashed some pieces of meat from the last kill in my pockets, and I stopped every now and again to rest, eat, and drink. My walking was slow. I kept to the stream when I was uncertain of the route, but most of the tracks I took were familiar and at night I stopped and slept soundly. I was so tired that I didn't even worry about predators—didn't even care perhaps. It was a full week before I reached the rendezvous point and my old rucksack was still hanging in the tree where I had left it, looking a little weather-beaten. I pulled it down and sat with my back against the tree to wait for someone to find me, and finally, and for a very long time, I cried. The pain and the grief for all that I had left behind cascaded over me and I cried and sobbed until I had no more tears.

I didn't know whether Levi still sent a vehicle out every two days, as we had arranged. It had been months since I had left my last note, and he knew how dangerous my plans had been. Maybe he thought I was dead and had stopped coming so regularly.

While I waited, I contemplated just how dangerous what I had done had been—and I scared myself with the realization of how close I had come to death. By rights, no human should have survived what I had been through. The environment and the weather conditions alone were enough to kill me, not to mention lack of food and the diet I had been eating. Add to that the wolves—the strength and size of the creatures, the battering they gave my body and the intimidation. Yet it was the wolves that had kept me alive. They had fed me, kept me warm, and kept me safe. I would not be writing this today if the young male had not protected me that afternoon and stopped me from walking down to the stream, as I had intended. The bear would have killed me; there was no question about it. The only thing the wolves hadn't been able to do was make my body tolerate their diet. It had obviously been able to put up with raw meat for a long while but not indefinitely. And now, as I sat and thought about returning to civilization and all that that might bring, I had a real craving for honey.

It was twenty-four hours before I heard the drone of an engine making its way up the track. It was a four-by-four from the camp, but the driver was someone I didn't recognize. In two years there had been a turnover of staff, so my appearance was not as shocking to this guy as it might have been. My smell, however, was another matter, but he was too polite to say anything. I didn't speak much on the way back to the Center. There was too much—and yet nothing—to say. I hadn't spoken to another human being in two years, and I was feeling strange and disoriented.

When Levi saw me, his usually inscrutable face looked horrified. I wasn't prepared for the strength of his reaction, but it told me that the change he saw in me went further than my appearance, as indeed it did, and when he held out his arms to embrace me, I broke down. Those two years had changed me in every way and the enormity of what I'd experienced was beginning to dawn. I had survived, but I had said good-bye to everything that I loved and to a world that I could never recapture. I felt weak and faint and emotionally confused. Not many of the guys had known me when I left, but those who had looked as shocked by the sight of me as Levi did. They could scarcely believe that I was the same man. He asked me if there was anything I needed. I said, "Honey," which someone quickly brought, and while Levi and everyone who had crowded round stood and watched, I ate my way through half a jar.

The events that followed became a bit of a blur, but I remember being driven down to Winchester for a shower and the incredible sensation of warm water on my body and thinking that this was what civilization was all about. It was a terrible shower, in a wooden shed with abysmal pressure, but it felt like the Ritz. I was a very strange sight with my clothes off. My face and hands were heavily tanned and weather-beaten, but my body was lily white and when I shaved off my beard, my face became two-tone. My body was so emaciated I looked like a cross between Man Friday and a homeless beggar. I was skin and bone and although an incredible amount of dirt had come off in the shower, some of it was too ingrained to shift. I looked as though I were wearing someone else's head and hands—but a head that had a pure white band around it where the beard had been. I wondered what people would think of me when I traveled home to the UK.

Everyone wanted to hear my story but there was so much to tell,

I adopted a kind of shorthand and kept to the facts. The biologists wanted data: how many wolves there had been, what their traits were, and their coloring, whether they had bred and how many pups, what location they had been in, where they hunted, what tracks they took. From everything I said, they agreed that these didn't sound like any of the wolves involved in the reintroduction program but were almost certainly wild wolves that had come into the area using the old corridors that Levi had spoken about. Everyone was pleased to have Levi's theories confirmed, but there were still people in the camp—mostly the biologists—who strongly disapproved of what I had done. They were as interested as the others in how I survived in that environment, how I managed to get into the pack, and how I kept my sanity, which at times I wondered myself, but they did not give me a hero's welcome. They were angry that I had put myself at risk and the wolves at risk, but others thought my achievement was amazing. And the Native Americans saw it as commendable but not that remarkable. Their people have been going out and living in the mountains alongside the creatures of the wild for thousands of years.

I was tempted to get on a plane right away. Now that I had irrevocably made the decision to leave the wolves, I had a real desire to be home. I was tired of being judged and condemned for what I had or hadn't done, but I was persuaded to stay at the camp for a couple of weeks to let my health recover and to try to adjust to normal life. But it was not easy. I knew that mentally and emotionally I was in for a long haul, but I was surprised by how long it took to get back to a normal diet, and how difficult it was. I longed to eat junk food—I was dying for pepperoni pizza and ice cream—but my system couldn't take it. That kind of food went through me without touching the sides and made me feel very ill. My stomach had shrunk so drastically I could eat only the smallest amounts of food—what I would eat as a plateful today would have lasted for three days then—

and for a good few weeks carbohydrates made me vomit or gave me diarrhea.

But the hardest thing was adjusting to the human world. The world I had come from, and felt I belonged to, was so simple and balanced. There was no deception, no malice, and no gratuitous cruelty. Everything was done for reasons that everyone understood, and although they could be rough and aggressive and fight for what was theirs, they also had a gentle, caring side to their nature and looked after their own with great tenderness, as I had seen and experienced. Keeping the family unit safe and fed was what mattered most to these animals, but they had respect for the creatures with which they shared their world. They killed to eat, never for fun and never more than they could use.

So many human beings, in contrast, take everything for granted. They are greedy and selfish and plunder the earth as though they are the only species that matters. And so much of our society is dangerous and uncaring. At the airport waiting for my flight I watched parents arguing with their children and disciplining them for nothing. I wanted to say, "Stop it. Enjoy your children; appreciate what you've got."

# CHAPTER SIXTEEN

# *Another Way*

The last few weeks had been an emotional seesaw and now that I was back, all I could think of was finding a way of helping to improve the lives of wolves in captivity. I had learned so much about them, so many things that I would never have known in a lifetime of watching them from a distance. Their behavior was so often misinterpreted and their needs neglected, and I had a burning zeal to make a difference.

I headed straight down to Plymouth to see Jan. I was completely out of money and I needed a job that paid me a decent wage but also one that allowed me to work with animals, preferably canids. I made inquiries and, using my Forces connections, I enrolled in a residential course in kennel management run by the army in Melton Mowbray, in Leicestershire. I started with the basic handler's course, then went on to the baiter's course, where the dog learns to take the intruder's sleeve, and finally took the kennel handlers course. It was about three months in all, and I learned everything from feeding and looking after the animals to teaching them and their handlers to attack.

Dogs are used by the army for all sorts of tasks: they go into war zones to sniff out explosives, they patrol secure units, and, like police dogs, are trained to arrest an intruder by taking hold of the person's arm. But unlike police dogs, these animals don't stay with their handlers in their homes and they don't have to differentiate between good guys and bad guys. Anyone who is inside the perimeter fence who shouldn't be is an intruder, and the dog is trained to attack and arrest that intruder.

It wasn't my style of training, but I saw it as a means to an end. It was a way to an income from working with animals. This was a tough military environment, where everyone from men to dogs obeyed commands without question. The man in charge was a sergeant major, a tall thin man named Sid Gillam, whom we nicknamed Blakey after the authoritarian character Inspector Blake in *On the Buses*, a British sitcom from the early seventies.

Blakey was rigid in the way he trained the dogs that came through his unit. The handlers were taught to dominate. This was not the place for my theories about allowing the creatures to dominate me. No one dared to challenge his methods—including me—although it was obvious to me that there was a kinder and a more effective way. Fear and intimidation had never seemed to me to be a good basis for a relationship, and these animals were so much stronger and faster than their handlers and their sensory perception was infinitely greater.

But I had leaned from the Native Americans that no man has the right to tell another what to do, so I kept my views to myself. My Indian brothers would tell me that it's good to have a dream but unless the world is ready to receive it, the dream has no purpose. Blakey belonged to a generation that was bound by rules and regulations and didn't question accepted practice. He was not ready for change—he didn't even use food as a reward when training the dogs, which civilian trainers had been using for years. These dogs were trained by brute force.

Blakey took himself and his job very seriously and we used to love winding him up—and it was so easy. Every morning at breakfast I used to steal a sausage and put it in my pocket, which meant the dogs

I was handling never left my side. They behaved immaculately—no force needed at all—and at the end of the training session they got their sausage. I came top of the class every time. Blakey guessed I was up to something but could never work it out.

Not long after I finished and had left Melton Mowbray, Blakey appeared in a television program in which expert dog trainers were paired with celebrities to help them train their dogs. Blakey's partner was the camp comedian Julian Clary, who had a little lapdog. It was a brilliant—and wicked—piece of casting. The two men could not have been more different. Blakey trained large dogs to go into war zones and come out winners, and there he was on the nation's TV screens holding Julian's ball of fluff on a pink lead. The poor man never lived it down. The next time I saw him I asked how Julian was, and he clipped me on the ear and told me never to mention that name again. But Blakey was a good man and I had a lot of respect for him. He was one of the few men whom I regard as having had a guiding influence on my life. As well as running the training center, he was a veterinary inspector and as such went around the barracks every three months checking that the dogs were healthy. So I stayed in touch with him, and to give him his due, when he came to see what I was doing with the dogs in my care he became convinced that his methods were not producing the right results. And years later he came to visit me in Devon to look at what I was doing with wolves.

My first job after training was as assistant kennel manager at Headquarters Land Command, just outside Wilton in Wiltshire. I was looking after about six dogs in the kennels at Erskine Barracks. The animals' job was to protect and guard the camp, and my job was to make sure that they remained in peak operational condition for twenty-four-hour duty. There were some wonderful characters among them, but they were not pets by any stretch of the imagination; they were working dogs—German shepherds—bred to go up against humans, and they were hard animals that needed a lot of careful handling. I felt very sorry for them. The dogs had six to eight weeks of training for this work; the handlers had just two, and in my view it should have been the other way round. Some of the handlers hadn't a clue what they were doing and the dogs ran rings around them.

There was a lovely young soldier we used to call Yim Yam because of his strong Birmingham accent. He wanted so much to be a handler, but he had had no experience with dogs at all. Every time he let his animal off the leash, instead of running and apprehending the training target, it ran past him and peed against a lamppost. But Yim Yam adored the dog, and every morning he would come into the kennels and say good morning to him and then go from one kennel to the next, greeting each of the dogs by name. One night I had been out drinking and decided to curl up in the kennels with one of the dogs rather than go all the way home. Early the next day, when it was barely light, this lad came in to say good morning to the dogs as usual, going from one kennel to the next, "Morning Shadow, morning Dusty, morning Kelly," and when he got to mine, he couldn't see me in the dark of the kennel, and I said, "Morning Yim Yam" in a very deep voice. The expression on his face was a picture. I think to this day he thought the dog was talking to him.

We had moments of good fun in the barracks. There was a sergeant major named Tony "Frangie" Frangos, who was from the same commando unit I had been with; he was very fit but a small man, and for some reason we were always playing practical jokes on him. I remember someone once put raspberry jam on his telephone receiver, and there was the occasion when we put his beret into the freezer the night before he had an important meeting with the regional sergeant major and all the bigwigs from the parachute regiment. Frangie sat there with his beret quietly thawing and dripping icy water down his collar, unable to say a word. Most shameful of all our exploits: The base commander had discovered that brass fittings, handles, doorknobs and knockers, and other valuable bits and pieces had been disappearing from an empty building on the site that was due for demolition. There was a suggestion that Frangie's men might have been responsible. He leaped to our defense with the ferocity of a mother tiger. There was no way his men would steal, this was an outrageous slur on his men's integrity, he could vouch for each and every one of us. "Don't worry, lads," he said in recounting the story, and then as an afterthought, "You didn't take that stuff, did you?" We had to come clean. Our lockers were stuffed with brass.

The real problem with the dogs we were handling was that the army didn't understand the importance of the dogs' natural rank and was asking animals to do jobs for which they were completely ill equipped. You could not put an alpha animal into an attack role. It couldn't cope. The alpha is the decision maker and the most valuable animal in the pack. Its whole being would be telling it to stay out of danger and to hide around the back of its handler and let someone else do the dangerous job. No low-ranking animal could do the job either because it wouldn't have the natural aggression. The perfect attack dog was the beta animal. He relished the task and was tenacious and fearless. By failing to appreciate the distinction, the army lost a lot of good dogs.

It was not much better at dog psychology. When a dog had the baiter's arm in its jaws, the handler would shout "Leave it," commanding the dog to let go, and then be enraged if the dog disobeyed. What no one seemed to understand was that this was working against the animal's natural instinct. In the wild, the wolf will hang on and won't release its grip until its prey is dead. That's how it survives and how it feeds the pack. The dog was being instructed to let go when it knew the prey was still very much alive and kicking, so of course it was confused—and it would have heard the shouting as encouragement from the pack. But I had to tread carefully. I was a new boy on the block and couldn't hope to change the culture overnight. Furthermore, what I had at the moment were just theories. I needed to put them into practice.

One of the joys of the job at the barracks was that I worked abnormal hours. It wasn't unusual to be at the kennels in the middle of the night because handlers were on duty twenty-four hours a day, and it was a good time to do some training with them when there were no distractions. This freed me up for a little moonlighting and it wasn't long before I found myself in demand as a dog trainer for civilians working at the camp and in the local villages. It was all by word of mouth, but I found it very gratifying to see how receptive people were to the things I was telling them—and it brought in some extra money. The traditional dog training at that time, even for pets, was still very much based on force and I turned that on its head. I used the animal's natural reward system, such as food and warmth, as motivation and their own forms of punishment, namely deprivation and cold, as a deterrent. I also insisted upon dog owners bringing the whole family to training classes because dogs see themselves as part of the family pack, even if there are just two people in the household, and training a dog to respond to just one member of that pack upsets its natural instincts. If small children are in the house, any confusion in the dog is potentially dangerous.

When things go wrong, dogs are very seldom the problem. The problems are invariably the humans who have bought the wrong animal for their situation and failed to train it in a language the dog understands. People often try so hard to do the right thing but end up with the dog ruling and destroying their life.

I had a couple with the most beautiful retriever that used to fetch balls and toys the owners threw for it in the garden. As time went by, the dog refused to give up the toys it retrieved and growled if anyone tried to take them away from him. No one dared challenge him and by the time the dog was two years old, he was the undisputed king of the castle. The owners had virtually been reduced to living in a cupboard under the stairs because the dog had gradually taken possession of the rest of the house. Every time they went into a room, he growled so aggressively that they hardly dared move. It broke the owner's heart but that dog had developed such a high level of possession that there was no alternative but to rehouse him.

The problem is that we go against nature when we ask a dog to retrieve an object and give that object to us. In the wild what they retrieve is theirs—and the way they indicate to their fellow pack members that something belongs to them is by lowering their ears and covering the object. If the ears go sideways like airplane wings, it means that others should stay away. But we have altered the looks of dogs so radically in our breeding that most dogs' ears now flop over and they can't use them to communicate. Instead they growl. If the dog is a high-ranking animal and growls when the owner tries to take the ball from it, and the owner backs off, then the dog quickly learns that that is the way to possess not just the ball but anything it wants to dominate. So we have to try to get rid of that instinctive behavior, but it's as much a case of educating the owner as it is of educating the dog—and usually that is much harder.

I remember the receptionist from a local veterinary practice ringing me once to see if I could help an old man, in his eighties, who was having problems with an eight-month-old collie crossbreed he had adopted. She said he couldn't cope; how much did I charge? I said five and a half pounds, which barely covered my petrol, but she beat me down. He was an old-age pensioner, she told me. "OK, I'll charge him four pounds." It was agreed and as I drove into the village following the directions I'd been given, I came to a huge house. If this is his, I thought . . . but it wasn't. His was next door, and even bigger. What's more, he owned most of the village. I was doing some serious muttering under my breath, but the minute I met the man I had a change of heart. He loved the dog but he was a man who could barely walk without assistance, and he had a dog that wanted to run for miles and herd sheep. They were a complete mismatch. But the man had a housekeeper, so I got him to take the dog on a lead into a paddock at the back of the house and I asked him to stand at one end of the field and his housekeeper at the other and gave them each a supply of food. Then I let the dog go and he raced from the old man to the housekeeper, and each time he reached one, he or she gave him a bit of food and moved a little closer toward the other, and the dog ran to the other and she or he did the same. The dog tore back and forth, slowly shepherding them into the middle of the paddock. It fulfilled his natural herding instincts and it gave him the exercise he needed. When the man and the housekeeper had reached the center of the field, the man put the dog on the lead again, and the three of them walked calmly back into the house.

In those days I was experimenting. People came to me with puppies to train and also with older dogs with behavioral problems, like the collie crossbreed and the retriever, and I applied what I had learned about wolf behavior to them all. But it was still early days for me—there were many things I didn't know about wolves—so it was as much of a learning experience for me as it was for the owners. But what I was telling people seemed to strike a chord and many of them found that their dogs became transformed. The timing couldn't have been better. There was a sudden and refreshing interest in dog psychology—people were beginning to look to the wolf as a means of understanding why their dog behaved the way it did. It felt as though the world was ready, but while other behaviorists based their teaching upon what they'd observed about wolf behavior from afar, mine was based on a unique perspective: I had lived with wolves.

Not that that qualified me to handle every problem. I was in the park one day near Salisbury with a couple in their sixties and their German shepherd, which they couldn't handle, when a very bossy woman—a Barbara Woodhouse look-alike—strode over to ask me whether I was a qualified dog trainer. I said that I wasn't exactly qualified but I did know something about dogs and was helping out a friend. She said she had a collie that was a nightmare. I gave her a card and said if she couldn't find a trainer, then she should give me a ring and I would see if I could help.

About ten minutes later her collie appeared in the park. I noticed it from the minute it appeared; the woman who had approached me was not far behind it and to my surprise the dog ran straight for me. Worse, it dived at my crotch. I swung round in the nick of time, and it sank its teeth firmly into the flesh on my inner thigh, a whisker from the crown jewels. The pain was excruciating—but not as bad as it might have been had I not reacted so quickly.

"You see?" said the woman triumphantly. "That's what he does!" I didn't offer to help.

# CHAPTER SEVENTEEN

# The Proof of the Pudding . . .

The Native Americans say that if you think of a captive animal as being in a cage, then so will the animal, but if you give that animal the impression that the cage is a means of keeping it safe and secure, and you enrich its life within it, then the animal will regard its cage as a haven, not a prison. It seemed to me that most wolves in captivity felt they were in cages. Those I had known bore little resemblance to their wild counterparts; they had had their spirits broken and most of them wouldn't have taken freedom even if you had left the gate to the enclosure wide open.

I was convinced that I could improve their lives by making it resemble life in the wild, but I needed credibility. I had had experience with wolves that went way beyond what most biologists could claim, but I had no initials after my name, so I set up an organization I called Wolf Pack Management. It was just me at that time but I thought it sounded impressive. I desperately needed to put my theories to the test. I enjoyed my work with dogs but my real mission was wolves, and as luck would have it, Wilton was very close to Longleat Safari Park, which still had a thriving pack of timber wolves.

Longleat was, and still is, one of the most highly regarded wildlife parks in the country, and I knew I couldn't find a better pack to study. The park is set on the grounds of a magnificent, stately home belonging to the 7th Marquess of Bath. The house is Elizabethan, completed toward the end of the sixteenth century, and is an amazing attraction in itself, but it's surrounded by the most fabulous parkland, designed by the great eighteenth-century landscape gardener Capability Brown. The parkland extends for nine hundred acres, with a further eight thousand acres of woodland, lakes, and farmland—unspoiled countryside as far as the eye can see—and that's where the animals live. The wolf enclosure couldn't compete with the space the wolves were living in in Idaho, but it bore no resemblance to the cramped enclosure at Sparkwell, and it was refreshing to see captive wolves—along with lions, tigers, and every sort of wild animal you can think of—living in such good conditions in England.

I went to see the head warden, Keith Harris, whom I hadn't met before, and I told him what I had been doing and asked whether I could put some of my theories to the test with his wolves. Despite the quality of the conditions in which they were kept and the health of the animals, Longleat had a problem: the wolves were not breeding. There was little understanding in the early days about pack management and the need to create four-year gaps between generations to ensure a successful breeding pattern. Like many other wildlife parks, Longleat had brought together a number of wolves at the outset, taking them from other parks that had surplus animals, and the current pack were of much the same age. They were getting too old to breed.

In the wild there would always be several generations in one pack and always young females coming through that would breed. They would breed to provide new pack members to defend territory, to hunt, and to continue the line. In captivity, the wolves had a square meal as often as they needed it, of good-quality food delivered to their door, and there was no threat to their territory. There was no reason for them to increase pack numbers and so they didn't. Wolves have an extraordinary ability to manage their own bodies and to decide whether or not to have young. Females will often have phantom pregnancies, or they will have genuine pregnancies that they can abort if they so choose. If she decides the timing or circumstances are not right for her to give birth, a female halts the pregnancy and absorbs the pups into her body.

I was confident I could improve the lives of these wolves and maybe even encourage them to breed, but it was hard to convince the management that they should pay me when their wolves were in every respect, apart from reproducing, healthy and happy animals. However, Keith Harris was interested in what I had been doing with the Nez Percé and agreed to let me work alongside their keepers, but it had to be on a volunteer basis. Because my primary interest was in helping the wolves and I already had an income from the army, I was happy with whatever terms they wanted to set out—and it was the ideal testing ground.

Visitors come into the park by car, hundreds of thousands of them every year. When it opened in 1966, it was the first drive-through safari park outside Africa, but because the animals are in the lush green English countryside rather than the African bush, and in enclosures of a few acres rather than a few hundred, they are highly visible and entirely unafraid of vehicles, so you can see the animals at very close quarters. It became the model for many other zoological parks around the world.

The Wolf Wood was beyond the tigers and the lions, in an area of perhaps four or five acres. In the center was a copse of mature trees, mostly oaks, and no thickets or ground cover. The whole area was grass covered and in one corner near the boundary fence was a small man-made pool for drinking water. I remember one day watching a young male wolf stalk a rook that was bathing in it. The wolf had been lying some distance away watching the pond and must have noticed that every time a bird came to bathe and splash about, it took longer than usual to get into the air afterward; the water on its feathers interfered with its aerodynamics and made it fly less efficiently.

He crept forward until he was about fifty meters away and I thought, what a silly wolf, thinking he could catch a rook, but he got it.

The only building was a simple brick structure that was used by the vets if and when they were needed; and the whole area was securely fenced and gated, as every enclosure was. During open hours, staff members would sit in black-and-white-striped four-by-four vehicles, painted to look like zebras, parked in each enclosure to make sure no visitors were tempted to get out of their cars. I used to feel sorry for the volunteers who worked in the park, taking the jobs because they wanted to work with animals and spending their days as glorified car park attendants.

Cars were part of the landscape; humans on foot were not, and docile as these animals might have looked from behind the windshield, in reality they were dangerous. Even I was not allowed inside the enclosure with the wolves—the park's insurance wouldn't cover me—so I spent all my time off from the day job parked in the enclosure studying the wolves and getting to know them from my vehicle, which was then a white Citroën van. The wolves learned to recognize the van and whenever I drove in, they would mark scent all over it. I didn't think anything of this until I noticed that the lions seemed to be taking a very close interest in my van. I would follow the keeper's vehicle out of the park in the evenings and the lions paid the keeper's vehicle no attention at all, but mine they ran toward, particularly the females. One evening one of these females took a massive swipe at the back of my car with her paw and with such force that the whole vehicle rocked. The only explanation I could come up with was that she objected to the scent of the wolves. The next night I tried hosing the van down before leaving the park and the lions didn't so much as look up when I drove through their enclosure.

At nighttime, when I wasn't allowed in the enclosure, I took up semipermanent residence across the valley from the wolves in a small copse, about five hundred meters away as the crow flies. It was a good vantage point from which I could watch and listen, and I felt very much at home as I settled down night after night with torch, binoculars, sandwiches, and a thermos of hot tea. I sat at the base of a big hollow oak tree, which also housed a couple of owls, and enveloped by the darkness and the noises of the night, I might almost have been a child again, at home in Norfolk being lulled to sleep by the hooting of owls and the other nocturnal creatures going about their business. There was something quite magical about sitting there in the middle of one of the finest landscapes in the country howling to a pack of wolves and having them return my call.

Having watched the pack's behavior for several weeks, I began what I call an enrichment program. I rigged up a sound system at a couple of vantage points outside the enclosure—one of which was the copse with my hollow tree—and at dusk and dawn, when these animals are most active, I played tape recordings of wolves howling that I had recorded in Idaho. The idea behind this was to fool the wolves into believing there was a rival pack across the valley, and I hoped that might induce the alpha female to produce pups.

The knowledge that there is a stronger or bigger pack in the locality, which might attempt to take over their territory, brings a pack together, in exactly the same way as human communities are brought together by the threat of an enemy invasion. And the instinctive action of any species that thinks its future security might be in danger is to breed. Let that pack know that there is an alpha female out there, who might challenge the resident alpha female, and she will either rise to that challenge or roll over and admit that she is past her prime and surrender the role to a wolf that is better equipped for the job.

This, at least, was the theory on which I was working. What I didn't know was what would happen in practice with a pack of wolves that had never known the wild. I was relying on their genetically inherited memory.

My equipment was rather Rube Goldberg. It needed to be

portable because wolf packs, obviously, move around, so in order to be realistic, the sounds of their howling had to move around, too. But the equipment also had to receive and carry sound over long distances. From a small electrical shop in Wilton I managed to beg a satellite dish that suited my purpose perfectly. I rigged that up to a tape recorder and a loudspeaker. It didn't look very elegant, but it was effective and I was able to take it to other locations within the park. But my base was always the hollow oak.

The tapes appeared to do the job and after weeks of uncertainty, Macha, the alpha female, was showing definite signs of being pregnant. There have been so many wolves I've known over the years and so many of them have been wonderful characters, but there was one in the Wolf Wood at Longleat that will be in my heart forever. Her name was Daisy, and she was the one Macha chose to act as nanny to her cubs. She was a dominant female, a beautiful animal who seemed destined always to be the bridesmaid and never the bride. That spring at Longleat I remember watching her waiting patiently for her leader to give birth—as we all were—and after sixty-three days of pregnancy, the moment arrived. Macha had taken herself underground into the birthing bowl she had excavated, and all the while Daisy lay nearby under the shade of a big oak tree waiting for the telltale squeaks that would signal all was well. The moment she heard those yelps and squeaks, she sprang to her feet and went eagerly to the mouth of the den, where she stood for a few moments listening; two pups had been safely delivered and were suckling contentedly. Daisy was clearly desperate to get at them, but she had to wait for another five weeks before she could take charge and do her job.

Five weeks is the normal length of time pups stay in the den after birth. During that period they see no one but their mother, who suckles them and keeps them warm, the two most important requirements to a wolf's well-being. No one is yet sure whether the pups are born to the rank they will hold as adults or acquire it during the first few weeks of life, that is, whether it is nature or nurture, but where they suckle on the mother is certainly significant and the mother can influence that. The pups that take—or are allowed to take—the teat closest to the middle will do better than those that feed on the outside. The milk in the middle is of better quality and they are kept warm by the closeness of their siblings suckling alongside them. These animals will hold higher ranks than the ones who are pushed to the edge, and as a result they will have a richer scent. And what begins in the first five weeks of life continues into adulthood. The high-ranking animals eat the richest food, smell stronger, and command the greatest respect.

What the pups also learn during those first five weeks in the den is who the various members of their family are, how the pack system works, and how each member needs to be greeted when the moment to meet them arrives. Every time the mother emerges from the den to feed, smelling of her cubs, she rubs herself against other members of the pack and carries their scent back into the den for the pups to smell. If the wolf she rubbed against was a high-ranking member, the mother will take the pup's head or neck in her jaws and very gently turn it to expose the youngster's throat, which she will then lick all over, teaching the pup that when he finally meets that high-ranking animal, he must roll over, exposing his tummy and throat, and be submissive. So entirely through scent she introduces the pups to the family and the family to the pups, and when they stumble out of the den, wobbly on their feet and still half blind, they know the character and social position of every member of the pack they meet and know how to behave.

At five weeks the cubs' mother starts the weaning process and they begin to move on to solids in the form of regurgitated meat. Initially it's their mother that regurgitates food for them, but then the nanny takes over and as they grow, they can induce any member of the pack to regurgitate by nipping the adult's lips with their very sharp little teeth. While the mother is nursing, she can't go far from the den and so other members of the pack bring food for her. They will often carry a piece of meat from the kill up to forty miles to feed the alpha female, and they will do the same for the nanny when she takes over the care of the pups. Alternatively, one of the wolves will take over the task of looking after the pups for a short period while the nanny follows a trail deliberately left for her to the site of the kill.

Bringing up the next generation is a collective task. The mother leaves the cubs so that as the alpha female she can get on with her job of leading the pack, and the educating and nurturing of the young falls to the nanny and in time the wider family.

Watching Daisy, who was so dedicated, so tolerant, and such a wise creature, I found myself contemplating my own childhood. Much as I adored my grandparents, I realized that I had felt hurt and angry that my mother had abandoned me to their care. It wasn't what happened to any of my friends or cousins. But watching how the wolf mother brought up her young made me see my life from a different perspective. So much about my childhood experience seemed similar to what I was witnessing here that all of a sudden it started to make sense. I hadn't been deprived—far from it. My childhood had been enriched by the patience and wisdom that comes with age—something my mother, as a young woman on her own, could never have provided. She'd had to go out to work, to bring home food, just as the alpha female did, and she left the child rearing to the member of the family she deemed most qualified. I felt that we were as one.

# CHAPTER EIGHTEEN

# Divided Loyalty

After I found the job at the kennels in Wilton, I rented a small bungalow on a farm just outside Salisbury, and Jan came to live with me there, along with two of her children from a previous relationship and a couple of Huskies I'd rescued.

Moving into this little bungalow together was everything I thought I wanted and Jan was a complete star. She had had no experience with dogs, let alone large, dangerous ones, yet she joined me working with the attack dogs at the barracks—and she immersed herself in wolves. She must have wondered many a time what she had taken on because it wasn't quite how she had imagined life would be. She had envisaged a conventional future for herself working in an office, driving a nice car, living in a neat semidetached house, and effortlessly paying off the mortgage. As she once said, her most exciting or dangerous decision before she met me would have been choosing which brand of orange juice to buy. All of that changed, and many were the times she would come out with me on a winter's night to sit in the pitch dark and the pouring rain, helping operate the tape recorder to try to convince the wolves we were a rival pack across the valley.

I couldn't have asked for a better girlfriend. She never complained about the bizarre lifestyle or the fact that I spent most of my evenings and weekends at Longleat. She gave me all the space I needed to do my own thing, and when we had children, she was a fantastic mum. But looking back, I realize that it was probably never a great passion for either of us. It was a relationship that, at the time, suited us both. We each provided what the other wanted—companionship, friendship, a home, and children—and although we thought we were in love, and were very loving and caring toward each other, I am not convinced that it was ever the real thing. But maybe I never gave our relationship a chance. I was so bound up in my work at that time, and so passionate about the wolves and everything I was learning and discovering about them, that I wonder whether any human relationship could ever have come close. If I had had to choose between spending a night in the wolf enclosure or at home, if I'm honest, I probably would have chosen the wolves.

We were together for eleven years in all and had four children—Kyra, Beth, Jack, and Sam—who are all great. Jan already had three children, although only two of them lived with us, so when she went into labor with Kyra, she'd done it all before and was very relaxed. She calmly ran herself a bath and told me to stop panicking. Moments later she shouted, "It's coming!" and was suddenly as panic stricken as I was. I bundled her into the car and drove at top speed to the hospital in Salisbury, phoning ahead as I drove to say she was about to give birth. I looked round at her lying across the backseat and I could see the baby's head. I thought I was going to have to deliver it in the car, but we screeched into the hospital entrance where two nurses were ready and waiting and practically caught Kyra seconds later, as she burst into the world kicking and screaming.

After Kyra was born, Jan had to stay at home and look after her, so our nights of sitting out under the stars—and the pouring rain—were limited. I was working day and night and becoming more and more obsessed about all the things I was doing. Even when I was at home, I was logging my findings, listening to recordings, rationalizing the information I'd been getting from this captive pack of wolves.

I was fascinated by them and equally fascinated by what their behavior told me about the attack dogs I was working with in the day job, and also the domestic dogs that people were bringing me for training. I could see that in our ignorance we humans were shamefully letting down our best friends and that we needed to radically change our thinking if we were to redeem ourselves.

I knew I had only scratched the surface and needed to learn much more if I was to help these dogs—and the place to learn was Idaho. I determined to go back to see my Native American family again and to be with wolves I could study at close range. England was home and where my family—my blood relatives—were; I would always feel the draw to come back, but my spiritual home was in the northwest of America. The tribes' people were my brothers, the wolves my adoptive family, and year after year I felt the need to sit at their feet and listen to their words of wisdom. Once there, the responsibilities of home and family seemed a million miles away.

My being away seemed to suit Jan. We became like a service family, much as we would have been if I had stayed in the army and been sent away for long tours of duty. Jan built herself a life around the children and her friends and family, who were based in Plymouth, where we eventually bought a house together. She was very independent and I think I disrupted the quiet order of her life on the occasions when I reappeared. She was probably happier without me and switched off so completely when I was gone that she found it hard to have me back.

I spoke to Blakey about going back to Idaho and asked if he would put in a word for me with the authorities, and he convinced them that further training among the Nez Percé would benefit the attack dogs. They allowed me to take extra leave that, added to my annual entitlement, gave me six weeks. It was long enough to make the cost of the journey worthwhile. I left not long after Macha's pups were born at Longleat, and although I longed to watch them grow and develop, I also longed to be among the mountains and the wild wolves once more.

Each time I went back to Idaho I imagined that my experience and seniority might earn me a better tepee. Yet time after time I was allocated the tatty one down by the edge of the forest away from the main body of the camp. To begin with, I had thought it was because I was the newcomer. Then I thought maybe being white, I was being punished for the collective sins of the white man who had persecuted the Indian tribes over hundreds of years. Finally, after the third or fourth year of being shown to this tent, I summoned the courage to ask Levi why I was always given the tent by the forest. In typical style he didn't give me a direct answer; he told me a story. It made little sense at the time but I came to understand what he was telling me.

One day, according to legend, an Indian squaw was collecting firewood for the village when she came upon a young wolf cub that was cold, hungry, and close to death. She looked around for its mother or other members of the cub's pack, but there were no signs and so, rather than leave it to certain death, she wrapped it in a blanket, put it into her basket, and took it home to her tepee. There she looked after it, fed it on warm fresh milk, and nursed it back to health. She raised it as she would her own child, feeding it meat from the hunt as it grew, and everywhere she went the young wolf trotted by her side. The two became inseparable; they went to collect firewood together and to fetch water from the river, where they would sit and watch their reflections in the early morning sun. In the cool of the evenings they ran and played together in the forest before going home to sleep curled up alongside each other.

One day when they went down to the river to collect water, they sat side by side, as usual, looking into the murky depths, but the squaw saw not her own reflection staring back at her, but the reflection of two wolves. Her own face had become that of a she-wolf. Greatly alarmed, she ran back to the village and sought out one of the elders of the tribe and explained what had happened, asking why she had been cursed in this way. The elder said, "This isn't a curse; it's a gift in return for your kindness. You must pack up your belongings and take them to the edge of the forest where you will live between the two worlds—the human world and the wolf world."

What Levi was telling me was that I, too, had been given a special gift and it would be my role in life to live between the two worlds.

As I returned to camp one day, I found a letter waiting for me from Jan. It had sad news. Soon after I'd left, Macha, the mother of the pups at Longleat, had died. I felt as though I had been told a close and dear friend had gone. I knew that the pack would have been howling for her, and I felt gutted that I hadn't been able to howl with them and share their grief. Instead, I went down to the enclosure with the captive wolves and cupped my hands around my mouth and howled alone and mournfully, hoping that somewhere, somehow, Macha might hear me and know that I was missing her. And as I lay in my bed that night, in that twilight zone between wake and sleep, I imagined that I heard her familiar voice say one final farewell.

Wolves don't share our emotions and can't afford the sentimentality we humans wallow in. The pack immediately restructured itself and, to my great joy, Daisy took Macha's place as the alpha female, and the following year it was she who was pregnant. I was back in Idaho on what had become an annual visit when she gave birth, but things had gone badly wrong. The keepers had found Daisy wandering around the enclosure with a dead pup stuck halfway out of the birth canal. She was in serious distress and needed emergency veterinary help. They darted her with a tranquilizer and then operated to remove the pup. One had been born, but they found several more dead inside her. She was not a young animal and there was a strong possibility that in another pregnancy this might happen again, and so, reluctantly, the decision was taken to sterilize her.

I arrived home shortly afterward to an impossible situation. The pack had an alpha female that couldn't breed. Somehow, she would have to be persuaded to surrender her role and allow a younger female to take the lead. The question was, could I convince her by the use of tape recordings? If I was able to convince her and the rest of the pack that she was being challenged by a stronger, younger lone female looking for a vacancy, then I hoped she might step aside for one of her own pack members, a younger dominant female like Zeva, who was one of Macha's early cubs.

With the help of Jan and one of the keepers, I first of all played recordings of a full pack from a couple of locations as I had done before, to give the impression that there were rival packs in the area, which would encourage the captive pack to pull together as a family. Then I played a recording of an alpha female from various points closer to the enclosure to suggest that she was moving around in the buffer zones between the territories of the three packs. The howl of a wolf that can't breed sounds very different from a breeding animal, and I knew that when she returned the challenge from this lone female, the pack would notice the difference and put pressure on Daisy. My fear, however, was that if Daisy refused to relinquish her position, and the rest of the pack wanted her gone, they would push her out and she would have nowhere to go.

In the wild that situation is solved by dispersal. The wolf that is no longer wanted leaves the pack and goes off in search of another pack to join. In captivity that can't happen and the wolf that would have dispersed is attacked. The other wolves bite it on the base of its tail where there are scent glands. If those glands are destroyed by creating an open wound, the animal loses its identity, and therefore all status, and is kept away from food and very often dies or is killed.

Fortunately, Daisy accepted demotion. We then had to persuade the pack to promote from within because the lone wolf they had heard looking for a vacancy didn't exist. I started to intersperse the lone wolf with recordings of a full pack again, which I hoped would have the effect of bringing them together. I also made sure that at their next feed, the wolves were given a whole carcass instead of hunks of meat that had already been dissected. In the wild, the kill is very important as a means of defining which animal holds what rank within the pack. The individual lumps of meat that wolves often get in captivity blur the distinctions, and this pack needed to work out its hierarchy.

It was another five days before the voice of a new alpha female rang out in answer to the challenge. It had been a long and nail-biting wait, but during the early hours of the fifth morning, in reply to my challenge from the lone alpha female, Zeva's howl pierced the silence. Her voice had taken on a new authority and she was defending her position and her patch with vigor. She was backed up by the rest of the pack, their howls indicating that they were firmly behind her. Even Daisy's voice could be heard among them rooting for her new leader.

It was the most thrilling moment for me and made all those nights spent out in the wet and the cold worthwhile. Unless this had all been coincidence, which seemed highly improbable, we had just witnessed an incredible breakthrough. We had restructured a pack from the outside; with nothing more sophisticated than tape recordings, we had demonstrated that it was possible to influence and alter the behavior and makeup of a pack of wolves and that had to be good news for biologists and for farmers who struggled to keep wolves from taking their livestock. I felt that what we had achieved offered great hope for the future.

Ironically, Zeva chose Daisy to nanny her pups when they were born and she once again fell into the role she had had many times before. She looked after them diligently and when they were eighteen months old, she lay down one day in the shade of her favorite tree and quietly passed away. She was a very special wolf who had touched me greatly and I was sorry to see her go.

# CHAPTER NINETEEN

# Finding a Home

News travels fast in the animal world and my success at Long-leat was beginning to be recognized. I was approached by a number of other wildlife parks and zoos wanting help and advice about how to manage their wolf packs. I also started working with the public. Jan and I would take visitors to one of the copses near the wolf enclosure for a howl-in as night fell at Longleat. I would explain to them why wolves make that eerie, spine-chilling sound by the light of the moon that's in every horror movie. I would give a number of rallying howls, as if gathering my pack around me, then Jan would howl, as if joining her leader, and from across the park would come the sound of the captive pack in full cry, defending their territory against us.

Human beings have long believed that wolves howled because they were grieving for a lost member of the pack. That's not true. It can be a mournful, grief-stricken sound, but they howl for all sorts of reasons and in different ways—with different intonations, just as we humans do when we speak—and there's a lot of information in a howl. It *can* be that they've lost a member of the pack and they howl to see if they can call it home, but they also howl to defend territory, to tell individuals or other packs where they are, and to rally the troops. If the howl is cut off short, it means danger—stay where you are, stop doing what you're doing, I'm taking charge. If it goes on for a long time and tapers off, it means quite the reverse—keep doing what you're doing. If it is low and deep, it is defensive, warning rival packs to stay away. The whole pack will howl together if they are under threat, and the mid-ranking wolves will even disguise their voices and use yips and yelps between howls to give the impression to the rivals that their pack is larger than it actually is.

Wolves whine and whimper when they are face-to-face. They howl to communicate from a distance when we might use a cell phone, and they can adjust the volume to make it short-, medium-, and long-range. If a pack member has gone hunting and fails to return, the pack howls to let the missing wolf know where the pack is in case he has lost his bearings. And if the missing wolf hears his pack calling, he will reply to let them know he's on his way. Each animal's howl is as distinctive to that wolf as the way it looks, smells, and walks; and once you start to study them and live among them, you quickly notice how different each wolf is. They are as unique as humans and their voices just as distinctive. Even in the dark I can tell which wolf is approaching by the sound of his footsteps and by his smell; and I can tell which animals within any pack are howling.

Each rank has its signature howl; the alpha's voice is deep and low and he or she howls intermittently: howls for five to ten seconds then pauses for the same amount of time and howls again. The pause is important because he is listening for a response. Depending upon what comes back, he will get the others to add their voices or he'll move and call from a different location. The beta also has a low voice but he howls continuously for three or four times as long as the alpha. And so it goes throughout the pack—the mid ranks, the mid to high, the low ranks, and even the omega all have individual voices.

This is how a lone wolf, looking for a pack to join, knows where and when would be a good moment to try. If he hears the pack calling for a missing member several days running and hears no answering howl, which suggests that the missing wolf might be dead, he knows that there could be a vacancy. Wolves are not sentimental. Their prime concern is survival, and in the wild that means being able to feed and defend their territory; a pack that is missing a rank is vulnerable.

Equally, they won't take in a defective lone wolf. I have seen wolves play terrible tricks, which amount to premeditated murder. The alphas have suppressed one rank in the pack from howling, giving the impression to the lone wolf that that rank was missing, and when he has turned up hoping to fill the vacancy, the beta wolf has killed him.

I thoroughly enjoyed what I was doing at Longleat. It was fantastic to be given the opportunity to put my theories into practice, and I enjoyed watching the faces of the public, particularly the children, light up when they heard the wolves howling. I am sure the park valued what I did, but the howl-ins were the only thing I was ever paid for. This meant I had to work around the clock trying to fit in everything I did there with the army job and the private dog training that I had to do to support us.

After a couple of years at Wilton, I moved to Warminster. I successfully applied for a job at the Land Warfare Centre and Battlesbury Barracks, which was much closer to Longleat, and the Longleat Estate allowed me to rent one of their cottages in the village of Corsley Heath. Warminster was a bigger job; there were more than twenty dogs in the kennels as opposed to the six at Wilton, so there was more scope to make a difference. Neither the day job nor the dog training was particularly well paid, though, and since Jan was pregnant again, money was becoming an issue.

I couldn't see an immediate solution until one day the BBC arrived at Longleat to make a pilot program about wolves. It was provisionally called *The Beast Within* and was presented by Philippa

Forrester. It was designed to highlight the similarities between the wolf and the domestic dog, and I was asked to take part. It was a subject that I knew like the back of my hand and we had a lot of fun doing it. We filmed in the park and I also went down to the BBC studios in Bristol. The program was a great success; everyone seemed very pleased with the result and with my part in it. They talked enthusiastically about a series being commissioned on the strength of the pilot. I felt confident that a new career beckoned—and television paid a lot better than anything else I had ever done. But time passed and I heard nothing; then one evening the television was on—and there was Philippa Forrester presenting the first of a brand-new series about wolves. Without me.

I was stunned and rang the BBC to find out what had happened. I was told by someone in the production office that they had contacted Longleat to try to book me for the series and been told that I no longer worked at the park and that they had no idea where I had gone or how I might be contacted. I was furious. Longleat knew exactly where I was: I was in the middle of putting their breeding program in order—it was a critical time for them—and I can only think that they must have been afraid they would lose me. It *was* a critical time and I can understand why they were worried, but I would have liked to have made the decision to refuse the job myself.

It was the beginning of the end. I stayed on for a few more months, but I knew the time had come for me to part company with Longleat. Things rapidly went downhill; they wanted more of me and I wasn't prepared to give it. I had been there for four years and had always slightly resented the fact that they had benefited from my research and my expertise but had never offered to reward me. They had provided me with the cottage, but it was very basic and I'd had to pay rent on it, and I had been scrimping and saving all that time. This was the final straw: they had deprived me of an opportunity to make some money and to make a bit of a name for myself. I told them I couldn't go on like this: they either had to put me on the payroll or I would have to go elsewhere.

If there was any lingering doubt in my mind, Jan removed it. One day she went into the dining room of our cottage where Beth, our newborn baby, was sleeping in her cot, and found a large rat sitting on top of her cleaning its whiskers. Jan had put up with a lot and been heroic in helping me with the wolves, but she had had enough. She wanted to go back to Plymouth, where her family lived, and I couldn't argue. So we bought a house together not far from her parents, and she took our two children, Kyra and Beth, straight there. Another child, Jack, was on the way. I told Longleat I was leaving and handed in my notice at the barracks.

It was no secret that my dream was to have my own wolves, and around this time I was offered a couple of male timber wolves by the Paradise Wildlife Park at Broxbourne, one of the places where I used to help out from time to time. They were nearly three months old and needed to be rehomed because their owner, a private collector in the West Midlands, had tried to socialize them but had left it too late and they would never be as tame as he wanted. They were perfect for me and I was dying to say I'd take them, but I had no land and so I couldn't commit. Then in the way these things happen, I was chatting to a couple of guys who had come to a howling evening. They were part of a group that staged medieval reenactments and were particularly interested in wolves because the forests of England would have been full of wild wolves in medieval times. They asked what my plans were, and when I told them I was hoping to find some land, they said I should get in touch with a friend of theirs, Stuart Barnes-Watson, an Australian who had just bought fifty acres in North Devon. He was another member of the reenactment group and like them was very much interested in history and therefore wolves. He was intending to create a kind of outdoor adventure and education center for kids to teach them forest skills and about the creatures that used to live there. They gave me his number and said I should give him a call.

I phoned him and very much liked the sound of what he was planning. I told him I had two wolf pups earmarked, and he couldn't have been more delighted by the idea of adding wolves to the mix. I went down to East Buckland to see him and to have a look around the place. It was a beautiful location with a pine forest leading down to a valley with a stream at the bottom, and we got on famously. He said I could choose anywhere I liked for the wolves. I went for an area at the bottom that reminded me of Idaho. It was steep and more thickly forested and obviously on a much smaller scale, but it was just as picturesque. I could imagine the wolves coming out of the ferns in the early morning mist—and how exciting it would be for the kids camping there—and I loved the way the sun dappled the ground beneath the tree canopy. It looked like a picture postcard. It wasn't going to be the easiest place to build an enclosure, but I couldn't have dreamed of a more perfect home for the wolves and immediately told Broxbourne that I'd take the pups.

While I was working on the enclosure, the pups, which I named Shadow and Pale Face, went to Linton Zoo, a family-run business in Cambridge. They happened to have a spare enclosure for a few months before some lions arrived, and offered to have the wolves, and to house me, free of charge, until we were able to move to Devon. In return, I gave talks when I was there and helped them with the other animals. I remember one of my tasks was to pluck hundreds of chickens that had been donated, and it was as if their feathers had been stuck in with superglue.

My accommodation was a portable cabin that became my home for two months. It was very basic and the nearest it had to cooking facilities was a microwave oven, so I borrowed a cash-and-carry card and went to the local wholesale store and bought Pot Noodles, which need no cooking and which I had always thought were quite tasty. But because you could only buy in quantity at a cash-and-carry, I had to buy the same flavor—so I lived off chicken and mushroom Pot Noodles for breakfast, lunch, and supper for two months. I never want to see another Pot Noodle as long as I live.

The enclosure was a nightmare to build. I had help from a couple of guys, but it nearly killed us. The only access was down a forest track, and the truck I'd hired to take the materials and equipment down kept getting stuck in the mud. In the end we had to carry it all down by hand—a distance of about six hundred meters. We dug a trench four feet deep around the entire perimeter because wolves are notoriously good at digging their way out, and fixed the wire to scaffolding poles that we cemented into the ground. That was the basic structure and it couldn't have been sturdier or more secure. I'd asked a local welder in Plymouth to bend the tops of the poles to forty-five-degree angles that faced inward, so there was no way any wolf could escape. We successfully begged, borrowed, stole, and fund-raised to get the money, but the greatest cost was in blood, sweat, and tears.

Stuart had put in an application for a license to keep dangerous animals at the outset, and when our efforts were finished, the various planning inspectors came to look. There was a vet I'd known at Longleat, someone from the police firearms department, and a man from the local council. They tested the fencing, asked to see paperwork about public liability insurance, and so on; they asked about safety procedures, about who held firearms certificates, and they wanted to be sure those people would be available in the event of a wolf escape. They covered everything and went away apparently satisfied, saying we would get their decision in due course. We were confident that the rest was a formality, and I went ahead with arrangements to collect the pups from Linton. Kim, the owner, was delighted because the lions were arriving any day.

Then on Christmas Eve I had a phone call; the county council had turned down our application. They said there had been objections locally to having wolves in the area. We could appeal, they said, but it would cost two thousand pounds. I couldn't believe it. I was in real trouble. I couldn't keep the wolves in Cambridge for much longer, I didn't have the money for an appeal, I didn't even have money to buy Christmas presents for my kids. I had nowhere to keep the wolves and no thought about what to do next. It was not a happy Christmas.

Fortunately, the local newspaper, *The Journal*, had been interested in what we were doing in South Buckland and when planning was refused, they sent a journalist to interview me. She wrote a big piece highlighting my plight, and the very day the paper hit the streets I had a call from Bob Butcher, who ran the Combe Martin Wildlife and Dinosaur Park near the coast, about thirteen miles away. He had read the story and said that he had space, and if I could put up an enclosure for my wolves, which he would pay for, he would give them a home free of charge. You couldn't see me for dust; I went to see him right away, unable to believe my luck. I liked Bob at that first meeting and was impressed by what he had done on the property and his obvious interest and concern for animals. The park had twenty-six acres in all set on the edge of Exmoor, and as the name suggests, it was a mixture of wildlife alongside a display of life-size animatronic dinosaurs that brought children to the park in droves. The wildlife collection was quite modest. He had birds of prey, snow leopards, meerkats, apes and monkeys, sea lions, and tropical butterflies. It was probable that the addition of wolves would boost trade, while the research I was known for would boost his credentials. The justification for keeping wild animals in captivity was to protect them and improve their welfare, and he seemed very keen to be doing the right thing.

The space Bob offered me was less than an acre, much smaller than the previous site, and it was very wet. It had been a pelican pond, and although there were a few trees, there was more pond than earth, but beggars can't be choosers; I could fix that and in other respects it was good. It was near the bottom corner of his property near the monkey house, with fields and open countryside beyond, which was hilly, wooded, and unspoiled. I agreed to take it and we shook hands on the deal. In return for housing the wolves, I undertook to give educational talks about them every day during the season, and Bob allowed me periods away from the park to further my research.

Kim Simmons of the Linton Zoo very kindly agreed to keep Shadow and Pale Face in Cambridge for another couple of months, and I immediately set to work with a digger with a swing shovel to move earth from higher up the hill and landscape an enclosure. Then the hard work started: digging a four-foot trench around the perimeter—by hand. It was backbreaking. We couldn't get the machinery down the hill, so there was no alternative, but every few inches my shovel would hit a massive tree root. There weren't many trees but those that there were had been there for a long time and had gigantic roots that reached over the entire area. I was working with a very entertaining Scottish welder named Arthur, who fixed the heavy-duty metal fencing to the metal posts. The highlight of our day was a huge breakfast in the local pub, the London Inn. But what I remember most about Arthur was that every time I touched the fencing while he was welding at the back of the enclosure, I got a tingle up my arm. I couldn't work it out until I noticed one day that the electric cable to his welding gear that ran from the monkey house was submerged in the pond. I turned to him and said, "Arthur, is that all right, mate?" And he said in his broad Scottish accent, "Aye, there's nay problem there. I do it all the time."

My first season at Combe Martin was a huge success. The local paper had followed up their story at Christmastime with news about where I was, and people started coming from far and wide to see the wolves. Every afternoon I gave a talk and went into the enclosure and howled, and without fail, the wolves began to howl with me. The children loved it and so did I; it was such a pleasure to see the looks on their faces and a great opportunity to demonstrate to everyone, young and old, that wolves did not deserve their demonic reputation.

The wolves seemed happy in their new home, but mine was more than eighty miles away, and it was no longer such an enjoyable place to be. My preoccupation with the wolves and building a home for them hadn't helped my relationship with Jan. She had been playing second fiddle to wolves for too long and the strain was showing. The drive to Plymouth was a good hour and a half and I had been doing it twice a day, so when Bob suggested that I rent a room in the house at the park, which he ran rather halfheartedly as a hotel, it didn't take long to agree. So that was where I stayed until the falconer at the park, who looked after the birds of prey, offered to sell me his damp, derelict old trailer that was parked on a piece of land alongside the road, just a short walk up the hill from the wolves.

I say parked, but its traveling days were done. If you'd tried to move it, it would have fallen apart. I paid twenty pounds for it—I was robbed! It was tiny, just big enough for a bed and a little gas cooker. It was in a shocking condition with mold growing all over the inside, and there was no toilet, so I had to pee into an empty putty bucket. But it was somewhere to lay my head and it was all I could afford. Bob had a shop at the park where visitors bought mementos and I sold bits and pieces there, which brought in a bit of money, but I no longer had a salary and I had exhausted my savings.

It was fantastic to have my own wolves, to be with them night and day, to freely interact with them, feed them, and study their behavior. They became the sole focus of my life. What I now wanted was a female for them. I wanted to breed a litter to see whether a captive pack would allow me to raise its pups, and if so, whether I could teach them about our world and theirs. Howletts Wild Animal Park in Kent answered my prayers with the offer of a three-year-old female named Elu that needed to be rehomed. It is common practice for wildlife parks to give one another animals that they no longer have space for or that are being picked on by the pack—animals that in the wild would be dispersed to find another pack.

She was a gorgeous animal, black in color, but when I went to see her, the first thing that struck me was how skittish she was; none of the wolves she was with had been socialized at all and practically climbed the walls when anyone went near their enclosure. My first thought was would my fencing be up to it—particularly those bits where the tree roots had defeated me? But she seemed to be a climber rather than a digger, and the keepers assured me that provided she had somewhere underground where she could hide, she would be fine. Fortunately, I had already built a den in the enclosure. I'd made a wooden frame that I covered with plastering mesh and finally plaster, leaving an entrance that was big enough for me to climb through should I need to get inside. I arranged a date to come back and collect her.

Three volunteers made the journey with me; I borrowed a decrepit old van from someone who worked at the park, put a big cage in the back, and two of them traveled in front with me while the other volunteer followed in a car just in case we broke down. It was a long trip: six hours each way. Howletts is very efficient and professional. By the time we arrived, the vet had been to see her, she had been darted, and she'd had a full medical examination—she was fit and in good condition and she was on a stretcher ready to go. We carried her to the cage; I gave her an injection to reverse the tranquilizer and bring her around, and covered the cage with a big tarpaulin. Some people keep animals sedated for travel, but in my experience it is better for them to be fully conscious, particularly wolves. We've lost too many animals that way, and if the cage is covered so that they can't see what's happening, it usually keeps unsociable animals reasonably calm.

We had driven for about three-quarters of an hour when we started to hear noises from the back—sounds of scuffling and the cage rattling—so we decided to stop for some coffee and investigate, and while the others got the thermos out, I went and checked on the wolf. She was wide awake and severely distressed. She was a pack animal and clearly didn't like being alone, and was doing all she could to bite and claw her way out. I wasn't worried about her getting through the cage; Arthur, the Scottish welder, had made it for me. The cage was so strong it would have held a rhinoceros, and it weighed about as much, but we still had more than five hours to drive and Elu was going to hurt herself unless I found some way to calm her.

I don't know what possessed me to do what I did next, though that's been the story of my life: I've done things no sane person would have dreamed of. I opened the cage, climbed in, and traveled for the rest of the journey to Combe Martin cramped into an area that measured two feet by four feet by five feet with a dangerous animal that had never been in close contact with a human being before.

My companions stood watching, their mouths gaping in disbelief. They then closed the cage door and pulled the tarpaulin back into place, leaving a little peephole so I had just enough light to be able to see Elu, and set off. The transformation in this wolf was incredible. As I climbed in she moved to the very back of the cage, but she didn't try to get away. She became completely calm and spent the next five and a half hours with her head resting on my shin and nibbling at my boot laces. She was even happy to have me stroke her and gently scratch her back end, as you would a dog. I still have bits of hair that I pulled off her that day as a memento. I was astonished by the trust she showed me and deeply flattered.

We didn't get back until late at night, when it was dark, so rather than immediately put her in with the boys in the enclosure, not knowing how they would take to each other, I put her into a bigger cage I had up near the trailer; and I went in there with her to keep her company. During the night she started communicating with the wolves down at the bottom of the hill, which was a really good sign. The next morning we transferred her into the small cage, and again I went in with her. The others loaded it—and me—into the bucket of a dumper and drove it down to the enclosure. She went through the open gate, walked straight past Pale Face and Shadow without even looking at them, and while they followed her, drooling like love-struck teenagers, she sniffed and scented around the perimeter, and showed no signs of wanting to escape. Pale Face and Shadow hadn't met a female since they were pups and she clearly exceeded all their expectations.

# CHAPTER TWENTY

# *Poland*

The biologists I worked with were always skeptical about the value of comparing wolf and dog behavior. They regarded them as two distinct creatures and didn't share my belief that unless we intervene, the wolf will eventually turn into the dog that we know today—and the dog into the wolf. I believe we can use them to help each other. If you look at the behavior of wolves as they get closer to human populations in countries like Poland and Finland, where there is less space than in northwest America, they are developing similar characteristics. Originally they were so frightened of humans they stayed in the forests and the hills and were rarely seen. When they started approaching farms, a farmer could scare off a pack of four or five wolves simply by showing himself. The minute they saw him, they would turn and run. Nowadays, they are so confident that if a man appears armed with a dustbin lid and a broom, that pack of four or five wolves will hold their ground and growl, and might even chase after him.

I became interested in Poland some years ago when a volunteer at the park named Angela, who, sadly, is no longer with us, asked me to go there, hoping that I might be able to help the local small landholders who were losing livestock to marauding wolves. Having been a research student in the forests of the northwest, she felt passionately that something needed to be done and she still had contacts in the region. I had never been to Poland and thought it was a great opportunity to learn more about European wolves and possibly interact with them. It is one of the few places in Europe where, despite being hunted and persecuted, wild wolves were never quite eradicated. They were hunted for sport in these forests until 1997, when the Polish government gave in to pressure from environmentalists and banned wolf hunting, but rather feebly policed the ban so poachers had a field day. Not surprisingly, there was little change recorded in their numbers. There were two other factors, I was told. The number of prey animals had dropped dramatically and with Poland's rapid economic growth, what was left of the wolves' habitat had become fragmented.

So in 2002, when the park at Combe Martin was closed for the winter, I left a team of volunteers in charge of the wolves and flew to Poland for the first of several short visits to learn as much as I could about the wolves, their habitat, and what was making them raid the farms. I flew to Gdansk, then took an eight-hour bus ride due east to the Romincka Forest on the Russian border. On the other side of the border it's called the Krásný Les, hence the name of the river Krasnaya that runs through it. It was the most amazing sight, a natural forest that looked as though it had never been touched. This truly was a place that time forgot. It was incredible to think that at one time, thousands of years ago, most of central Europe would have been covered in dense forests like this with massive trees, and they would have been home, as this one was, to species of wildlife that have become extinct in so many other places. Among dozens of other creatures there were elk, wild boar, red and roe deer, red foxes, even the odd lynx and, of course, wolves.

I stayed in the middle of the forest, in a lodge, busy during the season with people of all nationalities who came to hunt game. The walls were hung with antlers and there were photographs going back over years of forest life. The food was fantastic: soups, meats, vegetables, and serious cakes, all made by the woman who ran the place. It was food designed to keep you going in the forest, and none of it was expensive. The price list on the wall made me laugh. It had the price for every nationality and at the top was the German, which was a good few euros higher than any other. When I looked quizzically at Romick, one of the foresters who was my companion, he just grinned.

Romick didn't speak a word of English and I didn't speak a word of Polish, but I had a guide who spoke better English than I did, so between the two of them I learned everything he knew about the area and the wildlife within it. He was one of several foresters who managed the forest, all of them highly respected men in the community, like local policemen in ours. The jobs were handed down from father to son; they were managers of nature, keepers of the wild, and he was as pleased to join forces as I was. Our aims were very similar: my job was to help manage the creatures within his forest and his job was to manage the forest that gave those creatures a home. Despite the language barrier, Romick and I forged a tremendous bond. At dusk he would take me up to the high seat he had built in the forest, where we would watch the wolves and all the other wildlife without being seen, and all the way there he would be pointing at things and explaining, and I would answer as best I could. We managed to establish a way of communicating that went beyond words in the natural world. I respect this man deeply; he is a genuine, honest person, whose word is his bond and whose promise means everything. That, I discovered, was the culture of these people. A slipped word that means nothing to us means everything to them.

On a subsequent trip, I took along a few colleagues from Combe Martin to give them some experience of wild wolves. One of them, after a very drunken night on the local vodka, invited one of the foresters to come to England—something all of us do in a friendly sort of way to strangers we're having a good time with. It's an easy gesture that usually goes no further. The next time I went to Poland, this forester was noticeably standoffish. I was on my own this time and was mystified. I couldn't imagine what I had done to offend him, so I asked the guide if anything was wrong. "Yes," he said bluntly. "The last time you were here someone promised him a trip to the UK and it hasn't happened." That someone who had invited him had long gone, but I had no alternative but to buy tickets for this man and his son to visit me in Devon for a week. The son had to come because he was the only one in the family who spoke English. They loved the wolves and it turned out to be a good week, but it made me realize just how important it is to respect other people's cultures—and just how dangerous vodka can be.

Meeting one of the farmers who had lost animals to the wolves took me back to my childhood and immediately I had great sympathy for the man. Stanislaw had a wife and daughter and a small plot of land that stretched to the edge of the forest on two sides. They owned no more than twenty cattle that were so much a part of the family and so precious to them that each animal had a name. There were no fancy tractors or machines around, just a utilitarian working farmyard and rather shabby outbuildings. Nervous guard dogs that looked like a cross between a German shepherd and a Great Pyrenees ran around. The wolves had killed some of the dogs as well as the cattle, and although he had put studded collars on them for protection, the dogs had still been taken. That didn't surprise me—by the age of six weeks wolf cubs have learned how to avoid antlers on deer, so for them a studded collar would have been just another pair of antlers to avoid. What was interesting was that the wolves obviously didn't respect the dogs as being their own kind.

Stan and his family lived very simply in a traditional two-story, earthen-colored house. They kept chickens and geese, and it was clear that the farm was their life and their entire livelihood. Dressed in coveralls and a straw hat, he told me through the interpreter what had been happening. For a while a string of flags along the fence line had kept the wolves away, but that no longer worked and neither did their fences. One of his calves had been attacked just before my visit and he had some video footage that showed clearly which parts of the calf the wolves had taken.

To a farmer like this, losing a calf was like losing a leg. But losing an adult milking cow or a seasoned bull was even worse. The government paid compensation, but no money could replace an animal that had taken years of breeding to reach its peak. On small holdings like Stan's, farmers bred for succession so that there would always be a younger animal coming through to replace one that was too old to work. So if one of them was killed by wolves, it could take six or seven generations to replace it.

This man had more reason to hate the wolf than anyone I have ever met, and yet he didn't. You could see in his eyes that he had the utmost respect for them. His father, and his father before him, had taught Stanislaw about the wolf when he was a child. He knew that wolves created balance in the forest and kept the animals in natural harmony; he knew that they provided food for others as well as themselves and stripped out disease and illness. Even though they attacked his livestock, which he and his family could ill afford, he knew that he needed the wolf as much as he needed the cattle.

I visited two other farms in the vicinity with boundaries that went to the edge of the forest. They lived on the same subsistence level as Stanislaw and his family, and had suffered similar devastating losses, but like Stan, they were amazingly philosophical about it. They understood the value of wolves to the forest and would be happy to see them deterred rather than shot. One of these farms had a World War I cemetery on its land, and the calf they took me to see had been killed on the edge of it. While I was examining the remains, we heard a door slam and a car speed off down the track. Walking back to the house, four puppies came bounding toward us across the field. I was told by my guide that it was not unusual for people with an unwanted litter to dump them, and word had got out that animal experts were in the area. The puppies looked to me as though they were the result of a wolf mating with a domestic dog, which again I was told was a common occurrence. We took them back to the hunting lodge, and I was later told that the lodge had kept one for themselves and found homes for the others.

The third farm I visited, a mother-and-son business, was the poorest of the lot. She had been on the land all her life and was very old-school, and although she respected the wolf, she had had enough. The son had obviously had more education than his mother and seemed to have studied ecology and knew more about the animals in the forest. But what I remember most about the visit were the coffee and biscuits. The Polish are very hospitable people and in every home you go into you are offered food and drink, which you cannot possibly refuse. The old woman handed me one of the most disgusting biscuits I've ever put into my mouth and asked what I would like to drink. Because *coffee* was the only word I knew in Polish, I asked for *kawy*. The room fell silent and I wondered what terrible faux pas I'd committed. Everyone else, who'd been given refreshments at this farm before, asked for *herbata*, which I discovered meant tea. My coffee was like pond water and the only consolation was that by comparison it made the biscuit quite palatable.

What interested me, in looking at the carcasses of the animals the wolves had killed, was how little of the beast they had taken. I have been with wolves when they were starving and seen how quickly they tear up a carcass; if they are hungry enough, they will eat every last bit. These carcasses had not been the center of a feeding frenzy; they looked as though they had been dissected by a surgeon. In almost every example I examined, either from a recent kill I saw in the flesh or from one that had been photographed, strips had been taken from the thigh or the shoulder, or an incision had been made in the rib cage and the vital organs taken, or the stomach had been opened and cleaned out and a few choice pieces of meat taken, but the legs were still intact and the bulk of the animal had been left. Even parts of the dogs had been eaten.

The evidence simply didn't support the theory that the wolves were attacking domestic livestock for survival because there wasn't enough natural prey in the forest. Besides, the forest was bristling with deer and elk and beaver—all of which I had seen in the scats.

The other common theory was that farm animals were an easy meal for the wolves. I didn't buy that. I have spent nearly twenty years with these creatures and I have never seen them do anything that could be described as opportunistic. Everything they do has a purpose and that includes what they seek out to eat. They know so much about regulating their own bodies and about the world they live in and the value to the pack of the animals that share it with them. What they take, and when, depends on a host of variables like the time of year, the weather conditions, when pups are expected, their health, the cohesion of the pack, and a whole lot more. They know instinctively what their bodies need. I have even seen a pack of wolves eat the most putrid carcass that was practically liquefied it was so rotten, but they had worms and knew instinctively that eating bad meat would flush the worms out of their systems.

I have seen my own pack in Devon (more about them later) become practically addicted to the fatty stomach lining from the carcasses of the cows and sheep I fed them. They suddenly started eating that in preference to the meat. I couldn't understand it, so I ate it myself for four months and I found that during that period I was much better able to cope with the cold. The stomach lining of deer was completely different; it didn't have the fat content of the domesticated animals. They ate what their bodies told them they needed.

If I was right about the Polish wolves hunting according to need, then they were getting something from the cows and sheep—and even the dogs—that they couldn't get from any other source. I haven't done enough research to prove it yet, but I suspect that if the farm animals have been inoculated, the answer could be immunity to disease or even something as simple as the wormer the farmer has dosed his stock with. Or it could be the fat content in the stomach lining, as with my captive pack, that boosted their resilience to the long, cold, snowbound winters.

The irony is that the wolves would have discovered the value of domestic livestock without moving from the forest. For many years they received "meals-on-wheels." Hunters used to bring livestock carcasses into the forest to attract the wolves so that they were easy to find and shoot. After wolf hunting was banned, ecotourism took over, and the practice continued so that tourists could be sure of seeing wolves and getting the photo they'd been promised. It was only when Poland joined the European Union in 2004 that baiting was banned.

The solution to this problem could be simple. Once we know exactly what it is the wolves are missing in their natural diet, we could take the nutrients they need to them in some other form and they would no longer need to attack the cattle.

There is one other possible explanation for the raids, which is more difficult to remedy. They may not be wolves at all—they may be hybrids, like the four little pups that came bounding over to us on the farm. Wolves now live in such close proximity to human beings in Poland that it's inevitable that they breed from time to time with domestic dogs. It would explain why these creatures that look like wolves and live like wolves are prepared to come into the fields in broad daylight and have no fear of humans.

# CHAPTER TWENTY-ONE

# Making Contact

That first trip told me all I needed to know about the forest, the surrounding area, and the farmers. Next I needed to infiltrate a pack to see if there was any other explanation for why they were taking livestock when there seemed to be plenty of food for them in the forest. The problem was I didn't have time to do what I did in Idaho because I couldn't be gone from the park for that long. I had to speed up the process, and after the success of my experiment with a tape recorder at Longleat, I thought I might be able to use the method again in Poland. This time it would have to convince the wolves that there was a rival pack in the area with more males in it than they had in theirs. My theory was that it would make them want an extra male to boost their defense to ward off the rivals. And that extra male was going to be me.

I didn't get a lot of data from Romick. He knew every pathway and tree in the forest and he knew how many wolves there were but not whether they were male or female, young or old. So before I could make a convincing tape I had to find out how many male wolves were in the existing packs. I had to get out on the ground and establish contact. On this trip I had colleagues to help, and during the day they would go into the forest and look for tracks and scats and signs of any kill that would help me know which direction I should be heading in at night. I used the technique I had used in Idaho. I went into the forest as a lone wolf, howling to try to establish how many wolves were out there.

The European wolf is a lot more flighty than the wild timber wolves I lived among in America, probably because they see many more humans. The Romincka Forest is a national park, so there are nature trails through it and people go there to walk or to study the wildlife. As well as game and large mammals, there are dozens of smaller species and hundreds of rare birds and plants. The foresters come and go, as do loggers, and during the hunting season there are men with guns. Men, guns, and wolves are not a good combination. So the wolves have had a lot of interaction with people, but all of it has been negative. Even the scientists collecting data use snowmobiles to track them down and catch them with lassos. So where North American wolves are curious about humans, the Polish are frightened and therefore very shy—one sight of you and they will be gone. Romick told me through the interpreter that he didn't think I had a chance of even getting close.

I started preparing about a month before I left England. I adjusted my diet and cut out all perfumes, which included soap, toothpaste, deodorant, and shampoo. I wanted to look and smell as much like a wolf as possible—all of which went well until I was on the plane and the woman in the seat next to me sprayed perfume all over herself. I began to think traveling by sea might be the answer and locking myself in my cabin. I ate nothing but the food the wolves ate: venison, rabbit, and pheasant with some vegetables and only water to drink. I ate no carbohydrates and nothing sweet and stuck to that when I arrived in Poland, although it took a lot of willpower to resist those gorgeous cakes at the lodge.

Running as a lone wolf there was not as scary as it had been in Idaho. I knew the forest quite well by then, but it was still pretty hairy to be alone in it in the dark. There may not have been bears in

Poland, but there were wild boar and they terrified me. One night, before I set off on foot, I was in a high seat with a couple of other guys. We had night-vision goggles and were hoping to spot wolves in the forest below. There was no toilet in the seat, and as the night wore on I became desperate for a pee; I was so desperate there was nothing for it but to climb down and have one in the forest. I told one of the guys to keep the goggles on me and give me a shout if anything untoward appeared. Having held it in for so long, I was down there for quite a long time, enjoying the feeling of relief, confident that I was safe. All of a sudden I heard snuffling noises and the sound of something quite heavy on the ground not far to my left. I wondered what it might be; it was obviously nothing to worry about because if it had been, my colleague would have yelled at me. Just as I was about to zip up my fly, a huge boar with great tusks appeared in front of me. My feet didn't touch the ground as I ran for the ladder, screaming abuse and shaking like a leaf. "Why the hell didn't you warn me?" I said, but he didn't hear me; his back was turned. The other one had spotted a light in the forest and the pair of them were staring intently in the other direction, having entirely forgotten about me.

Boars in the Polish forests are about the size and weight of large sows but with tusks and a ferocious temper; they can be mean as hell, particularly if they have young. One of the foresters had a "tame" boar that he aptly called Wreck-a-neck, which was incredibly aggressive. My fear wasn't illogical. Local children who used the forest didn't worry about wolves, but they were afraid of wild boar. Not even wolves would take on a wild boar. They would take a young one if they were lucky, but I once saw three of them having a go at a female—she just ran at them and they scarpered. I often heard them crashing around at night and my heart would be in my mouth, but I never came face-to-face with one again.

After a week or so I had established what packs were out there and what we needed on a tape. They were very different from the North American wolves. Their packs were much smaller and they didn't stay together, maybe because they were looking for food. There were four packs in the area and two of them were just pairs. The largest pack had five individuals and that included pups. I worked out their territories, which was not hard—the ammoniac smell of their scent was quite eye watering in places; but they frequently seemed to go outside those areas and travel across the boarder into Russia. The border was marked by a series of white posts with red tops that stood about two feet six inches above the ground and in the winter were entirely buried in snow. It was very easy under those circumstances to get lost and more than once I found myself on the wrong side of the border trying to explain to a vehicle full of trigger-happy Russian border guards what I was doing there. I had learned that the trick was to shout *"Wilk! Wilk! Wilk!"* at them in my best Polish, while digging quickly through all my layers of warm clothing to find the official piece of paper from the Polish authorities that proved who I was and that I was there studying wolves.

Unhappily, the foresters wouldn't allow me to use a tape recorder inside the forest. They would let me howl, but they would not let me take in any sound equipment. So my colleagues played it from Stanislaw's farm. Wolves can hear from up to ten miles away, but whether they heard it and were influenced by it I will never know for sure. What I do know is that we established sound contact. I heard what I assumed was a lone female calling. I responded and she called back. Her call went from defensive to locating. She was asking for help and my call indicated my willingness to join her. We called back and forth for the best part of two and a half weeks. During that time I was letting her know my position by scenting and eating food left from the pack's kill, taking what a mid-ranking member would eat: fillet meat and stomach contents. I had a feeling that she was ghosting me, watching me, following me; and every now and then I would catch a glimpse of her.

One morning I came around a corner in the forest and there she was on the track ahead of me, not more than six or seven meters away. She stood and stared at me for forty or fifty seconds, which for an animal that had been shot at, chased, and persecuted was extraordinary; and then she was gone. She was the most beautiful wolf, in good condition, obviously well fed. There was no doubt in my mind that she was the wolf I had been calling to. And then one morning when I was kneeling over a stream in a clearing, splashing water onto my face and having a drink, I was aware that I had company. I turned around slowly and there, sitting no more than six feet away, was this glorious female.

Sadly, I didn't have time to stay in Poland any longer, so I will never know whether I could have got closer to her or infiltrated a pack in the way I did in Idaho, but I viewed this as a tremendous personal breakthrough. It showed me that no matter what human beings have done to them, if you go to wolves on their own terms, as I did with foxes all those years ago, and show them that you mean them no harm, then that trust will gradually return.

It was time for another experiment with tape recordings. I had promised Stanislaw I would try to find a way to keep the wolves away from his livestock, and with this limited knowledge of the wolves in the area, the farms, and the forest, I now felt confident I could show him how to help himself. My plan was very simple. I gave him a cheap tape recorder with some speakers—exactly what I had used myself when I had tried to locate the different packs. What we needed to do was convince the wolves that a rival pack already owned the territory around Stan's farm. If I could do that convincingly enough, my theory was they would leave it alone.

I showed Stanislaw how he must use the equipment. It was very basic. There was no point in going into that impoverished rural area with speakers that would shake Jamaica. The equipment had to be straightforward enough for people to be able to work it and cheap enough for them to be able to afford it. The tape I gave him had a recording of a pack with five males in it—one more than any of the packs I had heard in the forest—therefore a potential threat. They were giving a defensive howl, as if making it clear to all comers that the area around Stan's farm was their territory. I explained to Stan that there were different-sounding howls and that before wolves went into an area to hunt, they gave a locating howl to make sure they weren't stepping on anyone else's toes. He immediately said he had noticed the different howls; it was gratifying to see how in tune this man was with his environment. Before a raid, he told me, the howls were high-pitched and afterward they were low. That, I said, was because having made a kill, the pack gives a defensive howl to establish that the area is now theirs.

I told him that whenever he heard the high-pitched call—the locating call—he must turn on the tape and play it until he heard the howls of the wild pack recede, which I felt confident they would. He could see the logic at once and was very keen to give it a go, and when I went back to film a documentary in Poland two years later, he was delighted by how successful the tape recordings had been. He had used them exactly as I had told him to do and there had been no more attacks on his livestock. He was absolutely thrilled.

The joy of working with the Polish farmers, as opposed to the ranchers in Idaho, was that the Poles fundamentally respected wolves and Stanislaw was prepared to give anything a go. He didn't want to have to shoot the wolves; he just needed them to stop attacking his livelihood. Whereas the American farmers I met, sadly, seemed to believe that the only good wolf was a dead wolf.

Before I went home, Romick wanted to show me the primeval Bialowieza Forest, which is the oldest national park in Poland and a UNESCO world heritage site. It was due south of where we were. It was the most incredible place; it has eleven thousand different species of wildlife, including the European bison, and the plant life is equally amazing. But it gets hundreds of visitors, and the wolves appeared to be adapting their behavior in a slightly ominous way. As a consequence, perhaps, the foresters seemed to get closer to the wolves than they did up in the Romincka Forest, and one man that I was talking to told me he had watched two wolves walking down a track. At first he thought they might be dogs because wolves don't normally use tracks, but there was no doubt they were wolves—a male and a female—and while the female walked in a straight line, the male wove in and out of the trees from one side to the other, flushing out prey, which she then took. It was the way dogs hunt, not wolves.

# CHAPTER TWENTY-TWO

# A Harsh Lesson

I didn't really expect Elu, my female back at Combe Martin, to become pregnant that first year but I decided to move in with the pack two weeks before she came into season, just in case, so I could watch the courtship behavior and bond sufficiently with her for her to allow me to be nanny to her pups. To my surprise, although Shadow was the dominant male, it was Pale Face that mated with her. At the time, that puzzled me, and I had to wait five years for a possible explanation. It turned out that Shadow had a defective heart. He and a female wolf I had recently taken in from Dartmoor Wildlife Park, named Lady Penelope, were on their way to a collector in Oxfordshire, on loan as a breeding pair, when he unexpectedly died in transit. A postmortem revealed that he had heart disease. It's just possible that he always had heart problems and that was why Elu chose Pale Face to father her pups.

During the nine weeks of her pregnancy, Elu showed every sign she was going to be a good mother; although this was the first time, she instinctively seemed to know what to do. She got the boys to help her dig rendezvous holes for the pups. These are small burrows, in the vicinity of the den, that the cubs are taught to dive into if they are in danger. They are two to three feet deep and usually dug beneath a rock or tree root, so it is almost impossible for a predator to dig the

pup out. My relationship with Elu seemed to be going well. I mimicked everything I had seen Daisy do at Longleat when she was hoping to be a nanny, and Elu seemed to be responding to me. I had a
moment's anxiety after about six weeks when she started digging furiously beneath the roots of the biggest tree in the enclosure. I thought
she might be preparing to give birth in there rather than in the den I'd
built. If she had taken herself deep underground and something had
gone wrong, we could have had a problem. Luckily she didn't use it.

Two days before she gave birth, I had been off on a hunting trip
and came back to the enclosure with a few rabbits. It was midafter-
noon; Elu took one of the rabbits and went off into the den, where I
had dug a birthing bowl like I had seen wild wolves dig, and there she
stayed until, in the early hours of the following morning, I heard the
low, mournful howls of a wolf in labor. It was unlike any noise I had
ever heard a wolf make before. I had no idea what was going on or
whether she was in distress, and had no way of finding out. Every
time I or any others went near the entrance to the den, she gave a
deep, rumbling growl to warn us off. Judging by where the noises
were coming from she had ignored my birthing bowl and dug something for herself beyond it, obviously to be as far away from any
threat as possible, and was now completely inaccessible. But the
ground sloped, and in her digging she had come very close to the surface at one point; when she had turned, some of the earth had been
dislodged, leaving a tiny hole above her. I hoped that with a torch I
might be able to see what was going on beneath.

At first light I heard the first little whimpering sounds. My heart
pounding, I quickly ran up the hill to the trailer to find a torch and
when I shone it through the hole, I had to choke back tears. I was
looking straight down into her birthing bowl at four minute pups that
all seemed to be wriggling and squirming, and therefore were alive
and well. Bursting with what felt like paternal pride, I covered the
hole with a boulder to stop the rain getting in and sat back patiently to

let nature take its course. I wouldn't be on duty to look after them for another five weeks.

On the third day, Elu came out of the den and alarm bells started to ring. Normally a mother will stay underground with her pups for a full week. When I was with the wild wolves in Idaho, the mother had been in the den for over a week and was completely emaciated when she came out. I tried to convince myself that it was perhaps different with wolves in captivity, and the weather wasn't as harsh here as it was in the Rockies. But newborn pups need their mothers to regulate their temperature—they lose body heat very quickly—and they need feeding at least every two hours. When she was still out after three or four hours, I began to panic. I put pressure on her to go back in; I lined the entrance to the den with food, hoping the sound of her pups would rekindle her maternal instincts, but nothing worked; in fact, she seemed determined to stay as far away from the den area as she could.

If the pups were to be saved, I had to make a decision—and quickly, or there would be nothing to save. I went in and grabbed the tiny creatures; they were like furry little rats with their eyes tight shut, snuffling and grunting. Three of them were huddled together and were warm and looked reasonably well; the fourth looked quite different and was lying about two feet from the others and felt cold. Elu had clearly pushed her away and not wanted to know her. They were all suffering from a degree of dehydration, which you can test by pinching the skin. The longer it takes for the pinched skin to stretch out and disappear, the more dehydrated the animal. The skin of the fourth little pup stuck up like the crest on a dinosaur.

With the help of volunteers, we quickly took them up the hill to a little cinder-block shed next to my trailer that I'd prepared for a German shepherd puppy for someone at the park. The floor was already covered in straw and we rigged up a fake birthing bowl by putting a furry blanket with a heating pad under it into a box to replicate their mother as much as possible and then folded the pups into it. We bottle-fed them on a formula milk called Esplac, and the three boys that had been huddled together suckled as though it were going out of fashion, which suggested to me that Elu hadn't fed them for some hours before she'd left the den. The fourth little one, which I named Cheyenne, would barely open her mouth. I had to sit with her, tucked into my jacket to keep her warm, and painstakingly coax her to take the milk one drop at a time.

It is not unknown for wolves in captivity to abandon their pups. Sometimes the maternal instinct is just not strong enough and sometimes it's because they've had no role models to learn from. Howletts, where she was born, hadn't wanted any more pups, so they had kept the male and females in separate enclosures and Elu had never watched other mothers give birth or raise pups. When it happens, there are two alternatives: go in and save the litter, as I did, or let the pups die in the hope that the mother will learn from her negligence and be a better mother next time around. This does happen, although it sometimes takes the death of three or four litters for the female to realize that she needs to suckle her pups for five weeks if they are to survive; it is nature's way of teaching a harsh lesson. For me there was no choice; I had to go in.

After a couple of days I was needing to devote so much time to little Cheyenne that I needed help with feeding the others. That was fine during the day when there were volunteers around, but for the nights I appealed to Jan, who came to the rescue and agreed to help me look after them at home in Plymouth. I could make it to the house in under the two hours I had between feeds, so I fed them before I left, bundled them into a box on the front seat, covered them up and drove while they slept beside me; and she fed the boys at two-hourly intervals throughout the night, while I concentrated on Cheyenne. Come the morning, I took them all back to Combe Martin, and repeated the process the next night.

I named the boys Tamaska, Matsi, and Yana, and it was interesting to watch them develop their own characteristics. It didn't take long to see that Tamaska was the biggest and greediest. The boys were all doing well, and every now and again Cheyenne would drink half a bottle of milk in one go and I'd think she'd finally turned the corner, but it didn't last and I was forever taking her to the vet. The bills were mounting up and I was beginning to really scrape the barrel financially when a friend who owned a pet shop came to my aid. She generously said I could charge future visits to the vet to her account at the surgery in Plymouth. For two and a half weeks I nursed this creature, willing her to live, but we were making no progress. One day she started making a crackling sound as she breathed, which I knew was never a good sign. The vet said she had pneumonia and the results of some blood tests he'd done indicated she had no immune system. She died in my arms on the way home. I was heartbroken; but he said the only thing that had kept her alive that long was my round-the-clock care. In the wild, she would never have lived beyond the first day.

It taught me a valuable lesson. Cheyenne's mother knew that the pup wasn't going to make it and had deliberately pushed her to one side. She didn't have the luxury of helpers to feed the other pups while she concentrated on the weakling. Nature told her to go with the ones that would survive. I was interfering in something I knew nothing about, but I would never do it again. I buried Cheyenne in a box in what is now another wolf enclosure near my trailer and I planted a tree for her. I mourn her to this day.

# CHAPTER TWENTY-THREE

# We Are What We Eat

The three remaining pups now needed a mother and because Elu had lost interest in them, it was down to me. Having hoped I might be chosen as nanny, I was now facing an altogether different and more difficult role. Was I up to it? I knew I could keep them alive—that was the easy bit—the challenge was to prevent them turning into domesticated wolves. I wanted them to grow up with as many of the instincts and characteristics of their wild cousins as possible, because for me, the justification of keeping wolves in captivity was to further our understanding of what makes wild wolves behave the way they do and by understanding that, to help prevent them from clashing with humans.

There was a shocking incident in Canada a few years ago when a hiker, a student on his own in the Saskatchewan forest, was attacked and partially eaten by wolves. Some suggested that it was an opportunistic kill. As I've already explained, I have never bought the line that wolves do anything because it's the easy option. Humans are fellow predators, they are not prey, and everything that wolves have taught me about their world in all this time tells me that these creatures would not take a man—or any food source—just because it happened to be there and was convenient.

The dominant female will direct the hunters to go for the food sources that will provide them with what they need at that particular time in their lives, and that plays an important part in maintaining the social ranking within the pack, too: they are what they eat. The richest bits of the kill and the vital organs always go to the alpha pair, and their scent, and therefore authority, is very different from that of the lower-ranking members who eat less well.

The pack is quite capable of ignoring an injured animal that they could effortlessly bring down, and instead will run after a healthy creature for a week and a half if they need what that animal can provide. There might be a rival pack in the area, for example, and they need high-octane food to be able to defend their territory. Equally, if the alpha female is close to delivering her pups, she might deliberately select an older animal or one that's not as fit as the rest because she wants to calm the pack's energy levels so they won't be too boisterous and unruly around her young, which would endanger them. This intelligence is passed down from generation to generation and is amazing to watch in action.

The dominant female can identify and select the animal she wants, out of a herd of three hundred, by the scent it leaves on the ground. It might be a moose with a cut on its foot that has become infected. Every time that foot touches the ground it leaves the smell of pus. She knows it has been weak for some time and so she follows it. She smells the grass and the bushes where the animal has stopped to graze and nibble leaves along the way, and she can smell from the scent of its decaying teeth that it's not a young animal. So before she gets anywhere near this moose, she has built up a mental picture of it. As she gets closer, she switches her attention from the ground to the air. She could still be two miles away but she opens up her nostrils, takes a deep breath, and her nose fills with particles of dust mites and hair that are on the wind, and all her senses confirm that this animal is the one she wants. And so they go on to make the kill. She starts to run and the hunters follow, which gets their adrenaline up, and when she draws level with the beast she's chosen, she indicates which one it is with her tail and they bring it down, even if other animals in the herd are closer. They obey their alpha.

The pack that killed the hiker was living in an area where a lot of trees had been felled and forests cleared, which meant that the prey animals were losing their habitat. These wolves had started eating migratory salmon instead, which is something wolves enjoy from time to time, but it is not part of their regular diet and does not have the properties of meat. I thought this might go some way to explain why they had attacked a man, so I carried out an experiment with my wolves at Combe Martin, which is one of the values of having animals in captivity. After a few months on a diet of fish, they were all eating exactly the same quality of food, and the social structure of the pack fell apart. There were no longer any distinct ranks, so there was no one to make the decisions, no one to do the disciplining, and they behaved like unruly hooligans. So I think the most likely explanation for why that pack attacked the hiker was that there was no one to tell them what to do—and what not to do.

That still left the question of why they started to eat him. Both wild and captive wolves will kill other predators. I've seen wolves kill bears and bears kill wolves and wolves kill mountain lions and coyotes, but I have very seldom seen them kill a fellow predator for food. They will eradicate you if they see you as competition for food and they'll kill to protect their young—and they would kill humans as readily as any other animal under those circumstances, but they wouldn't eat us.

My theory is that maybe they no longer recognize us as fellow predators. It's arguable that because of our modern diet—a lot of which is carbohydrate and junk food, not to mention the people who are purely vegetarian—we smell more and more like prey animals. We behave more like prey, too. Our ancestors would never have run away at the sight of a wolf or a bear or a mountain lion—their heartbeats wouldn't have raced, they wouldn't have broken into sweats or rolled their eyes like frightened zebras. These animals were a familiar sight and because they shared a world—as the Native Americans continued to do for much longer than our forebears—they knew better than to come between a mother and its cub or to walk too close to a den. The smell of fear is very exciting for a predator and it's only prey animals that transmit it so readily. So if there was some confusion about the hiker, and the pack's instincts were telling them they needed meat to restore the ranking system, I can see how they might have started to eat him.

Foresters say the same thing about bears. The first time a bear attacks, it is always protecting its young or a food source, but having killed a human once and realized how much it smelled and behaved and even tasted like prey, that bear will see humans as another source of food and kill again.

The problem is that with every advance we make, humans take away a bit of their world. Wolves have all this extraordinary intelligence that is passed down through the generations about how, where, and when to hunt, what to eat, and suddenly they come face-to-face with mankind, who has upset the balance. The natural food supply they have been living on for hundreds of years disappears and in its place someone builds a farm or a ranch with cattle. It's inevitable that they are going to stay ever closer to man if he is providing the only source of food that is left.

We have assumed the role of the dominant creature on this earth and yet we have no idea how to manage the creatures under us. We don't know how to maintain the balance that regulates everything—which animals do naturally. Rats and vermin are fine in the wild. They feed on carcasses and their numbers are limited by the availability of food; nature doesn't allow them to get out of control. Encourage them to come into the cities by throwing food into the gutter and leaving bins overflowing on every street, and their breeding, not surprisingly, goes haywire. If we could begin to be responsible, the animals beneath us would become responsible.

We are out of control and too comfortable in our ways. We eat too much of the wrong sorts of food—food that is so low in value we have to eat mountains of it to get any goodness. The Native Americans used to eat nothing but high-value foods and only in moderate proportions. There was scarcely a fat one among them, and they were some of the strongest, fittest people on earth. Now they are eating white man's food and they are becoming obese like the rest of the Western world—and poisoned by the chemicals we use on the land. The incidence of cancer seems too high to be a coincidence. The basket weavers who still work in the traditional way, which involves running the reeds through their mouths, are developing cancer of the mouth. Other sorts of cancer are rife.

We have so much to learn from animals. If only we would pay attention, they could teach us how to save the planet. We need to go back to being keepers of the wild and learn about their world and heal the wounds we have inflicted on nature. Everything has a place in this world and we can't be naïve enough to think we can safeguard ourselves if we let other species fail. The Native Americans believe that what happens in the wolf world happens in ours and vice versa. They say, "He, me." We need to work together and then everything else will fall into place. The animal world works together; nature doesn't have to be cruel. Wolves have rivals but they need their rivals in order to keep driving the prey in their direction. And no animal kills for fun. I've seen predators and prey peacefully drinking alongside one another at a watering hole; it was as if the animals had agreed to a truce so that none of them would be forced to drink when the insects arrived and made life uncomfortable for them all. They were cooperating with one another to such a degree that I expected Noah to turn up at any moment with his Ark.

# CHAPTER TWENTY-FOUR

# Knowing Your Place

A full pack of wolves—and one that is eating as nature intended—will always have an alpha pair, which are in their prime, and these have always been thought to be the only ones that breed. They make the decisions for the welfare of the whole family. Then there will be a beta, or enforcer, and a tester, which is the quality controller. After that come mid- to high-ranking wolves and mid- to low-ranking wolves and an omega animal whose role is to break up fights and defuse tension within the pack. We tend not to use the alphabetical terminology so much these days because it suggests too big a gap between the top and the bottom, which doesn't truly exist. So the alphas are now often called the decision makers. They get the job because they have the most experience; and the minute either of them falters, he or she will be replaced, as Daisy was at Longleat. For years people thought that alphas were the biggest and boldest animals in the pack, the ones that came forward, and the dominant ones who ate first and wouldn't let the others near the carcass until they had had their fill. Living with them, I realized that this was completely wrong. They are the thinkers, the most intelligent animals in the pack, and therefore the most valuable.

Most of us are never going to live with wolves but an awful lot of us live with dogs, and it is useful to translate wolf social structure for the dog world because, as I discovered with the army dogs, most of the problems we have with Man's Best Friend are caused by our failure to understand the similarities between the two animals. The difference between the DNA of wolves and domestic dogs is .2 percent. After thousands of years of selective breeding, we have created every shape, size, and color that man could possibly want—from the St. Bernard to the Chihuahua; we now even have a breed that doesn't inflame our allergies. But underneath the gleaming coats, clipped toenails, and adoring brown eyes, those creatures are very similar to the guys I spend so much time with. They have been domesticated, of course, but fundamentally their instincts are the same. They are pack animals, just as wolves are, and we take them out of their world and are surprised and angry when they don't fit perfectly into ours. And usually that's because we buy the wrong animal for our situation or we feed it the wrong food, which interferes with its ability to socialize.

People often think it's good to have an alpha dog, believing the alpha is the bold one that comes to say hello when you go to choose your puppy from the litter. That is not the case. The alphas stay at the back of the kennel because they have a strong sense of self-preservation. They never put themselves in jeopardy. If a situation becomes dangerous—if a bear is marauding around the den, to put it into wolf context—the alphas won't get involved and will watch other members of the pack being killed rather than risk their own lives. They are half of the breeding pair, and the continuance of the line is all that ultimately matters.

If you take an alpha puppy home with you, he will be a very quick learner, easy to train, so that one day, when he sees the time is right, he can take over the pack. And he'll be looking for that day, for a sign of weakness in you that suggests you are no longer capable of doing the job. That could be at six months, nine months, or two years, and unless you are constantly one step ahead of him, your lovely biddable dog will turn into a willful so-and-so who pays no attention to anything you tell him.

Sometimes he will just become "deaf" outside of the house. Owners say, "He's fine at home but the minute he gets into the park, he doesn't listen to a word I say." This is because the dog's sensory powers are infinitely greater than ours. He knows exactly what dogs and what people are in the park because he can see farther than we can, hear things we can't, and smell everything that has passed that way in the last day, so he assumes control, knowing that you are not capable of keeping you both safe.

The beta, or what we now tend to call the enforcer, *is* the puppy that comes boldly over to you when you go to view the litter. He's the disciplinarian, the bouncer, the bodyguard; he is pure aggression. He doesn't think; he just weighs in. He doesn't need to think because that's not his job; the decision makers do that for him. His role is to protect the pack and to make sure that pack members keep pack rules and don't take food that doesn't belong to them or behave above their rank. And if the threat is from outside, he will deal with it, fearlessly.

In a wolf pack this animal has one of the most important jobs, but if you choose this puppy to take into your home without being aware of what you have picked, it could be disastrous. You and he may differ in what you view as a perceived threat. It could be another dog in the park, a neighbor, or a child who has come to visit. From your point of view, his aggression will be inexplicable, but he will have picked up something you haven't. He might also take to enforcing what he sees as pack rules in the house. If he's been taught he's not allowed to sit on the sofa or go upstairs, your children may find they're not allowed to either. And if the dog disciplines your child in the way it would discipline another dog, it could result in a serious wound. We don't have the thick fur that dogs and wolves have to protect them. I hate to think how many dogs have been condemned to death for biting someone for no better reason than that the humans in their life failed to understand the pack system and how that particular dog should have been handled.

Then there's the tester within the pack, the quality controller. He is a mid- to high-ranking animal, and his job is to keep all the others on their mettle; he makes sure that they can do the jobs they say they can and if they don't come up to expectations, then the enforcer is the one who hands out the discipline. If it reaches the stage where discipline doesn't work and the animal starts to lose his authority and can no longer be of use to the pack in any capacity, the beta wolf will banish him. In a dog, the tester can be a very trying pet because he will be pushing and testing your ability on a daily basis, making sure that you deserve to be the one who makes the decisions for you both.

Mid- to low-ranking individuals are naturally nervous and suspicious. Their role in the pack is to keep a lookout for danger; they pace around the den or go high up onto the hillside to give an early warning of anything the alpha pair might need to know to ensure the safety of the pack. They make good pets because they have no need to discipline or teach anyone anything. All they need is a bit of food every now and again and they will be happy, and they will take orders from anyone. These ranks don't seek you out when you visit the litter; they are the ones that will be hiding in the corner—they are the good old underdog. The only problems might be excessive barking and fear aggression, but those can be prevented—as can all the traits that are useful in the wolf pack but a nuisance in human society.

There are three specialist roles within the pack. The hunter, the nanny who is usually a grandparent, and the defuser, and these guys all get a lot of respect from the others. The hunter is very often female because they are lighter and faster than the males, although if the quarry is a big animal like a bison, moose, or elk, the female will run it to exhaustion but it will need the bulk of the male to bring it down. So they often set up an ambush. The hunters do the chasing and the killing but they are not the ones who decide what to kill—

that's the job of the alpha female. She runs with the others and selects the beast she wants by singling it out. The hunters then take over and do the deed. What that animal is varies, depending upon the time of year and the quality of meat she knows the pack needs. In dogs, the hunter is usually a wiry-looking character, lean and muscular and quick on his feet, and he has great stamina. He's the one that's always watching for movement, stalking birds and pouncing on leaves or feathers.

Nannies are chosen by the alpha female to look after her pups and they are usually wolves that have been alphas themselves when they were younger. They can be male or female but are usually female and take over from the mother at between five and six weeks, when she goes back to her duties with the pack. The nanny guards the pups, disciplines them, and feeds them, in the early stages by regurgitating. She teaches them how to defend their food, how to hunt, and how to interact safely with the rest of the pack.

The role of the defuser, or omega wolf, is to keep the pack on an even keel, to absorb the energy and aggression of the others. Wolves fight among themselves often, and often violently, particularly at mealtimes and in the mating season—as I discovered to my cost in Idaho—when tension is high and the whole pack is on edge. It's the way they challenge and reestablish the pecking order. The defuser gets into the middle of the scrum and takes the brunt of it but never loses his cool, never shows aggression himself, and eventually calms things down. He doesn't get many thanks for his troubles; he is always the last to eat and has the fewest privileges, but his role is essential to the well-being of the pack. In the dog world, if there are dogs fighting in the park, this guy will dive straight into the melee and might make a lot of noise but will actually break up the fight.

Knowing which of these animals you have given a home to goes some of the way toward ensuring a happy life together, but the rest of it comes down to how you handle the particular dog you've bought and how you train it. Most trainers and behaviorists base their methods on wolf behavior and they acknowledge the importance of the pack, which of course I have no argument with, but as I have said before, to really understand what's going on, you have to be there. Observing wolves from afar can easily lead one to the wrong conclusions, and I think in many cases this is what has happened. Owners have been taught that they must take on the role of the alpha dog, and despite the miraculous results for problem dogs that we've all seen on our television screens, this doesn't always work and isn't always a long-term solution for the owners involved.

I don't mean to put down dog behaviorists in any way but I do believe passionately that it is important to mimic wolf behavior accurately, and the fact is that not every animal can cope with its owner taking on the alpha role.

# CHAPTER TWENTY-FIVE

# *Back to Basics*

In the past, scientists always argued that it is false to make comparisons between wolves and domestic dogs. Given my firsthand experience of both, I profoundly disagree. I feel strongly that what I have discovered about wolves is not just relevant, it's vital when it comes to handling the wolf in your living room.

If you have that nervous, low-ranking animal that hides in the corner and tugs at your heartstrings—the one that most of us are suckers for—and you behave like an alpha or even a beta around that dog, you will destroy him. He will fold himself up his own backside, because in his world the distance between the alpha animal and his rank is colossal. He is valued for what he is by the pack, but in the wild the two don't mix with each other. It would be like asking the president and a shoe-shine boy to share a house together. Don't buy that pup just because you feel sorry for him; think long and hard about where and how you live because that animal will be naturally vocal. Remember that in the pack it's his job to alert everyone to danger. So if you live in the middle of a busy town or city, he will bark around the clock and drive you and everyone in the neighborhood mad. Unless you are able to convince him you know what's going on, he will tell you about anything that moves within a three-mile radius of your house—but over flat ground and with the wind in the right direction it can be anything up to ten miles.

It's not impossible to turn this animal into a relaxed city dog, but it is all in the training and the way you manage him from the day you collect him. Ideally you should get him in the summer when the weather is good, the evenings are light, and the atmosphere is clear. Take him out as much as you can and as far as you can, expose him to all the sights and smells and sounds and keep him close, reassure him about anything that seems to make him tense, give him long strokes down his back and breathe deeply, which is how his mother would have calmed him. Let him see that there's nothing out there to be afraid of and he will be reassured—a sound that is familiar is not alarming to a dog or a wolf or even a human being. Anything he hasn't heard before will set him barking, so if you don't put in the work with him when he's young, then when a factory alarm goes off five miles away and rings all night, which you can't begin to hear, he will tell you about it.

Don't go down the shouting and screaming route. You'll be wasting your breath and only encouraging him. He'll think you're backing him up with your own barking. Dogs can only hear tone and pitch, the equivalent of the different sounds we hear by tapping a cup that is full, half full, and empty. And they only understand the command words they have been taught. These have to be short words or phrases like *sit, stay, down, come, leave it,* and *quiet;* and they have to be said in a tone and pitch that's authoritative, bearing in mind that tone and pitch can be distorted by the wind and weather if he is some distance away. So when the dog starts to bark, you would say "Quiet!" with a definite sharp cutoff that means stop. If you wanted him to continue doing something, like coming toward you, you would allow your voice to taper. You would teach him by giving him a reward every time he did the right thing. The command reassures him that you can hear the sound, you know what's happening, and you are going to make the decision about what action to take. He's only too pleased to hand over the responsibility because decision making is not his job and he doesn't want it.

The first thing, though, is to establish why he's barking. There might be times when you need to be warned about a stranger approaching or something unusual happening across the street. The days of thinking a bark is a bark is a bark are long gone. Dogs have a complex language, like wolves, and their bark says different things and can be pitched to carry over many miles. For example, you might have a house with a garden, which the dog regards as his territorial boundary. The dog is in the house and hears someone coming; he gives a deep growl, followed by a single bark, followed by another growl. He's telling you that someone's out there but is still some distance away, so there's no need to panic. If the person keeps coming, he'll give you an update—three barks and then a long growl. If you do nothing and the person comes into the driveway and breaches the boundary, you get the full machine-gun effect. If, however, you get up before the final stage and go to the window to see who is coming and give the dog the command, he will relax. Spending the first six months of the dog's life giving him this sort of training can make all the difference between you and your dog living happily ever after— or not.

Many people, of course, don't get their dogs as pups. More dogs are rescued than bought from breeders, and often they've been mistreated. We look at the crime sheet and discover the animal was chained up, beaten, and starved, and being all emotion, we long to give him a new start in life; but as soon as he pees on the carpet or does anything antisocial, we don't give him anything of the sort. We put it down to his past and go straight back to that dark place that he was desperate to escape, usually dragging him with us. Humans are always looking back; dogs, like wolves, live in the present. He thinks new pack, new rules, new leader—I'm happy. And contrary to the saying "You can't teach an old dog new tricks," I believe you can by going back to that period in the dog's life when he was at his most receptive to education.

The wolf and the dog develop in small circles. In the beginning that circle is in and around the den or the whelping box, where, while suckling, the pup learns the basic principles from his mother—he picks up her calming signals, discovers the reward system, learns his pack value, and how to communicate with his own kind. When he stumbles out into the world at five weeks and begins to mix mother's milk with regurgitated meat, that circle of learning increases and he starts to learn how to treat other pack members, how to defend his food, what to do and where to go if he is in danger. As the months go by, the circle goes on getting bigger until at nine months he has the social and survival skills he needs.

As I have said earlier, diet plays a very important part in wolf society and can entirely alter the nature of a pack, as the fish experiment proved. The alpha female knows this. Before she introduces her pups to the rest of the pack, she ensures that the pack members' energy levels are down by feeding them older individuals from the herd or calves that are still suckling because the milk content in the stomach of those animals has a calming and soothing effect on everyone. They become placid, gentle, and forgiving, almost like overgrown pups themselves. The aggression and fighting that usually breaks out around mealtimes disappears and they tolerate everyone. When you see them like this, is not hard to believe the myths and legends about human children being suckled and adopted by wolves. A lactating female, whose pups have not survived, might welcome a surrogate to nurture.

So to reeducate an adult dog, you would feed him on the sort of diet he had in his first few months of life: a mixture of milk and minced or very finely chopped meat, which would be similar to the regurgitated food he had during that intensive learning period. A couple of months on that and he should be calm and pliable and ready to listen, whereupon you could train him more or less as you would a puppy, heavy on reward and light on punishment. Force should never be used on dogs, in my view, because it doesn't work; and kicking a dog is only likely to make it attack, because kicking is how prey animals defend themselves when they are being hunted.

The most effective way to teach a dog is by example and the most effective punishment is to deny the animal warmth. That is how dogs and wolves are taught and punished in their own world—they get pushed away from the security of their mother's body.

It is impossible to overemphasize the importance that diet plays in maintaining the structure of the pack. Wolves eat three categories of food: that which they take for basic fitness and health; survival foods, which would include animals with a high fat content to keep them warm during harsh weather conditions; and sociable foods, which keep the structure of the pack.

In order to keep their status, the alpha pair have to have a very high percentage of internal organs in their diet as well as some movement meat, such as leg or rump, and a little bit of vegetable matter to keep them healthy, which because their prey are always herbivores, comes from the stomach content. The beta ranks, the enforcers, eat exclusively movement meat along with some vegetables; the mid- to high-ranking animal, which would be the tester, eats a percentage of nonmovement meat from the neck or the backbone with about 25 percent stomach contents. The mid ranks have fifty-fifty meat and stomach, and the mid to low ranks have 75 percent vegetable matter from the stomach and 25 percent meat.

What has happened to the dogs that live in our world is that we have upset the natural balance. We feed them all, irrespective of the rank they hold, the same sort of food—mostly dried all-in-one or tinned, which we mix with biscuit (no canid in the wild has ever eaten wheat)—and therefore confuse the natural pecking order, making it difficult for the animals to differentiate themselves. We compound the problem with our training, such as making a dominant dog sit or lie down in the park in front of lower-ranking animals.

We have also, with our desire for the cosmetically perfect animal, removed the features that in the wild these creatures use to communicate with one another. We have dogs now with no snouts, so they can't be disciplined in the way canids have done for thousands of years. We have dogs with ears that flop over, which deprives them of another vital way of communicating with their fellow dogs. And until recently when it was banned in the UK, we docked the tails of certain breeds, thus taking away their ability to communicate via scent, an important part of their language, which they use by moving their tails.

# CHAPTER TWENTY-SIX

# Family Values

After Cheyenne died, I kept Elu's three boys in the shed for the next couple of months and during that time they moved from milk to milk and minced meat—I was doing my best to create what their mother might have regurgitated. They lapped that up and very swiftly moved on to mince alone and finally chicken wings, which they instantly defended against one another, growling and snarling. At about this time I realized they needed some space, but there was no way I could put them back in with Shadow and Pale Face. So with the help of six volunteers, I built a new enclosure of about half an acre up next to the trailer at the top of the park. I put the two boys in there and put the three pups in the enclosure at the bottom, where they had been born, and I moved in with them.

Suddenly I was responsible for everything. In the wild there would be others who would look after the security of the pups while the nanny role was just to help with the education, and to mind and monitor them. Now it was up to me to keep them warm and safe and fed, and to drive them into the den at night. All the things they had come to rely on from an adult were now in my court. I was the adult but nowhere near as well equipped to deal with it as the adult wolves. Yet it seemed to work and when I went into the den at night, they followed. But there were many ideas I had for their training that seemed like good ideas at the time but which, as they became adults, I wish I had forgone. One was dear old Tamaska, the beta rank who was big and bold and supposedly scared of nothing and always went forward and was a rock among wolves—yet had a complete terror of thunderstorms. As a small pup he would freak out at any sign of an electrical storm. He would scream like a big baby and come running to me and I would pick him up—this was in the shed, long before we moved to the enclosure. He would need warmth and I would hold him in my arms and wear him like a neck scarf, and the warmth from my neck on his belly would calm him down. When he was calm, he would wriggle his way down and try to suck on anything that he thought would give him food. Normally that would be the end of my nose, which resembled a teat, and he would suck on it for about fifteen or twenty minutes, until he fell asleep, at which point I could put him back with the other pups.

Having a cute, fluffy, three-to-four-week-old little bundle sucking on the end of my nose was a wonderful experience and everyone admired it, but what I didn't realize was that as their primary teacher, everything I taught them they would take into adulthood. So even now, as a full-grown adult weighing something like 130 pounds, Tamaska can still be found during a thunderstorm sitting on my lap under a tree and sucking my nose. Only now he's too big to actually suck my nose, so he just gets his incisors around it and holds on tight. So what I would say to anyone with a dog is be careful what you teach them when they are small.

Something else I might have avoided with the benefit of hindsight: after we had fed the pups, in the early stages, I used to take them underground into the den to keep them warm. By six months or so, they were quite big, seemed to cope with the weather better, and preferred to lie under a tree. It was only if it had been raining solidly for four or five days and we were all wet through that we would go under cover to dry out and warm up. Each of the pups established his own place underground. Matsi, Yana, and I would all go to the back and lie in a huddle, but Tamaska, who was the biggest, would lie at the entrance with his head and shoulders in the open air and his backside toward us. This was fine when he was small but as he grew and ate more and more raw meat, he developed a serious wind problem. There was very little air at the back of the den and when he got going, he was breaking wind every fifteen minutes and the smell at the back was horrendous. We were between the devil and the deep blue sea: Did we stay out in the wet and the cold or did we get dry and risk being overcome by the noxious smell? Sometimes it was so bad that even he would whip around and sniff, as if to say, "God, who did that?"

If I had to own up to having a favorite of the three, it would be Tamaska. He is such a character; but they are all family and I try not to single one out. My role among them was a strange one. I was there to teach each one of them to fulfill his role as an adult wolf yet I was never their leader; that was the unusual thing about this experiment. The only individual I would ever be above was Matsi, who was a wary, shy little animal, but with the other two, I had to build them up to be above me in the pecking order. I taught by example in the hope that when the time came for them to lead, they would remember and be the balanced animal that I had tried to be myself. I didn't chastise them; I just showed them how I expected them to behave and if ever I did need to discipline them, it would be by denial of warmth or food or water, which is how pups are disciplined in the wild. Everything I did was designed to teach them how to be wild wolves, not semidomesticated. If I needed to display my strength, I did it through games, and if ever I felt angry, I would just walk away and lie down. I didn't want my aggression to interfere with my teaching.

I taught them how to defend their food and to recognize that each had his own source of it on the carcass. By six weeks they were already beginning to show signs of the ranks they would eventually hold and when I started to introduce rabbit at that age, I portioned it and gave each of them a different part of the animal according to the characteristics they were displaying. Matsi as the lowest would have the stomach contents; Tamaska, who was clearly destined to be the beta, the thug, would get the movement meat, the legs and rump; and Yana, who undoubtedly had the brains, would have the internal organs. When I brought in a carcass, I did my best to get Yana into the rib cage, so she could get the heart, liver, and kidneys, and keep Tamaska on the rump and the shoulder. But he was so greedy he would start eating any bit he could get and I had more than a few battles with him. I had to try to intimidate him by snarling with my lips pulled back to show my teeth—my weaponry—and my tongue protruding, just as the wolves did themselves. If that didn't work, I'd snap to the side of his mouth to get him to move over. Everything I did mimicked what I had seen wolves do in the wild; and many were the times when he decided he didn't like the place he'd been moved to and he would come back at me. My nose and lips were riddled with puncture marks where his needle-sharp teeth had caught me, and he somehow managed to repeatedly peel strips of skin from my nose with his molars. He once got my entire bottom jaw in his mouth; his bottom teeth had me under the chin and his top incisors were sunk into the soft tissue under my tongue. We were growling and snarling at each other and at the same time I had him round the scruff of the neck; it was a real tussle and battle of wits. Had he been any older, I wouldn't have stood a chance, but for that brief period in his life, I held a higher rank as nanny, and he needed to learn where his place was. I used to joke that Tamaska and I had so many fights you'd have thought we were married.

Another important lesson was how to prevent the three of them from seriously damaging one another in their play-fights. With their weight, strength, and jaw pressure, wolves have to be very careful not to accidentally kill another member of the pack. The minute one is in pain, he will let out a high-pitched squeal, and a balanced animal will always let go. I can vouch for the fact that they do; human skin is no match for a wolf's and many are the times I've had to protest. I had to teach these guys to do the same, but it was quite hard for me to inflict pain on them. The only way I could do it was by biting them on the ear or the lip. So we would get into play-fights and I would nip them just hard enough to hurt, and the moment they squeaked I released my grip, pushed them onto their backs to expose their vulnerable underside, then I held my mouth over their throats, in classic wolf pose, to indicate that I was trustworthy.

Balance had to be taught, too, which I did through games involving hunting. Dogs go into what we call a play bow; with wolves it's called a prey bow because from that position, crouched low, they can jump six feet in any direction. A lot of our games started with a prey bow, bouncing from side to side and running and chasing each other around. If things looked as though they were getting too rough, I would drop down into that prey bow position again and everything would stop, which calmed everyone down so that we could make sure it was safe for everyone for the fight to carry on. I was trying to teach them how to switch from high energy to low so that they never went beyond the danger zone. They could have a mock fight but they couldn't end up hurting one another as a family.

What I discovered through all these games and mock fights and mock prey drives was that the intensity of interaction pushed up our adrenaline and pheromone levels, which gave them—and me—an edge over other animals in the pack. If I couldn't make Tamaska move off the kill, I would just have to go and have a mock fight with Matsi for ten minutes, and when I came back, Tamaska would move without my having to do anything very much, because my blood was up and he could smell the change in me.

Another very important lesson was self-preservation; they needed to be able to read body posture, to understand vocal communication, and to know how to protect themselves. Any sound a wolf makes that is high in tone is encouraging, so if there was danger in the area and I wanted the pups to come to me, I would attract them with a high-pitched whimper, and having brought them to me, I would calm them down with a deep whimper. There was another noise that meant danger, which could come from land or air. If a buzzard was soaring overhead or a helicopter or plane, I would make a staccato "uff uffing" noise, and they would instantly come running to me for protection. Anything low in tone is discouraging, so at close range a low throaty growl will be a warning, and as I learned from the wild wolves, you then need to look at what their weaponry—bared teeth—and body posture are telling you. One of the ways in which the ranks differentiate themselves is by the height at which they carry their weaponry. A high-ranking animal holds his up high and expects to be greeted by other ranks with theirs down, at the level that accords with their rank. If the lower-ranking animal doesn't show the respect he should, the dominant animal will growl. The same thing happens with dogs that meet in the park; they very quickly establish a pecking order and if one doesn't give the other the respect he should, they snap and snarl and sometimes fight. If that lower-ranking wolf still refuses to avert his weaponry, the growl will intensify until finally the dominant animal will snap beside the other one's face. The snap is its last warning before he goes for him and holds him down with his mouth, growling all the while. He will then let go, stand back, and repeat the growling, by which time the lower-ranking wolf should have lowered his body and be showing signs of submission.

A similar process happens over food. Adult wolves indicate possession with their ear posture. To an outsider watching wolves feeding, it looks as though the teeth are the thing you need to watch out for. You'd be wrong; it's the ears. They tell you exactly what you can and can't have. If an animal is standing over a carcass and has his ears flattened like wings out of the side of his head, he is telling you that he is a higher-ranking animal than you, that the piece of meat belongs to him, and if you come near it, you will be in trouble. Dare to move in and he will growl, baring his teeth with his tongue thrusting through; the growl will intensify, he will snap as the final warning, and then he'll go for you. If, however, an animal that is higher-ranking than he is comes in from the right, for instance, he will turn his right ear sideways and back, indicating to that animal that he can come in and feed, while keeping his other ear horizontal to protect his own portion. I needed to teach this to the pups but of all the lessons, this was almost the most difficult because I didn't have their ears. I had to cover the meat with my whole head, but they seemed to get the message.

But possibly the hardest lesson for me, as a human with human emotions, was teaching them to prioritize. As a pack, if they are faced with danger, they have to safeguard the highest-ranking members. They will even sacrifice a whole litter of pups if faced with an either/or situation, knowing that they can have more pups next year but if the highest-ranking wolves die, the whole pack could be doomed. And if it came to it, the highest-ranking pups, as future leaders, would have to be safeguarded ahead of the others. It was something I battled over; it didn't seem right with my human sentimentality to let a healthy, fit animal perish because another held a higher rank. But this is what I had to teach them. We played games of tag. I would run after them nipping at their backs and their legs, making them twist and turn, as if a rival wolf was after them. I'd teach them to hunt playing the same sort of game. But in this particular lesson, I steered them in the direction of the rendezvous holes and the only way they could get away from my nips was by diving underground. Then I'd leave them, partly because I had no alternative. It was as if they were tailor-made for a three-month-old wolf cub. I couldn't have got them out for love or money. So they learned that this was where they went to escape. The hardest bit was having to teach them to seek safety in order of priority; keeping Tamaska and Matsi out and making sure that Yana went in first.

I was glad it was only a lesson.

# CHAPTER TWENTY-SEVEN

# *A Life Apart*

I lived with these guys continuously for eighteen months—eating with them, sleeping with them, and wrestling with them. I didn't have a proper meal during that time, a cup of coffee, or a sandwich; I didn't change my clothes, shower, or wash my hair. I didn't lie on anything softer than the hard ground. I peed in the enclosure as they did, using my urine to scent. The only difference was that while their scats were left where they fell, I bagged my poo for the volunteers to dispose of hygienically. My only luxury was toilet paper that they left for me in the area between the two entrance gates. I didn't once leave the enclosure and I never once wanted to. I was as happy as I had ever been, and totally fulfilled. These guys were my family—I knew them better than my own children—and the longer I was with them, the less I wanted to leave them. I was a hundred percent comfortable in their world. They were constantly challenging—as children are—but watching them grow and become more confident, seeing their characters develop and their different talents and skills come to the fore, and knowing that they valued me and that I'd played some small part in all of that was an incredible feeling.

My contact with the outside world was minimal. I had no idea what was going on beyond the wire fence of the enclosure and no interest. I had a walkie-talkie so I could communicate with the volunteers, but all I used it for was to discuss when I wanted them to bring food into the enclosure and what sort it would be so that I could prepare the pups to associate our hunting games with the food we ate. And occasionally, if I felt they were getting a bit overconfident, I asked some of the volunteers to howl or play tape recordings of different-sized packs howling to give mine the impression that we were not alone.

After they were past the first few months, when they needed to eat little and often, I had them on a feast-and-famine diet, which is how they would have lived in the wild. The obsession with teaching them wild ways, when clearly they were destined to spend their lives in captivity, was for a purpose. I hoped that they might teach their own young what I had taught them and so on through generations, so that one day if ever wolves were released into the wild again in Britain, the descendants of these boys might know how to take care of themselves. My dream was that they would know about their world but also enough about ours to be able to survive in it.

In those first eighteen months we ate every two days. Day one was spent preparing for the hunt, playing games, psyching ourselves up, and feeding either at dusk or at dawn of day two. Matsi was the fastest and nimblest of the pups, and showed the greatest interest in our hunting games, so even though he was male, I trained him to be the hunter; and I played the role of the alpha female, choosing what I wanted him to hunt. I taught them how to cache food, which is a very important part of survival in the wild, as I had discovered in Idaho. They know that times of plenty don't last and they need to guard against those times of the year when there's nothing about or the pack can't hunt. I stashed pieces of meat in the mud around the pond beneath the water level, which acted like a refrigerator, and occasionally I would stretch the time between a carcass coming into the enclosure to three or even four days, but would then show them how to dig up the cached food to eat in between kills. Along with the meat, I buried bits of the carcass, like deer antlers and legs and bits of rabbit, cow, sheep, and pheasant wings to use as learning tools.

On that preparation day, depending upon what the volunteers had told me was coming up on the menu, I would dig up a piece of the same type of animal and use it to excite their interest. If it was pheasant, I would hold the wings up in the air and flutter them and dip them up and down so they had to jump for them—anything to try to teach the pups about the food they ate and in this case, that pheasants couldn't be caught on the ground. I would even get the volunteers to throw them over the fence into the enclosure so it looked as though they were flying. I would take fish into the pond and make the pups wade into the water and dive for them. If a local farmer had been out lamping and had delivered a whole lot of rabbits, I would dig up a piece of rabbit fur or a foot or an ear, and dangle that in front of them, or if someone had come in with a venison carcass, I would dig up a deer leg.

The leg would have the hoof attached and was always very well preserved. I would run with it, twisting and turning and changing direction as though I were a prey animal, and they would chase after me, trying to bring me down. In the early days they tried to grab me from behind, in which case I would kick out at them with this hoof and catch them beneath the jaw, teaching them a valuable lesson— that if they went for a deer or an elk from behind, it would kick them. When I did it, it made them stop in their tracks, but they were just sore. They needed to know that a powerful kick in the throat from an elk fighting for its life would kill them. I used the antlers to teach the pups about the dangers of approaching a quarry from the front or not being fast enough to move out of the way if the deer turns around. I had seen wolf nannies do this in the wild. If they came anywhere within reach, I stuck the sharp horns into their sides. It didn't take them long to work out that the safest way to get me to the ground was by working together and attacking as a unit, and coming in a triangular pattern from the side. Only when they did that, did I give them the meat.

After eating, I would teach them to give a defensive howl to protect their kill from any other wolves in the area that might think of muscling in. And I would teach them to use what they had eaten to scent every few meters around the perimeter of their territory, which was effectively turning the key in the lock. In the wild it would be every few hundred meters. Day two was spent relaxing and digesting before starting all over again. I fed them at dusk and at dawn to teach them that these were the natural and most successful times to hunt. The minute the volunteers brought that day's kill into the enclosure, my battle to keep them to the areas of the carcass that were rightfully theirs began—and as they grew bigger and stronger, the more of a battle it was and the more bloodied I emerged at the end of it.

I ate what they ate, putting my face into the carcass and ripping out the raw flesh with my teeth alongside Yana, while growling and snapping at Tamaska to keep him off the rib area, which was ours. But after about nine months of eating it raw, I began to worry, after my experience in Idaho, about the effects it might be having on my health. So for the last nine months I got the volunteers to flash-fry my share and put it with some vegetables into a polyethylene bag and tuck it inside the carcass. The only problem was I had to be quick in finding it; the three wolves were very interested in my portion, particularly Tamaska. He was mad about the taste of this cooked meat for some reason and it was a case of the student becoming the master; if he got there first he moved me off, snarling and snapping like a good 'un, and there was no way I could take it from him. He gobbled up my food time and time again, and I'd have no choice but to go back to the raw meat.

After eighteen months I started leaving the enclosure for about an hour at a time, as if going out on hunting trips, as would happen in the wild, returning with a kill. At first I went no farther than the top of the hill, from where I could see what was going on, and I could see they were very agitated by my absence. If they called to me, I called back to let them know where I was and what was going on and for the first couple of times they were so distressed they didn't stop howling, but they soon associated my disappearance with food. On one occasion Tamaska gave the most extraordinary howl, one that I'd never heard before. It was like four little barks and a howl but it sounded as though something was wrong, so I went running back to the enclosure and found there was a white plastic bucket in the primate enclosure nearby that was being blown about in the wind and making a noise he didn't recognize, and it was distressing him. He was giving a long-range warning call that I hadn't yet taught any of them. He'd learned the rallying howl and the short-range defensive "uf uffing" noise, and he had simply put the two of them together to call me back from a distance and tell me there was something wrong. That was an exciting day for me—once again I felt that the student had become the master.

Hard though it was to tear myself away, I knew that these guys had to be a pack on their own and to be less dependent upon me. So although I continued to live with them for another six months or so, I started spending longer periods of time away from them. And it was on one of those occasions that I met Helen Jeffs, and my life took an unexpected turn. I had always thought that there might be someone one day who would drag me away from the animals and back into the human world, but I hadn't expected the pull to be quite so sudden or quite so strong.

One evening when I was out of the enclosure, a mate of mine turned up at the park saying that there was a two-for-one offer on meals at the local pub, the Station Inn, and against my better judgment I agreed to go with him. Helen was there with a friend of hers. It wasn't a pub she usually went to—in fact, she would say she normally wouldn't have been seen dead in it—but they had had a particularly bad day and felt like a drink on their way home. I would call it a chance encounter; she would say it was meant. She recognized me—I was quite well known in the area, and there weren't too many men around smelling as I did, with more than eighteen months' worth of growth on my chin, long unbrushed hair, and scars all over my face. I wasn't wearing the coverall I wore with the wolves nor the shoes I wore in the enclosure; I left those outside my trailer during breaks so that they wouldn't be contaminated by any other smells, but even without them I must have stunk to high heaven.

Helen was interested in what I was doing with the wolves, so we chatted for an hour or more while our two mates chatted, and we agreed to meet again. She was gorgeous, with big blue eyes and long blond hair, and reminded me of Michelle, my first love back in Norfolk. She was a year younger than I was and worked with children in a local school. She was married and had an eight-year-old son but the relationship with her husband had been over for a long time, and although they shared the roof over their heads, it was a matter of convenience. Her situation was very similar to mine with Jan. There was an immediate attraction for both of us; and while I was technically still with Jan, and a moment of rash optimism had even brought about a fourth child, Sam, born shortly before the pups in March 2004, our relationship had been over for a very long time and Jan had found someone new.

Helen lived in a bungalow across the valley, quite a drive by road but no more than a mile as the crow flies, and for the next few months, as my time with Yanu, Tamaska, and Matsi gradually drew to a close, Helen and I communicated with each other by howling across the valley.

# CHAPTER TWENTY-EIGHT

# A Curious Coincidence

Shortly before I moved back to sleeping in my trailer, someone tried to poison the three wolf pups. I went into the enclosure at the end of one day to spend the night with them as usual, and Yana was behaving as though he was stoned, off his legs, drunk. I had never seen anything like it in a wolf, and if I hadn't been so worried, it might have been funny. He couldn't walk straight and he kept bumping into things. He collided with trees and rocks and the fencing once or twice, and kept wandering in and out of the pond. I pulled him out a few times because he was standing there shivering, but he just went straight back in as if he were sleepwalking. He didn't respond to me in any way; he didn't even seem to notice that I was there. He was completely out of it and obviously freezing cold, although it was not an especially cold night.

I had no idea what was wrong. I stayed with him that evening and yet again he wandered into the pond and I had to fish him out. He couldn't hold his temperature, and by the early hours of the morning I was at my wit's end. I suddenly had a harebrained idea, the only way I could think of warming him up: I picked him up and with herculean strength born out of panic, I managed to get him through the gates, fending off the other two wolves, and carry him up to my trailer, where I put him into bed with me. I put the heater on and lay under the quilt with him, holding him close to my body to try to give him some of my heat. He was a full adult wolf at that stage, in appearance at least, yet he was so out of it, he could do nothing but lie limply beside me.

His body seemed to draw the heat out of mine and within a couple of minutes *I* was freezing, so I had to keep jumping out of bed, wrapping myself in a blanket in front of the heater, and after I had warmed up, getting back under the quilt with him, letting him absorb my heat again. This went on for the remaining hours of the night until he started to come to shortly before dawn and, still not recognizing me, tried to bite me. I grabbed his jaws and decided that even if he didn't know who I was, he might know my voice. In the wild, I had never used my human voice and I rarely did with these wolves, but they had heard me talking to volunteers in the park when necessary and speaking on the phone occasionally. It was the only thing I could think of doing, so for the next couple of hours I spoke to him about everything and nothing; I told him about the weather and about what was going on in my life and everything I planned for the future. I exhausted every subject under the sun.

When he did finally come around properly, he proceeded to tear apart my home, which was not entirely surprising for a full-grown wolf that was now compos mentis and had found himself in a confined space he didn't recognize. Fortunately, I managed to get a chain around his neck to lead him out into the field, where I walked him round and round and round until he was exhausted.

I then took him back to the trailer and gave him buckets of water. He was still a little bit shaky but I hoped that the water would flush out whatever was in his system, which is what eventually happened. It was after midday that I felt he was safe enough to return to his brothers down in the enclosure. Analysis of Yana's feces showed a heavy concentration of the barbiturate phenobarbital, which is widely used as an anticonvulsant for epilepsy. I can only think that someone threw a piece of meat laced with the drug into the enclosure and that Yana, being the alpha male and first to feed, ate the bulk of it.

The Native American people say that after an experience like that, Yana and I would have a unique bond. They used to say that if a hunter and a bear spilled each other's blood, they would become the same person and the hunter wouldn't be able to shoot that bear, no matter where he saw it. I never really believed in that legend until a few months later when Helen and I were in bed in the trailer and I had a really sore left hand. I kept rubbing it and examining the fleshy bit by the V of the thumb, expecting to see a cut or a thorn or some kind of explanation, but I couldn't see anything. I asked Helen to have a look for me but apart from its being red, she could see nothing. It felt like one of those thorns that get under the skin and become so inflamed and so sore that you can't bear to touch it or try to get it out. The pain got progressively worse as the evening wore on and was so intense that night that I barely slept. The next morning we went down to the enclosure. Helen was slightly ahead of me and came running back up the track.

"You're not going to believe this," she said. "Yana's limping; he's holding his left foot up."

I said, "He's probably taken a bite in the night," and went and had a look at him, not giving it a second thought.

When I rolled him over and looked at his foot, he had a thorn in almost the identical place corresponding to where I had felt the pain in my hand. The thorn was just below the surface but I managed to get my nails around the top of it and pull it out.

I said to Helen. "He's got a thorn in his foot."

I didn't immediately make the connection because I was too busy with Yana, but she said, "Oh, my God."

"What?"

"Your hand last night. The thorn."

Now that could have been the biggest coincidence of my life. Or it could be the Native American belief that if you help a creature and look after him, you will become as one and share similar feelings.

# A Soul Mate

My relationship with Helen progressed rapidly, although most of our time together was spent around the wolf enclosure or in my terrible trailer. She was under no illusion about what she was getting herself into, but that didn't seem to faze her—and I admired and loved her all the more for that. She was prepared to spend the night in the trailer with no hot water, pee into the putty bucket, and get up to leave at 5:30 in the morning so she could be home for Arran, her son, before her husband left for his shift at work. I was always up at that time anyway to look after the wolves, so it was no problem for me but it wasn't her idea of fun. She would shower at home, have some breakfast with Arran, and the two of them would go off to school together. Her husband had no problem with what she was doing—I had even been up to the bungalow to meet him and Arran and we were all very friendly—but it made a very long day for her.

This arrangement couldn't work long-term, and after Helen and I had been away for the weekend to a hotel in Minehead—and I had enjoyed my first bath in years, having had only the cold hose outside the trailer—she decided she had had enough of getting up at 5:30. She needed a place of her own where she could live with Arran and I could join her on nights when I could get away from the wolves. She rented a chalet in a holiday park in the village, and I went there as often as I could but not as often as I might have liked.

I was very busy at the park. I had been offered two young European wolves that a private collector didn't want and, I suspect, would have had put down if I hadn't taken them off his hands. The man had more money than sense; he seemed to me like a rich man with toys. I have no problem with people splashing around their money if the toy is driven by an engine, but when it's driven by a beating heart, I do. When I went to see the wolves it was quite clear what had happened. The man had a brat of a son who had been kicking a football around inside their enclosure and had induced a prey drive in these young wolves and one of them had finally given him a nip. The names of the disgraced three-year-olds were Totto and Nanook. I hastily adapted another enclosure near the trailer for them, so there was no chance of their interbreeding with the timber wolves, and brought them home to Combe Martin.

They settled in soon enough but their experience had done them no favors. They were very quick to nip and I had to go into their enclosure with rabbits and rodents in my hands for the first week or so to teach them that I was the provider of food, not the food itself. Not long afterward I was offered their brother, Zarnesti, whom I had known at Broxbourne when he was a small pup. He was the one whose mother had rolled or trodden on him soon after he was born, crushing his jaw and giving him a comical look, like Goofy. And he was the one who had evoked emotion in the disabled child.

That brought the total number of wolves to nine, which I now had in three enclosures: Shadow, Pale Face, and Elu were together; the three pups—Yana, Tamaska, and Matsi—were together; and there were the Europeans. I was not looking to expand, so I gave Elu a contraceptive injection for the second year running to ensure she didn't become pregnant. It was designed for dogs but had worked well on Elu the first year, so I used it again. What I hadn't allowed for was the wolf's extraordinary ability to regulate its own body; these are animals that can absorb a litter of pups if they feel the environment is no longer safe to give birth in. Elu worked out what was going on and held her season back until the contraceptive had lost its potency and then she mated. Nine weeks later she delivered exactly what she had had the first time around, but this time the female survived. I called her Cheyenne, and the boys Nataa, Tejas, and Nanoose.

Elu's maternal skills had not improved, and once again she abandoned the den and I had to go in and rescue the pups; once again I was up all through the night for the next five or six weeks bottle-feeding four hungry mouths. This time, as soon as they were on solids, I handed them over to Yana, Tamaska, and Matsi in the hope that they would do a better job than I would.

Although the pups had been unwanted, they turned out to be very useful. I had been in touch over the years with Bernard Walton, a television producer who had made the *Talking with Animals* series for the BBC. He now had his own production company, Aqua Vita Films, and when he heard about what I had done with the first set of pups at Combe Martin, he wanted to make a documentary about them, and about me and my career and the research I was doing in Poland. The new pups were perfect for the purposes of reconstruction and we filmed them extensively. We also traveled to Poland, Finland, and America to film wolves and talk to wolf experts, including Levi Holt. The film was shown on the National Geographic Channel in America as *A Man Among Wolves*, and in the UK on Channel Five as *The Wolfman*. In the interests of balance—and to add controversy—Bernard invited a panel of scientists to voice their opinions about my hands-on approach.

Most of the scientists were scornful, if not downright disapproving, which didn't surprise me. The young scientists seemed to be blinkered, frightened of questioning accepted wisdom and jeopardizing their careers—as they always have been—but one of the most re-

warding conversations for me was with Doug Smith, who is the biologist in charge of the wolf reintroduction program at Yellowstone
National Park. We sat on the hillside at Blacktail Deer Plateau, looking out over the park in all its glory, and for the first time I felt comfortable and at ease, hopeful that there might be a middle way. I had
never before been able to sit down with a biologist and bat ideas back
and forth. Although it was just for a TV program, at the end of it I
felt we could see a mutual glimmer of hope, or as Doug put it, the silver bullet we were both striving to find.

He acknowledged that howling and scent were the secrets to wolf
behavior and two of the least researched aspects of it. He knew that
each wolf had a different howl but didn't seem to know that collec-
tively there were different howls that meant very different things.

Yellowstone has a fantastic program that set the standard for
other reintroductions, including Idaho's, but in my view mistakes
were made. They looked at this glorious park with its thousands of
acres and picturesque forests, valleys, and streams and thought it had
everything for the wolf—and that the sight of wolves majestically
roaming free would be a moneymaker with the public. But setting
eight wolves down in all of this was just one part of the equation.
After the wolves had run the prey out of the park, they had no alternative but to follow into the surrounding countryside, which brought
them up against people and livestock. What wolves do in the wild is
to fragment into rival packs, like players on a chess board, so that
they can bat the prey back and forth between them, which keeps
them and the prey within their own territorial boundaries. And if that
can't be done by real packs, my belief is it can be done by playing tape
recordings of packs, which will turn around the prey animals and
make it unnecessary for the wolves to stray outside the park. But it's
the scientists who run the reintroduction programs, and they guard
their patch jealously; they don't want an unqualified maverick suggesting there might be other ways of doing things.

Doug and I also had a long chat about the similarities between the dog and the wolf, particularly in social positioning, something I had brought up time and again in Idaho but which had been a taboo subject. I had always felt that the key to the wolf was the dog, and vice versa—that the way to get people to understand and respect the wolf was by comparing it to the animal they had in their living rooms. But the biologists wouldn't listen to me. I was told that they were different animals and there was nothing to be gained from comparing them. Ten or twelve years later there was Doug, one of the most respected wolf biologists in the world, saying much the same as I had said, and he was being taken seriously. Just think: if the biologists had listened ten years earlier, many, many problems might have been avoided.

The last time I went to the Wolf Education and Research Center in Idaho, they were having terrible problems with the captive pack I had spent so long with. They were down to just three animals, which didn't surprise me—the pack had become so celebrated that even members of the public knew their names. Years ago, dogs were like wolves but by bringing them into our homes and domesticating them, we changed them.

Humans are not intrinsically pack animals. We like to have family but we can survive without them, on our own if we have to, and by associating with us for all these years, dogs have learned to do the same. What happened to the dog is now happening to wolves in captivity. They are turning on one another, fighting and sometimes killing their own, and packs are gradually dwindling in numbers because in captivity, where there is no territorial threat and no chance of famine, the wolves have no need of family. In the wild they can't survive without every rank pulling its weight—the pack is all. But because of their increasing proximity to man, even in the wild, wolf behavior is changing.

The wolf is an adaptable animal—the Nez Percé taught me that.

Their people came close to extinction themselves years ago and they looked to the wolf for inspiration and guidance to bring them back from the brink, because wolves had rescued themselves many times before. Nature, including wolves, will always find a way. I have to believe that eventually some balance will return and humans will stop dominating and start listening. Biologists have used wolves to earn letters after their names; the Nez Percé have always seen them as symbols of survival and hope. Their attitude is that if the wolves can come back onto the land, then so can they. Just to be sitting there on the plateau with Doug Smith was a breakthrough. He had tried science and discovered that it didn't hold all the answers. Unlike some of his colleagues, he was prepared to listen to other ideas. I had to hope for the wolf that more would follow his example.

*A Man Among Wolves/The Wolfman* was shown in March 2007 and caused quite a stir. It very nearly won an Emmy Award but was narrowly beaten by *Meerkat Manor*. National Geographic flew me to the United States to do a whole lot of publicity around the launch and, suddenly, everywhere I went people seemed to recognize my face. Helen came with me and we had the time of our lives, staying in a lovely hotel with the biggest bath I'd ever seen. I spent more time in the bath than anywhere else; I thought I'd arrived in heaven. One evening Helen and I ventured out on our own. We went to see a show on Broadway and on the way back to the hotel afterward, feeling and looking like a fish completely out of water, I could see a gang of young guys in hoodies ahead of us, shouting and gesturing at passersby. They were heading our way and I began to think of all the TV dramas I'd seen about muggings and rapes on the streets of New York. I told Helen I was going to push her into a doorway and that she must then run, and I would do my best to fight them off. As they came level, my heart was pounding—there were four, five, six of them. Wild wolves, bears, were nothing compared to the terror I felt now. The biggest and the meanest looking brought his face up close to mine, thumped me on the shoulder, and said, "Yo bro! It's the Wolfman!" And as he gave me a high five and asked how it was going, I thought, what were you doing sitting in watching the National Geographic Channel on a Friday night?

Helen was becoming an indispensable part of my life. The more I saw of her, the more I realized that I had never been in love before. I hadn't understood the meaning of the word. The excitement, the laughter, the need to be with her, to know everything about her, was a whole new experience. We had so much in common. Her passion was for children and mine was for wolves, seemingly two very different subjects, but there were so many similarities in our aspirations and our outlook on life. She was a learning support assistant, but her views on child care, especially disabled children, were almost as alternative as mine were in the study of wolves. She had come up against the educational establishment in the way that I had come up against the scientists and she had felt some of the frustrations in her job that I had felt in mine. The more I saw of her, the more I was convinced I had found a soul mate, someone I wanted to be with—the *only* person I'd ever wanted to be with as much as the wolves.

After several months, Arran expressed a desire to go home and live with his father. He was a sensitive boy and I suspect he felt that his mum had someone to be with but his dad was on his own. Helen was devastated. I told her that Arran was too young to know what he wanted, that she should make the decision for him, but she wouldn't do it. She had always listened to what he said and had respected his views even though he was a child and, all credit to her, she let him go, although it caused her weeks of heartache. But it was the right decision. I thought it would be a flash in the pan, that Arran would be back in a couple of weeks, but not so; he is still living with his dad but Helen sees him a lot and everyone is very happy.

Once it was clear that Arran was not coming back, we started to think about moving in together. One good thing that came out of the television series was that Bob decided that my tatty old trailer was making the park look untidy, so he gave me another, larger one with two bedrooms and a shower and toilet. It wasn't the height of luxury—the hot water system didn't work properly and eventually stopped completely, and there were no cooking facilities to speak of—but it gave us a little more space and at last we were able to say good-bye to the putty bucket.

Helen was getting more and more involved with the wolves and the work I was doing and getting less and less enjoyment from her job. She spent every spare moment with me in the evenings and at weekends, and was such a natural with the animals that after a little while I asked her to join me full-time. And so she gave up the chalet, with its kitchen, bathroom, and hot and cold running water; gave up a good job and security; gave up a normal life; and came to live in a trailer with a gas ring and a man who stank of wolves. I have such admiration for this woman.

By chance—Helen would say nothing happens by chance—the morning she agreed to join me I had a meeting to discuss ideas for a new television series. Bethan Corney, the commissioning editor of Channel Five, who has always been a great supporter, was looking for two hour-long documentaries to take the story of my life with the wolves further. The question was, how? She had driven down to Combe Martin with my newly acquired agent, Hilary Knight, and Kath Moore, an executive producer with a company called Tigress, based in Bristol, who were to make the films. We were sitting around the table in the trailer nursing coffee mugs when I mentioned that Helen had decided to come on board full-time to help at the park. Kath asked what work she'd be doing. I said that first of all I would have to teach her how to be with the wolves. Her eyes opened wide and in that moment the theme for *Mr. and Mrs. Wolf* was born. About three months into the filming for Channel Five, Animal Planet in America joined the project and extended the brief for the U.S. market.

They wanted twelve half-hour programs that went out under the title *Living with the Wolfman*.

Helen always felt that her place was to be with children. She had worked with them all her life and watched their hierarchy in the classroom and on the playground, and the more we talked, the more we realized how similar they were in this respect to wolves. I felt that if I could train her and make her comfortable with the pack, she would make a perfect wolf nanny. I was interested in discovering whether wolves were gender specific, as I thought they were. The wolves that I had had the closest interaction with had always been male, and I suspected that Cheyenne might open up to Helen, as another female, in a way she didn't with me. She was almost two years old; if she became pregnant, the challenge that we all knew would make good television was whether I could teach Helen enough about the wolves in the nine weeks of Cheyenne's pregnancy. And could we then persuade Cheyenne to choose Helen as the nanny for her pups?

# CHAPTER THIRTY

# The Miracle That Is the Wolf

The filming started in late February with the courtship, with the males endlessly fighting with one another as they had done in the wild. I had put Cheyenne into the main enclosure with Yana, Tamaska, and Matsi, fully expecting her to take Yana, the alpha male, as her mate. He was her half brother, but wolves breed with their own family members in captivity, as they do in the wild, and there is no evidence that it causes any problems with the bloodline. Her full brothers were in the enclosure next door, which had a connecting gate so we could segregate them if necessary, but at this point they were all running together, a pack of seven animals. Nataa, Nanoose, and Tejas were too young to mate and even if they had come close, one of the adult males would have run them off.

Wolves are so shy about mating that they usually do it away from the rest of the pack, as I discovered in the wild, or under the cover of darkness. I had never properly witnessed mating, but this time we were hoping to capture it on camera, so as soon as I knew from her behavior that Cheyenne had become receptive, I spent all my time with her watching and waiting—expecting Yana to make his move.

He did nothing of the sort. In the middle of the afternoon, shortly after they had fed, Cheyenne chose Matsi, the lowest-ranking animal in the pack. I couldn't believe it. It was a complete shock; it went against everything I had been told. The biologists all say that the alpha will suppress any other hopeful candidates. We were watching something very interesting and I suspected that she must have chosen him for a reason. Early the next morning she mated with Matsi again. That night, although it was difficult to see under the trees in the dark, it looked to me as though she was finally allowing Yana his due.

The following morning I was up at the trailer with the film crew, snatching a quick cup of coffee and a bacon sandwich, when Linda and Roger, two staff members at the park, called my mobile and said, "Come quick; you're not going to believe this." We ran down the hill to find Cheyenne and Tamaska, the beta, knotted together. In the space of two days, Cheyenne had mated with all three possible candidates.

To the best of my knowledge, this has never been witnessed before, and at some stage we will carry out blood tests to find out which males fathered which pups. There is evidence of dogs producing two different breeds in the same litter; for example, some of them might be pure Labrador and some clearly a Labrador-collie cross, so it must be possible for wolves to do the same. I have a theory that she might have selected her partners because of their rank, knowing instinctively that her young would have exactly the same rank as their fathers—designer pups, if you like. It could, of course, have been just the result of an inexperienced female, but it could also have been something far more clever, which would turn current thinking on its head.

The next big question was whether Cheyenne was pregnant after all this mating, which because of the filming schedule, we needed to know. The most reliable way to tell is with ultrasound, but I wasn't prepared to put Cheyenne through the stress involved, so about fourteen days later we tried two alternatives: We sent away a sample of feces to a lab, which normally tests lions and big cats but was prepared to see what came up with a wolf, and we tried a human pregnancy test, which again was not guaranteed to be accurate, but we felt might give us some idea. When Helen and I went into the drugstore in Combe Martin to buy it, everyone looked at us knowingly and we quickly had to explain it was for a wolf and not us.

Collecting a sample of urine was the next challenge. I had to run around after Cheyenne, who had the run of two enclosures, with a little pot and throw myself onto the ground every time she looked as though she might be about to squat. Against all the odds, I succeeded, and we carefully took the sample up to the trailer and dipped in the testing stick. I thought I detected a faint cross but I couldn't be sure.

We had to wait another three weeks for the results from the lab about the feces, but in the meantime, she was showing all the signs of being pregnant: she had started to put on weight, her teats had begun to swell, and she'd started digging a den and constructing rendezvous sites that I'd witnessed the alpha female do in the wild. When the lab finally said they were as sure as they could be that she was in pup, it was all systems go. We had only a few weeks left to convince Cheyenne that Helen was experienced enough to be a nanny.

Helen had been going into the enclosure in the intervening weeks but now everything had to be stepped up. Every day I took her down to the expectant mother, her mouth stuffed with little bits of chewed raw beef and mince that she could regurgitate on demand when Cheyenne nibbled her lips—the first thing the pups do to their nanny. I did the same alongside Helen, and Cheyenne had such an appetite and nibbled so greedily at our lips that we both looked as though we had been sucking on a cactus. After weeks of doing this, our lips were so sore we could no longer drink hot coffee from a mug.

Finally the birth day arrived. The den was already fitted out with infrared cameras positioned to cover every angle Cheyenne could possibly get herself into. Outside the enclosure, in the little stadium the public sat in during the season to listen to my talks, the film crew had set up a monitor so we could all see what was happening underground. Cheyenne went into the den and was restless but otherwise there was no sign of activity. Bearing in mind her mother had gone into the den two days before giving birth, I wasn't expecting much. Helen and Jude, a volunteer who had come to us from the primates unit, took the first shift while I had something to eat. I went down to take over at about 11:00 p.m. At about 1:00 a.m. she started to get restless again and scratched out a birthing bowl, partially covering one of the cameras in the process. I called Helen and Jude, and a little later we started to hear sounds that suggested she was going into labor and then watched the most incredible sight: she tore the fur away from around her teats to prepare them for the pups. I had never heard or seen of wolves doing this before. We were witnessing something truly extraordinary.

Between four and four-thirty in the morning the first pup emerged, a very dark-looking creature, which she picked up rather roughly with her teeth. I had a moment's anxiety and said out loud, "Ease up, Cheyenne," but the pup squeaked and she relaxed her grip on it immediately and gently eased it over to her underside, where it started suckling. We all heaved a massive sigh of relief and allowed ourselves to relax. She had one live, healthy, suckling pup and seemed to know what she was doing. Numbers two, three, and four arrived with the same ease and we were over the moon. Success. Helen started to do a piece on camera for the video diary she was keeping. Cheyenne was suckling, licking, and cleaning up her pups. We could all go and get some sleep; our girl had done good—we had expected four pups and she had delivered. They were textbook births.

And then I realized that Cheyenne had started to push again and was producing nothing. She was becoming distressed. She howled and grunted and moaned, and the noises she made will probably haunt Helen and me until the day we die. She did that for the best part of an hour and a half, but it can take that long for a final pup to be born so I tried not to panic. After two hours and still no sign of anything, I became seriously worried. At first light I decided to try to get her out of the den and walk her around a bit to see if that would get things moving. Helen and Jude called her and she came out and sat on the bank for four or five minutes, licking her back end, then went back underground, circled, lay down and started pushing again, getting more and more distressed as she did so. I knew there was a very real possibility that we might lose her. If the pup inside her was dead, it would soon start to poison her system, so I called the vet, who took an agonizingly long time to come.

He agreed that the pup still inside her was probably dead and wanted to dart her so he could ease it out and let her return to her live pups. We called her out a second time and the vet darted her, but it didn't do more than make her groggy. He darted her a second time and she still didn't go down, and in her semiconsciousness she gave me a nasty bite on the hand. The vet couldn't dislodge the pup manually. He was going to have to do a cesarean section, which meant taking her to his surgery, a twenty-minute drive away.

We had an agonizing dilemma. The worst-case scenario was we would lose Cheyenne; if we didn't, she would be gone from the pups for so long during the operation and the travel back and forth that we would lose the pups, and if we removed them and fed them while she was away, she would probably reject them when she came back.

I decided to go in and get the pups and take them with us to the vet's. So while Helen and Jude loaded Cheyenne into the cage in the van, I went into the den. Cheyenne had dug six or seven feet beyond the den I had made, exactly as her mother had done before her, making sure nothing larger than she was could get at the pups. I had to wriggle through this narrow tunnel, which was a very tight fit. At one point the tunnel dipped down, almost like a U-bend in a drain, possibly dug to catch water and prevent the birthing chamber from being flooded. As the ground went down, there was a bulge above that I thought might be concrete. I bumped it inadvertently as I snaked my way beneath and it turned out to be loose earth she had excavated, which collapsed around my face. I couldn't breathe and I couldn't move. I yelled for help in the hope that someone might hear me, but everyone was so busy above ground getting Cheyenne loaded that no one did—except for Helen's young son, Arran. I could hear the panic rising in his voice as he shouted for someone to come back to the den; then, thank God, two of the keepers came and I felt hands pulling on my feet, just as I was beginning to find breathing difficult and think I'd never get out. The den had collapsed completely by this stage and I had no option but to dig the pups out of their chamber. I put them into a box, covered them with a sweater to keep them warm, put the box on the front seat of my four-by-four with little banana-shaped bottles of formula milk, and raced after Helen, who had had to set off without me because Cheyenne was beginning to come around.

By the time I arrived, Cheyenne was on the operating table, so I left the pups with all our helpers to try to get some milk into them, and went to see how their mum was doing. It was as we had suspected: Cheyenne had a large female pup dead inside her and there was no way it could ever have come out naturally. Luckily, we had been in time—Cheyenne was still alive and the C-section was successful—but we still had a long way to go with the pups, and I was looking at at least another twenty-four hours without sleep.

I can't explain why I did what I did next. I reckoned that if the pups had suckled once from their mother, a bond would have been created, however fragile. It would be a lot to expect of Cheyenne: she had been through a great deal of trauma, she'd had the worst birthing experience imaginable, and her den had been destroyed. Nevertheless, I went back to the park ahead of Helen, taking the pups with me, and went into the enclosure and started to re-create the den and to make it as much like Cheyenne had made it as possible. I was completely shattered by this time. I was running on pure adrenaline but I couldn't accept offers of help because if my plan was to have any chance of success, the den couldn't smell of anyone but me. I was hoping to put the pups back underground and encourage Cheyenne to join them. The odds of succeeding were not good, but I knew that if the den smelled of anyone else, she wouldn't go near it.

One by one I placed the squirming, squeaking little bundles in my newly created birthing bowl, just as Helen was backing down the track in the van with Cheyenne in the back. We maneuvered the cage into the enclosure and opened the door, and a very groggy and blood-stained wolf staggered out, looking very sorry for herself. She tried to run and immediately fell into the pond, so I went in and pulled her out. We were now both soaking wet as well as everything else. The boys were shut in the adjoining enclosure and she desperately wanted to join them. She seemed to have no memory of the pups or of anything that had gone before the anesthetic; she just moved shakily back and forth, up and down the fence line. I didn't know what to do. If I opened that connecting gate, she would never look at the pups again.

Then I had a flash of inspiration. I went up to her and started whimpering and whining in a high-pitched voice that she knew from all the time I'd spent with her. I rubbed myself around her, trying to create a bond in the way that a couple of wolves do when they need each other, and she started to respond. Very slowly I started to back away, calling her all the time, until we were around the back of the pond and halfway to the den. Slowly, slowly we edged forward, getting closer and closer until we were within maybe ten meters of the den entrance, and then she turned and ran back to the boys.

Valuable minutes were ticking away. I couldn't afford to go through that procedure again. I could hear the pups urgently squawking underground, in need of warmth and food, and if I didn't get her down to them soon, we were going to lose them. If I could only get her close enough, my hope was that she would hear them, too, and their cries might trigger her maternal instinct. So I stayed by the den and whimpered and whimpered until my throat was starting to seize up. I hadn't had anything to eat or drink all day and I still had mud all around my mouth; I had been on my feet for nearly forty-eight hours and I was exhausted. Finally, she started to come toward me, and kept coming, coming until she was about one and a half meters away. I backed away, still whimpering, until my head was right by the entrance; she came and put her mouth to mine as if asking for food, and at that moment I saw her hear the pups. Her head tilted to one side and then to the other and her ear flickered, as if listening intently. Shakily she put her head and shoulders inside the entrance and I was willing her to keep going—I was even tempted to give her a push—but she backed out again and went and sat under a tree.

I started up the whimpering a second time and once again she staggered over to the den entrance and licked around my mouth, so I put my head inside and she put her head and shoulders inside with me. Slowly, I backed away. She had her head and neck and shoulders in, and this time I held my shoulder under her back end to try to keep her from backing out. The noise of the pups calling was almost deafening by now, and suddenly the pressure against my shoulder vanished; I fell forward and she disappeared underground.

I waited a few seconds. I could still hear the pups calling, but I had no idea what was going on—would she come out again or lie on them and crush them? My heart was in my mouth and I crossed every finger I had. As I made my way out of the enclosure, Helen came toward me in floods of tears. She had been watching the monitor.

"What's happened?" I said. "Has Cheyenne eaten them?"

"She's feeding them!" said Helen, laughing through the tears.

I just thought, "Oh, my God." This is the miracle that is the wolf.

# CHAPTER THIRTY-ONE

# Pushing the Boundaries

I had been very excited by the prospect of teaching Helen to interact with the wolves and of her becoming a part of my world; and I liked the ideas behind the documentary. It would be a great showpiece for the research work we were doing. But I didn't kid myself; I knew Helen and I had a huge mountain to climb. She had to learn in a matter of weeks what I had taken years to discover, and so much of what kept me safe with these creatures was my experience. By expecting this to work—expecting the pack to be conned into thinking Helen was more experienced about their world than they were—I was pushing every boundary. Although I had spent my life pushing boundaries and doing things that common sense told me were foolish, it had always been *my* neck that I'd put on the line. This time it was the neck of the woman I loved—and if I had been able to turn back the clock and have those months over again, I would never have done it.

During the months of filming, I had a glimpse of the anxiety Helen had suffered in all our time together. Every day she felt sick with worry about the state I would be in by the end of it, not knowing whether I would be cut or bitten or bleeding and needing to be patched up or even taken to Accident and Emergency for stitches. Quite often I was concussed. If I got a really hard blow to the head—

the sort that left me reeling and seeing stars—an hour or so later I'd suddenly come to and find Helen hovering over me, ashen faced, asking if I was all right. She'd tell me that I'd been unconscious for the last ten minutes. And many were the times I'd pee blood.

Now we had reversed roles and both of us found it unnerving. I became the one who lived with the terror of something going wrong. She was the one facing the daily interaction, and although I was in the enclosure with her for most of the time and reassuring her that there was no danger, I knew I was bluffing. I was telling her she must lie down on the ground, on her back, and expose her neck and vulnerable underside. I couldn't guarantee that one of the wolves wasn't going to accidentally bite too hard or nick a vein with his canines. If he punctured one of the big veins in her neck, she could be dead in seconds.

At the start I had been quite confident and in the beginning things went well. My plan was to introduce Helen to the wolves in stages. First she met Cheyenne, on her own, because unless she accepted Helen, the whole experiment would be over; and their first few meetings looked promising. Helen had to show Cheyenne respect as a higher-ranking member of the pack and she did everything I had drilled into her. She then met the young males, Nanoose, Nataa, and Tejas. She had to convince them that she was of a higher rank than they were, which was more of a challenge. They were like boisterous teenagers, spoiling for a fight, and she was very frightened, but she managed to hold her own with them and at the end of the day they all howled together to cement the relationship. The wolves she was going to have to work with really hard were the expectant fathers: Yana, Tamaska, and Matsi. To be successful, she had to be accepted by the entire pack.

Then something happened that gave me a reality check. I had taken a deer carcass down to the enclosure. Helen had been helping me feed the animals but had not come in with me. She was standing outside chatting to a volunteer. The whole pack's energy levels were up; I think there must have been a bitch in heat in the area that had come close to the enclosure. Whatever it was, the atmosphere around them was very tense—almost explosive. Feed time is always highly vocal with all the wolves snarling and snapping and defending their own places on the carcass. To anyone unfamiliar with the scene, it looks as though they are out to kill one another but they never are. It's the classic situation where their bark is worse than their bite. Until it isn't.

I was in my usual place on the carcass between Tamaska and Yana; both were growling and snarling as they tore at the fur and the ligaments. I was growling as I ripped away at my section, making it clear to all comers that this was mine, when suddenly I pulled back and raised my head. A split second later Tamaska and Yana went for each other; their jaws locked and their bodies turned into a spinning bundle of black-and-tan fur. Had I not pulled back when I did, I would have been in the middle of it and some of the worst injuries I have sustained over the years have come from being caught in the cross fire.

Helen had watched with mounting horror. She wanted to know how I had known that such violence was about to erupt, and she wanted me to teach her how to recognize it so that she would be prepared when she was in there on her own. I felt physically sick. I couldn't begin to tell her how to do what I had just done. It was instinctive and had come from years of experience. It wasn't something I could teach her and it wasn't something I could do for her. And at that moment I realized that what I was putting Helen through was too risky. I had thought I knew enough to be able to keep her safe, but at that moment I knew I didn't. I always believed that Steve Irwin, the Australian wildlife expert who was known as the Crocodile Hunter, was killed because he allowed himself to be taken outside his field of expertise. He was killed by a stingray barb while filming in

the Great Barrier Reef. I had great admiration for Irwin, but croco-
diles were his field, and I thought it was dangerous when he was either tempted or persuaded to move out of his area of expertise. I
remember watching him on television as his wife was playing with
dingoes on Fraser Island but, to the best of my knowledge, he knew
nothing about dogs—he was out of his depth but was doing it because of the demands of television. I could see that one of the dingoes
was about to snap and a moment later it did snap at his wife; Helen,
who was watching with me, said, "How did you know it was going to
do that?" I couldn't answer. It was just a feeling that had come after
years of experience with these creatures. Television or not, this was
Helen's life I was playing with, and I needed to play safe.

There were other times during the course of filming when I
thought I'd made a big mistake. I was consistently torn between
doing what I knew would make great television, which was important, and what I knew was safe for Helen. Sometimes I ambushed her.
She was terrified of meeting the older boys; it had built up and up in
her mind until it had blown out of all proportion. I knew that if I told
her in advance that I planned to introduce her to Matsi in a couple of
days, she wouldn't have eaten or slept a wink. She would have worked
herself into such a state that she would have gone into the enclosure
smelling like a different person and giving out all the wrong signals.
Matsi is probably the most unpredictable of all the wolves in the pack
because his job, as the tester, is to expose weakness. If he detects the
slightest hesitation in another wolf, or a person, he alerts the alpha
and she dispatches the beta, the bully boy, to deal with the problem.

So I sprang it on Helen. Her confidence was at an all-time high,
having managed to cope well with the three teenagers, and Matsi was
in a good mood. I had spent a few hours with him earlier that morning and he was calm and relaxed. He had met Helen from the other
side of the fence many times, so he already had a lot of information
about her. It was a beautiful, still day. Everything augured well for a

successful encounter. All I needed now was some old-fashioned deception. I told her we were going to meet the youngsters again; when she saw Matsi in the main enclosure with them, she started to panic. I said that all she had to do was lay down some scent so that he could first get to know her through that. With a hint of hysteria in her voice, she said, "But what if Matsi comes over to me?" "He won't," I lied, "because the camera crew will also be in the enclosure, with all their equipment, and he'll be too nervous." I knew that he would make a beeline for her but gambled that once she was in there, she would deal with it, just as she had dealt with others. I had noticed already that her tendency was to panic a few hours before an event, but to be as cool as a cucumber when the crisis was actually upon her. Besides, I was going to be there with them and I wouldn't let things go too far.

As Matsi came toward her, I could see tears begin to well up in her eyes and her bottom lip start to quiver. This was the first wolf she had truly feared meeting. Not only was he a big, heavy, fully grown adult male, but Matsi had a reputation and Helen had heard the stories. Not so long before, there had been an accident in the park. Matsi had taken all the flesh off someone's fingers. The victim was a staff member and what she had done was completely out of order, but sometimes the more experienced staff can read the animals and get away with misjudgments. She had put two fingers through the wire fence to give Matsi a scratch, mistakenly thinking he was another, more docile wolf.

Matsi, being the tester, had spun around and grabbed the girl's fingers in his mouth. She started screaming at him and tried to pull her fingers away, whereupon he closed his teeth around them and pulled against her, neatly stripping them to the bone. I hadn't told Helen the story to frighten her but to remind her that although these creatures were behind bars, they were still wild animals and you could never afford to be complacent around them. They live for the moment and you can't take anything for granted; you are only as good as the last time you were with them. It doesn't matter that you raised them with a bottle; that was then, this is now, and unless you can prove your worth to them every single time you meet, you are in trouble. Wolves are not sentimental.

"Don't you dare!" I said sternly, as her composure started to slide. She glared at me and her jaw set in the way it did when I knew she was cross. I thought, good, let her hate me if necessary, just don't let her break down in front of Matsi. My hunch was right. Matsi leaped up at her but she stayed completely calm and held her own, and after giving her a thorough investigation, the tester of the pack turned and walked away. The relief on Helen's face was obvious and I breathed a huge sigh of relief. I don't like gambling at the best of times.

Moments later I was knocked flying by the three adolescents who cannoned into me. They were in the midst of a rowdy rough and tumble and I hadn't been watching carefully enough. I was in my usual position, down on my haunches, and it was my head that took the brunt of it. Everything went black for a second, and then I saw stars and felt as though I'd been hit by a train. Apart from practically knocking me out, the blow had dislodged my microphone, so I had to leave the enclosure briefly to let the sound engineer reattach it. While I was out, Matsi moved in on Helen. I was powerless to help.

Watching her with Matsi's jaw clamped round her throat was, without exception, the most terrifying moment of my life. It wasn't that I didn't trust Matsi. I had absolute faith in him. What I didn't trust was Helen to keep her cool. If that staff member had kept her nerve and remained quiet and still when Matsi had her fingers between his teeth, he would have let them go without harming her. The damage he did was terrible, but those were just fingers; now Matsi had his teeth around Helen's neck. If she had screamed or tried to pull away—if she had moved so much as a muscle—he would have done exactly what he'd done to that staff member, but the consequences would have been entirely different. Helen would have been dead.

My biggest fear in this whole exercise was Helen's reactions. Helen is *the* most emotional person I've ever met, and trying to make her turn off her emotions was the single most important lesson I had to teach her during that period—and also the hardest. Time and time again in the enclosure I could see the telltale signs. There was a little area between the double gates to the enclosure where she would psych herself up before going in with the wolves and I could see the transformation come over her as she went from emotional Helen to wolf pack Helen. I always had to wait for that change, when she'd say, "Okay, go," then, as I opened the second gate, I used to say to her, "Forget human; think wolf!" It was very difficult for her and I was incredibly proud of the way she managed to hold it in, but the minute we came out through that first gate she would collapse into tears or laughter or a mixture of both, and everything she had held back would come cascading out.

She held still. And the look of naked fear on her face still haunts me. Powerless as I was to help her, I stood at the wire on the outside of the enclosure and, trying to keep calm, told her not to move. By the grace of God she listened; she trusted me and she didn't panic. And having held her throat for what felt like an eternity but was in reality probably no more than a minute, Matsi let her go. Strangely, despite her fear, Helen didn't realize quite how serious the situation was until she saw the look on my face. That was what really freaked her. But she passed the test; Matsi approved and, despite my fears, he and Helen formed an incredibly close bond; they were similar characters—both deeply suspicious and slow to trust. The next hurdle was Tamaska.

# CHAPTER THIRTY-TWO

# *Breakdown*

The meeting between Tamaska and Helen never happened. Two weeks before the end of the filming schedule Helen collapsed. She had reached a point of total exhaustion. At the outset, we had agreed to film for two or three days a week, which, given everything else that was going on in our lives, would have been doable, but as time went by, pressure came from Animal Planet to get the series made ahead of schedule. That put pressure on Tigress, and they in turn put pressure on us. They were gathering material for twelve half-hour programs for North America and two hour-long documentaries for Channel Five in the UK. That represented several hundred hours of footage and they needed our involvement in most of it.

Our filming commitment increased to six and sometimes seven days a week. We began at seven-thirty most mornings and were frequently still at it until nine-thirty at night, by which time we were shattered. The filming placed other strains on Helen. Doing a crash course in becoming a wolf nanny meant a complete change of life for her. She had already adjusted to living in a shoe box, but now she had to change her diet. Like most people, she enjoyed convenience food like pizzas, pasta, and hamburgers, and she loved cakes and sweet things. She wasn't mad about liver and couldn't get kidney past her throat. In order to smell acceptable to the pack, she had to eat what a high-ranking wolf would eat—and that meant liver, kidneys, and heart as well as some good-quality meat and plain vegetables. What's more, she had to chew the offal, partially cooked, so that she could regurgitate it for Cheyenne and the pups. And she couldn't even cheer herself up with a drink.

Another major change: she had to work out at the gym to increase her body strength. I made her do weights, pull-ups, and push-ups as well as the treadmill. She hated it; she had never taken this sort of physical exercise in her life but it was vital that she did. She had to be able to hold her own against the wolves for her own safety. I was strong but even I had to work out and was going for daily runs to keep up my stamina, as I always had and still do. Without that level of fitness you don't stand a chance wrestling with a 130-pound wolf that is all teeth and muscle; and fit as I am, there's no guarantee that one of them is not going to break my neck one day.

Our schedule would have been exhausting enough if filming was all we'd had to concentrate on, but it wasn't. The filming came on top of our normal day's work. I still had to do what had previously taken up all my time. I had to look after the wolves, check on the perimeter fences twice a day, and maintain a bond with them all—including the European wolves, which were not being filmed. I still had to enrich them with recordings of other packs, still had to feed them every few days and organize carcass deliveries, and I still had to fulfill my commitments to Bob Butcher. The filming disrupted the busiest season at the park and he was increasing the pressure on me to meet and greet visitors, many of whom had seen me on television and had come hoping to see me give a talk and do my normal demonstration. I hadn't seen my children for twelve months and was feeling increasingly uneasy; Jan and I were going through a custody battle. Meanwhile, Helen and I were living life at 110 miles an hour; we were doing sixteen- to seventeen-hour days, and it was too much. It left us no time for each other, no time to talk. We had no escape from each other either and no life outside what we were doing. It placed an unbelievable strain on us both and on our relationship. We felt as though we were sliding ever closer toward the abyss. Something had to give.

It must have been about three-quarters of the way through the filming when the cracks started to show. Helen was working up to meeting Tamaska, the enforcer, and she knew that was the big one. Matsi, the tester, had been tricky, but the tester doesn't do the disciplining. His job is simply to highlight your failings to the other animals. It's only if you panic that he reacts, and that's when the danger, and life-threatening situations, arise with him. Her meeting with Yana, the decision maker, had had its own challenges, as Helen found out, and she had to give him the respect he deserved as the boss, but he was never going to be the biggest threat. As the alpha male he was self-preserving and would always be more likely to threaten Helen with his voice or his body posture—and bring in another pack member to do the business.

Tamaska was the one who did the business. He was the one she couldn't afford to make a mistake with because there was no forgiveness in him. Under pack rules he had the right, and he certainly had the power, to mete out whatever discipline was necessary and I had no right to interfere. If he went for Helen, the only hope I would have to save her would be to distract him momentarily, and get him to have a go at me. That would have bought her a few seconds to get out of the enclosure, but no more. I would have had to grab hold of him, which would have gone against everything I believed about these animals, and take his bites, which would have been serious and probably fatal. The more I watched Helen, the less confident I felt about her ability to cope with this final introduction. I was beginning to worry. Every day she was looking more and more tired and pressured. The diet, the fitness training, and the emotional strain—everything was getting to her and taking its toll.

It reminded me of the commando training I went through. Anyone with a reasonable standard of fitness could quite easily go through one of those tests we did, but if they had to do it day in day out, sometimes twice a day, over a period of eight to ten weeks, as we did, that's when the cracks would appear and that's what was happening to Helen. The physical and mental exertion of her days with the wolves, coupled with what was going on emotionally between us, was too much, and shortly before she was due to meet Tamaska, it all fell apart.

I can't remember the precise incident that sparked it. It was something petty and irrelevant, like whether I had flushed the toilet or remembered to buy milk at the shop. Whatever it was, as Helen said, it was the straw that broke the camel's back. Everything had built up and up and we desperately needed a break. I don't think either of us thought it would be permanent; she said she just needed to get away from the wolves and from everything that went with them. Even though we had been together and she had been a part of my world for nearly three years, we still saw things very differently. Her way of dealing with what had happened was to get back to normal life; mine was to go down to the wolves. We both reverted to the worlds we knew. It felt as if we were in a long dark tunnel and every fragment of light at the end of it had been blocked off. We'd had bigger rows than this before and come through them. This wasn't even a full-blown row. It was just a discussion that couldn't be resolved. Helen went to bed that night and I slept on the sofa, and when things were no better the next morning, we came to the conclusion that we needed a break and some space.

It was September. We had been filming for more than seven months and we still had several weeks left to go and, of course, we were under contract. But there was no way we could carry on that day, and when the film crew arrived, ready to go as usual, we told them things had broken down and we couldn't work. I needed to get out of the trailer, so I left them to it and went off into town. By the time I came back, the crew had vanished and so had Helen. Later, she sent me a text message telling me that she couldn't come back to the trailer; she had to sort herself out.

During that time I discovered the horrors of the celebrity world. When the Americans heard about our breakup, their solution was to get the cameras on each of us as quickly as possible, to stick a microphone in our faces and ask us how we were feeling—which, feeling the way we were, was the last thing either of us wanted. Tigress came to our rescue. They had become good friends by this time—we'd been through a lot together—and their attitude was, that may be what you do in the States, but it's not the way we do things over here. These guys need time to try to sort things out between them and once they have, we'll pick up the story up again. I don't think Animal Planet liked hearing that—they seemed to relish the soap-opera element of our lives—but without that breather I don't think we would have been able to carry on at all. We were given a week.

Helen has since told me that those were the worst days of her life; she didn't know how she was going to get through them. They were unbearable for me, too, because I sought solace in the wolves, thinking I would find comfort under the cloak of darkness with them. I spent every night after she left down in the enclosure with them, but they missed her as much as I did. They called for her throughout the night, a haunting, spine-chilling cry for a lost member of the pack, a rallying call showing her the way home. I longed for her reply to come over the valley, as it once had, but nothing came back; there was just silence. They called like this for about five nights and little by little it broke my heart. I wanted her back. I couldn't face the thought of a future without her. She had shown me a world I hadn't known existed, a world of love and laughter, a world that Helen inhabited. A world I wanted to be a part of, but she had closed the door to it.

Helen and I didn't speak to each other in the intervening time, but Kath Moore contacted us separately and we agreed to let Tigress film our split. They would conclude the series for Animal Planet by following Helen on her journey to a new life and show me and my future alone once more with the wolves. That was difficult enough for me, but what was worse was having to film "pickups" together. Filming is not always done sequentially and there were scenes we had to do together to drop into footage about our lives before the break that had already been shot. Pretending to be a couple for the cameras was one of the most difficult things I have ever done. It was agony for both of us.

What we needed more than anything was time apart to come to terms with what had happened. Maybe one day we would be able to salvage something from the relationship, maybe we could be friends, but we wouldn't know that until we had taken time to reflect and allow the wounds to heal. But we weren't afforded that luxury. The filming contract that had seemed so exciting in the beginning had turned into the worst kind of nightmare and was forcing us to be together.

And it wasn't over yet. What the contract also held us to was publicity. We had to travel to the United States together to promote the launch of *Living with the Wolfman*. So when we finally had a break from filming as the happy couple, we had just a few weeks off before we were sitting laughing and joking alongside each other on the sofas of all the major chat shows in New York. Once again it was all pretense. Helen had to talk cheerfully about the joys of living with the Wolfman, and I had to howl and snarl and generally keep the audience amused. Animal Planet decided that they wanted to keep the breakdown in our relationship secret. It would come out in the last program and they intended to use it as a cliff-hanger for a second series. Would the split be permanent or would we be able to patch up our differences? It felt as though our heartbreak was being used to push up the ratings.

Our last trip to New York had been so happy. This couldn't have been less so. It was a crazy time for us—and confusing. I don't think either of us really wanted to live without the other, but we just couldn't see a way of being together and making it work. Separate cars came and collected us to take us to the airport, although we were coming from just a few miles apart. We traveled separately on the airplane, stayed in separate bedrooms in the hotel, and were living separate lives but chatting together on television studio sofas as if we were inseparable. Going back and seeing all the old haunts from the last visit and remembering the fun and laughter then was unbelievably painful. This was tougher than anything I'd had to cope with in the wild. The battle for survival, the physical pain, the bites and gashes and blows to the head and every other part of my body were as nothing compared to the hurt I was feeling now. In all those years I had kept my emotions hidden away. Now they were laid bare. I couldn't see a way forward.

Every day it was a battle to get up and I had to remind myself to breathe in and out. I was more depressed than I had ever been and my mood had a tremendous impact on the wolves. They had never seen me display such emotion and I was worried about how they would react. But they were the ones that pulled me through. They had called and called but when there was no longer any hope of a response, they stopped calling and started restructuring the pack. They had grieved for their loss, for Helen, but life had to go on. If the pack couldn't recruit, it had to restructure; we all had to move forward.

One morning, soon after we arrived from New York, I was surprised to get a call from Helen on my mobile phone. She asked whether I would let out her dogs for her. "Why?" I said. "What's up?" Her voice sounded strange and she said she couldn't get out of bed. I went straight over and I was shocked when I saw her. She looked like an empty shell, and as we talked she seemed to drift—one minute she was with me and the next she was far away in a world of her own. I didn't know what was happening or what to do. I had never come across anything like it; this wasn't the Helen I knew lying in this bed. She was like a complete stranger and it was very scary. I dealt with the dogs and then I rang the film crew. We were still making the last episodes of the American series. I said, "There's no way on this earth that Helen's going to be able to film today." I said I'd see how she was tomorrow. They said they couldn't keep losing filming days like this. It was costing money; Animal Planet was on their backs. The first two episodes had now been shown and they were running out of time. They said I had to sort it out or call a doctor.

In retrospect, that was the best thing they could have said. I managed to get Helen into the GP's surgery and he took one look at her and sent her up to the hospital to see a specialist. The diagnosis was complete physical and mental exhaustion: her system had shut down.

Helen didn't get out of bed for the next two months. Even the slightest activity exhausted her. I did the odd task for her but otherwise I kept away. I wasn't the person to nurse her; I knew that having me around would only make things worse. Besides, I still had filming to do and the wolves to look after, so Jude stepped into the breach. They had become good friends and because she worked at the park, she could act as a go-between for Helen and me and would alert me to anything Helen might need.

The last days of filming were very difficult. Helen had made her last appearance—she was flat on her back and going nowhere—so Tigress had to use clips of her that they had already shot to make the final programs work. I was worried about Helen, and for my own part, I was just holding on, existing, but time was now of the essence. We had stretched Tigress and Animal Planet to the limit emotionally and financially but thanks to everyone pulling together and helping to make the best of a bad situation, we got through it—we had the series and the two one-hour documentaries for the UK in the can. Suddenly, after ten months of pressure, of long days and camera equipment filling the trailer, it was all over. Christmas was looming, and I was on my own.

I had been invited by friends who run one of the local pubs to have a meal with them, but first of all I celebrated with the wolves. A turkey dealer had delivered a whole lot of substandard birds that he'd been unable to sell and these were the guys' Christmas treat. The only problem was they hadn't been plucked and it was very muddy down in the enclosure that day. The pups hadn't seen turkeys before and they went mad, pulling them into pieces as white feathers flew everywhere. When I came out, with only thirty or forty minutes to go before I was due at the pub, I was so filthy I looked as though I had been tarred and feathered.

The hot water hadn't been working in the trailer for months, so I stood under the hose, trying to make myself look respectable enough to go out and thinking, on Christmas Day at the age of forty-three, that my life had to change.

The decision to go out was a mistake. I agreed to go, thinking it would do me good to get out of the trailer, but it was disastrous. Helen and I had been to the pub many times together, so it brought back painful memories, and every other table was taken by couples. They were all laughing and joking and pulling crackers and having a good time. And I was sitting at a table for one, feeling about as low as I had ever been.

# CHAPTER THIRTY-THREE

# I Have a Dream

With the help of a therapist, I learned a lot about myself in the next few months. The Nez Percé had said that I belonged between two worlds, but what I came to realize was that I had been with the wolves in their world for so long I had almost forgotten how to be human. My aim had been to bridge the gap between those two worlds, to try to find acceptance for wolves in a society that didn't want them or understand the value they have in bringing balance and prosperity to the natural world. But as the Native Americans said, being able to speak for the wolf is pointless unless you can communicate with the people who need to hear you. I had forgotten how to do that. I was so close to the wolves I had lost sight of why I was doing it. In order to make a difference in their world I had to regain a foothold in ours.

Helen and I had overstretched ourselves with the filming and that had put unbearable pressure on us both, but I knew that the real cause of the breakup, and possibly even Helen's breakdown, was me. She loved the wolves; she was almost as passionate about them as I was, and she didn't bat an eyelid when it came to dragging carcasses around or hacking off the heads and hooves of the calves that came from the abattoir. (We can now feed whole sheep and deer but ever since the BSE [bovine spongiform encephalopathy] crisis in the eighties, we are no longer allowed to feed heads or hooves to the wolves.) That's what I loved about Helen: the fact that she wasn't squeamish and didn't mind getting filthy. I don't think she even minded living in the trailer with dead rabbits being flung onto the roof of it in the middle of the night by Derek, the slaughterhouse man, after his lamping expeditions. Whenever I asked him why he did it, he said he was hoping to catch Helen outside one night in her nightdress. I don't think she minded giving up the creature comforts she'd been used to. What she minded was my inability to give myself completely.

I had been with Helen physically during the years we had been together, but mentally I had always been in the enclosure with the wolves. One was a world devoid of emotion; the other was full of it. I knew I turned my emotions off when I was in the wolf world, but I had always thought I turned them back on when I walked up the track to the trailer. It was clear to me now that I never had. I never truly left the forest and I realized that if I wanted to have human re-lationships in the future, whether with Helen or my children or any-one else, I needed to come back to the human world.

I had also become obsessive. I couldn't separate the dangers I knew existed in the wolf world, where life is a constant battle for sur-vival, from the dangers I perceived in the human world. I was like a Vietnam veteran or someone suffering post-traumatic stress disorder. When Helen and I would take out Arran for the day, I behaved like a male wolf protecting his pack. I could see danger everywhere, even walking down the streets of Barnstable, the local market town. I could never relax until they were back in the safety zone of home. I couldn't enjoy the outings we made to the park or the zoo or the beach because I was always on edge, fearful if either of them wan-dered down to the water's edge without me or ran and played in the sand. I was like a misguided collie dog that needed to herd everyone together, all the time, to be sure they were safe. I had a morbid fear of not being there when danger struck, which in the animal world is the biggest crime a protector can commit because it threatens the whole pack. If Helen was going out I would always need to know where she was going and when she'd be back, and I don't think she could take it anymore.

My world was wolves and I had taken her into it and nearly suffocated her. I had no other needs in my life; Helen did and I hadn't recognized that. She needed to live a much more normal life than I did; she needed to go out, to see friends, to shop, and to go to the beauty parlor from time to time to have her eyebrows plucked or her nails painted. She wanted to sleep in every now and then, but I got up before dawn every day so I could run to meet the rising sun as the Nez Percé did. Helen was the love of my life. When I was growing up, I'd always had the romantic dream that one day someone would take my breath away and when it didn't happen like that, I settled for something different. Finally, Helen had come along and I had been so desperate to keep her and protect her that I had almost killed our relationship.

As she rested, and the new year progressed, she gradually grew stronger and sent me the occasional text. There were various things we needed to discuss and sort out. There were financial issues and also things she had left in the trailer, including clothes, that I needed to return, and she had a suitcase with some of my things in it from when we had last been away together. One day she phoned. She had a problem with one of her dogs and asked my advice. At the end of the call I said, "If you ever need the twenty-four-hour dog help line again, just give me a shout," hoping she would pick up the underlying message, which she did. She then had a long conversation with her mother, talking through the feelings she still had for me and saying how she hoped that there might be some way we could resolve our problems. She also spoke to Arran, who gave her every encouragement.

We met again in early February and had a cup of coffee together. Helen had also been in therapy. Our time was taken up analyzing what had gone wrong between us, identifying what had caused the pressure cooker to blow, and we came to the conclusion that even though we shared a mutual interest in the wolves, and a desire to understand and help them, we had not allowed time for our individual needs. We went over this ground again in the next few meetings, acknowledging that although we led abnormal lives, we were normal people—Helen being more normal than I am—and we had normal needs.

It is still early days; Helen has taken a job with the National Health Service and is renting a small house in Barnstable and seeing more of her friends than she did when we were together. We speak daily and see each other as often as we can, but we both know it would be a mistake to go back to where we were. We are taking our time about everything else, but I hope that one day we will be together again. After a long battle in the custody courts, I now see my children every other weekend and because I wanted somewhere better than the trailer to take them, I am renting a small cottage. I've had enough of that kind of life.

I have made contact with my mother again, and one day I would like to bring her down to Devon. I went back to Norfolk recently to confront my fears and discovered that they were more manageable than I had expected them to be. I also visited my grandparents' graves in the churchyard at Great Massingham, and realized just how wrong my memory had been about when they died. I saw old friends, and for the first time I was able to see my childhood through my mother's eyes, visualizing how hard life must have been for her and how brave she was to have brought me up as a single mother in those days, in that environment. My behavior must have puzzled and hurt her. She still won't tell me who my father was, but she must have her reasons. Someday I would like to introduce Kyra, Beth, Jack, and Sam to their half sister, Gemma. All these years they haven't even known she existed. I'd like to get to know my grown-up daughter, too.

Meanwhile, my long-term plan is to find a property to buy with space for the wolves—an acre of natural forest per wolf, ideally—and to run an education and research center. My dream is to prove that having wolves roam the forest is beneficial to the environment and therefore to humankind. I would bring in naturalists to identify the animal and plant life in the area before the wolves arrive, and then invite them back in three or four years' time to see how it had changed. I believe we would find that the prey animals had become healthier and had increased in number. Having predators in an area stimulates females to breed stronger animals and more of them; and being kept on the move, keeps them from decimating any one area, as they currently do in so many places. The vegetation would flourish, bringing birds and a wide variety of wildlife into the area.

There is a story the Inuit tell about when their ancestors first started to hunt and kill the caribou, which they believed had miraculously come to them from the sea. The animals sustained them well until the people started to take too many and the herd became weak and diseased. So the Inuit prayed for a creature to safeguard the caribou and keep it healthy, and what came from the sea this time was the wolf. After the wolf weeded out the old, the sick, and the injured, the Inuit were left with strong, healthy animals to hunt—and more of them. Neither animal, of course, came from the sea. The caribou would have been a migratory herd, and wherever the prey goes, so goes the predator, but thereafter, in Inuit eyes, the wolf had mystical powers.

There is still so much research to be done. No one yet knows what would happen if wolves were released into the wild in the UK. In Scotland they are talking about trying to control two to three hundred thousand head of deer with wolves. If we can prove that wolves create more life than they take—as I believe we can—releasing wolves on their own would be futile. You would have to release them as part of a much larger program along with other predators. More research needs to be done about diet to find out exactly what effect different food sources have on these animals and to get to the bottom of what it is that the wild wolves in Poland get from domestic livestock that they don't get from their natural prey. And human beings would have to be prepared to have wolves roaming the forests once again. That is probably the greatest hurdle: people's fear, which is based on myths and legends that have been instilled in them through centuries. If I walk down the beach with a German shepherd, people are immediately frightened because it looks like a wolf. If I have a Jack Russell terrier, everyone thinks, how cute! The fact is that the Jack Russell is far more likely to bite than the German shepherd.

In all the talks I have given at Combe Martin, I have tried to dispel the falsehoods that people believe about wolves. Children need to be taught how to behave around them, to stay calm, never to turn and run, which is exactly how they should behave with dogs. I have a friend in Devon, Charlie Richardson, who breeds a dog called a Saarloos, which is a cross between a wolf and a German shepherd. These dogs look like wolves and have many of the wolf's characteristics but are better adapted to being around humans. They could be introduced to children at various facilities to teach them about wolves.

We know that wolves can connect with humans in a way that sometimes no human is able to—like Zarnesti with the disabled child who had never displayed emotion. I have seen several similar scenes over the years. A tall, thick-set man once came to the wolf enclosure at Sparkwell. He had a wife and three children with him, but you would never have known they were together. He stood well apart from them and while I chatted with the family, I noticed that he and Dakota, the female wolf, had connected. She was staring at him through the fence and every move the man made Dakota mirrored. He bent over, she went into a play-bow; he skipped to one side, she skipped—it was the first time I'd seen a wolf do this. We all stopped chattering and watched. I was then called away but when I came back, I found the family hugging one another and in tears. The man, I learned, had been a rugby player, fit and athletic, but he had recently had a back injury that meant he would never run again. His sporting life was over and he felt everything he had lived for was gone. He had been profoundly depressed and had withdrawn from everything, including his family. He had always loved animals and his family had brought him to the park in the hope that the visit might lift his spirits. Whatever happened between him and Dakota that afternoon, the wolf brought him back. Through his tears he was apologizing to his wife and to his children and holding on to them as though his life depended on it.

And we are beginning to learn, as has long been suspected, that wolves can detect illness in humans, too. Over the years I have run wolf encounter courses at the park for people to get closer to the wolves than normal visitors do. Before these introductions, I always ask if anyone has an ailment or whether women are pregnant or where they are in their cycle, because all these things can have an effect on the wolves. If a volunteer goes into the enclosure with a cold or an injury, the wolves know immediately and their behavior is more challenging. Centers that have socialized wolves the public are able to walk with report the same behavior. The wolves immediately single out people who have any kind of weakness.

Helen brought a middle-aged man down to the enclosure one day who looked perfectly healthy and had been asked all the usual questions. When he went close up to the fence, one of the wolves started trying to nibble and lick his hand through the wire, not in an aggressive way but obsessively, as though he couldn't get enough. This was very unusual, not to say abnormal, and I looked at Helen and said under my breath, "Is everything okay with this guy?" She said he hadn't said he had any problems, so I put it out of my mind and just thought the wolf must be having a curious day. When he'd finished, I stayed in with the wolves, while Helen took the man back up the hill, and on the way he became short of breath and started to pant and wheeze. She asked if he was all right and he said that he hadn't mentioned it before because he didn't think it was relevant, but he had a blood disease that made him very short of breath at times. This sixth sense of theirs could be harnessed.

Another aspect of my dream is to help the Nez Percé. The U.S. government doesn't believe they can manage the land. I would like to bring some of their people to the UK to give them an opportunity to demonstrate that they can, that their methods of purifying the land work, so that one day they might get back some of what was once theirs. We could have summer camps to show children—future generations—how to respect and use the land, how to value nature, and how to turn polluted streams into those pure enough to drink from by the use of plants and rocks and animals. I think people have a growing thirst for getting in touch with the land again and finding natural means of healing the planet. I would love to be part of that.

One other important ingredient would be dog-training courses to help people understand the creatures they share their lives with. As the old adage goes, there is no such thing as a bad animal, just bad teaching, and so much misery is caused by buying the wrong dog and misunderstanding it. Dogs are no different from wolves, and I have seen so many dangerous wolves come through rescue centers. If you get a wolf that has been brought up badly by humans then you have a modern-day werewolf. It looks like a wolf but has all the characteristics of an undisciplined, poorly educated hoodlum.

That is my dream. I hope you share it.

I am sorry that so many scientists disapprove of what I have done. I believe their fear that I would make life more dangerous for the wolves, by infiltrating a wild pack, was unfounded. Time and time again during those two years in Idaho, it was clear that knowing me didn't mean the wolves let their guard down. They didn't regard all humans as harmless any more than they regarded all wolves as benign. The cubs were taught to trust only those creatures that were part of the family. They were fearful of other wolves and, by the same token, they were fearful of human beings. I would argue that the benefits of what I did far outweighed the dangers for that pack. I discovered more about wild wolf behavior and communication by eating, sleeping, and living alongside those animals in the Rocky Mountains than I could ever have done with binoculars, however powerful. My hope is that we pool our discoveries and the scientists and I join forces.

The wolves I ran with were all wolves that were likely to come into contact with humans and, therefore, needed to know something about our world. I would never try to infiltrate a wild pack in the Arctic or in the wastes of Russia, where there were no farms or villages nearby, no livestock being attacked, and no conflict. There would be no reason to interfere and no justification. Those wolves don't need us and we don't need them. My interest in learning how to speak for this noble creature, whose language no one else seems to understand, is where the two worlds collide. I hope that one day we humans, who have lost our way in so many respects, might be able to learn from the animal that once walked alongside us and taught us so much of what we knew about survival, loyalty, and family but seem to have forgotten.

# Acknowledgments

My Native American family believes that our breath is sacred. It connects us to the Great Spirit (Creator). Therefore, our words are just as sacred and should not be used lightly. It is important to choose them carefully and use them wisely.

In honor of my Native American family and the many people who have contributed to this book, I hope I have chosen my words wisely.

First, Hilary and Katie at Hilary Knight Management. For your support and loyalty to duty, also going above and beyond an agent's obligations, thank you.

To Jane Turnbull and Daniel Conaway for their support and help in finding me the right publisher; to Julia Pastore at Harmony Books; and Carole Tonkinson and Kate Latham at HarperCollins; thank you all for showing such faith in this book.

To the dedicated and selfless staff at Wolf Pack Management: Roger Cooke, Linda Cowen, Jude Cross, and Wendy Jamieson-Butler. Thank you, my friends, for your endless support. It may not have always been easy but it was certainly worthwhile.

To Penny Junor for committing my innermost thoughts to paper. I always believed it would be virtually impossible to put my life into words, to relive the miracle of living with wolves through one man's eyes. You truly are worthy of your reputation among authors.

To my family and friends, who are responsible for shaping my childhood and making me the person I am today. Grandfather, I hope you are looking down on me and are as proud of me as I have always been of you.

To my mother. Sorry for all the doubt through the years, not only for not knowing how hard it must have been for you to raise an angry and unforgiving young boy, but also for the sacrifices that you made through the years. I know you can't talk to me of my father, but I hope for the short time you were together, you loved a lifetime's worth.

To my traveling father: Sir, I have never known you. I feel inside that you are a traveling soul, and I know that my mother loved you because of the strength she has found to deal with your absence. Thank you for your wisdom.

To my family: for my children, thank you for making my life complete. Watching you grow and take your place in this world, I know that you will help restore its balance. For smiling through Christmases and birthdays without me and often with homemade presents. Never once did I hear you complain. You are my life!

To my wolf family: I have always said that every day with you begins and ends with a miracle. For your patient teachings and sharing with me your family secrets. I hope I never let you down. Give me your wisdom so that I may know how to help your children to live peacefully in this world.

Finally, to Helen: thank you for your strength, my angel. You always believed in me and had the strength to stand by my side. Without your courage I never would have been able to take the steps that I did. I am sorry if I ever let you down. You and Little Man (Arran) will be in my and the children's hearts forever.

# Index

# About the Author

Shaun Ellis is the star of the hit Animal Planet show *Living with the Wolfman* and the National Geographic Channel documentary *A Man Among Wolves*. Ellis is a British wolf behavior expert who conducts research in a unique and sometimes controversial way: by living with wolves and becoming part of their world. He has lived among captive wolf packs in England and spent seven years on and off the Nez Percé reservation in Idaho studying wolves. It was in Idaho that he first was able to get inside a pack of wild wolves and live among them.

Ellis is the founder of the Shaun Ellis Wolf Pack Foundation (www.wolfpackfoundation.org), a nonprofit organization based at Combe Martin Wildlife Park dedicated to helping wolves worldwide. By studying wolves' behavior and ecology from inside the family unit at a very close range, Ellis and the foundation aim to teach the human population how to live alongside wild wolf packs and so conserve the species worldwide.

www.ShawnEllis.org